WHO TO EAT?

ISSUES OF ADMISSION TO THE LORD'S SUPPER

A LUTHERAN VIEW

ERIC W. GRITSCH

EDITED BY
LAWRENCE R. RECLA STS

ALPB BOOKS
DELHI, NEW YORK

The American Lutheran Publicity Bureau
wishes to acknowledge with deep appreciation
BONNIE BROBST, Eric's wife, who provided the unedited
lecture notes, references and the biographical sketch,
FREDERICK J. SCHUMACHER, who shepherded the
publication of this book from beginning to end,
DOROTHY A. ZELENKO, who scanned the original typed
documents and converted them to digital files,
LAWRENCE R. RECLA STS for editing the material and
providing the fall 2012 photo of Dr. Gritsch at the altar,
WILLIAM FENSTERER for his proofreading of the text,
JEFFERY NEAL LARSON for his ongoing pen & ink artwork
used on the covers in this Handbook Series, and
MARTIN A. CHRISTIANSEN for book layout and design.

— Paul Robert Sauer
Executive Director

American Lutheran Publicity Bureau
P.O. Box 327
Delhi, New York 13753

ISBN 1-892921-30-8

Eric W. Gritsch, *Who Gets to Eat? Issues of
Admission to the Lord's Supper: A Lutheran View*
(Delhi, NY: ALPB Books, 2015), 75 pp.

TABLE OF
CONTENTS

Editor's Comments

The original documents are nine lectures and printed essays from the late 1970s of the Reverend Dr. Eric W. Gritsch. The task was to edit those materials into a format more suitable for reading in a book. To that end I printed First Corinthians 11 in its entirety and printed the text for biblical citations along with chapter and verse notations. Upon occasion Dr. Gritsch expanded footnotes beyond the simple citation and often I included those comments in brackets in the text itself or simply printed them in their entirety.

Dr. Gritsch had an Appendix (with its own footnotes) to his lectures tracing the history of infants being precluded from communion in the LCA (Lutheran Church in America) and a response by then President /Bishop of the Upper New York Synod Edward Perry. I have chosen to begin with that so the reader has a perspective of the historical context of the impetus of the detailed study and position of Dr. Gritsch.

One of the facets that I have most admired since first beginning a relationship with him in 1965 was his commitment and focus as a pastor. The impetus and focus in the issue of admission to the Lord's Supper regardless of age, was the desire of several seminarians at Gettysburg Seminary to have their children receive.

From that pastoral concern, all of us benefit from his endeavors as a church historian and theologian. I was humbled to be quoted on Eric's Requiem bulletin, "From his teaching, I learned the history of our people, the church. From his actions, I learned how to be a better pastor. From his life, I learned how to be a better man."

These days theological disputes are often best described as competing slogans hurled ad hominem. The win being determined by volume, number of adherents, or the necessary sensitivity requisite to those whose feelings would be hurt were they not to prevail. Dr. Gritsch invites us to a reasoned debate with the presentation of the various historical positions the Church has practiced and espoused. He has the integrity to include all positions, not just those supporting his conclusions. While I am at some divergence with some of his conclusions, I am convinced that everyone, clergy and laity, would be informed and humbled by attending to his presentation. Some might even be convinced to the contrary of their initial inclinations; all would be the more respectful of others' conclusions.

Thanks to Bonnie Brobst, Eric's wife, who provided the unedited lecture notes and references and the Biographical Sketch, Honors, and Publication List and thanks to the Reverend Frederick J. Schumacher, who guided the publication of this from beginning to end.

THE HISTORY OF THE LCA
(LUTHERAN CHURCH IN AMERICA) ROAD TO PRECLUSION OF INFANTS FROM COMMUNION

Infant communion began to receive attention in 1962, when the Joint Commission on Confirmation submitted a report to the first convention of the LCA. The report suggested, in the context of a study on the significance of confirmation, that "the prerequisite for admission (to the Lord's Supper) is not confirmation, but baptism..." Some members of the Commission concluded, "The matter needs further study."[1]

A subsequent study of the relationship between confirmation and first communion stressed the significance of infant baptism as the full initiation into the church as the body of Christ. The Joint Commission on the Theology and Practice of Confirmation, in its study report to the ALC, LCA, and LCMS presidents (December 1967), asserted that infant baptism "incorporates fully into the church and makes the baptized one fully a member of that church, the body of Christ" (First Corinthians 12:13 "For in the one Spirit we were all baptized into

---

1. LCA Minutes, 1962, pp. 132, 135.

one body — Jews or Greeks, slaves or free — and we were all made to drink of one Spirit"). Infant baptism is a covenant which is described as "an unconscious, hidden relation, the depth of which no man can plumb."[2] At the same time, the Joint Commission, on the basis of findings derived from child psychology, recommended

> ...that the latter part of the fifth grade would normally be the most strategic time at which children should be admitted to Holy Communion, provided they have been brought up within the church (Christian home, Christian fellowship, church school) and have received instruction for first Communion. Admission to first Communion would have to be deferred for those who have not had these advantages. This will put the burden of decision and of pastoral care upon the pastor which, however, he should be able to share with the home, the church school teachers, and the entire congregation.[3]

The 1970 LCA Convention adopted the recommendations of the Joint Commission, thus separating confirmation from first communion and admitting children to first communion at age ten, or the fifth grade level. It is significant that admission to the Lord's Supper was based almost exclusively on findings derived from the psychology of education rather than child psychology.

For example Martin L. Maehr (University of Illinois) in an unpublished paper presented to the Colloquium on First Communion and Confirmation at Gettysburg,

---

2. Klos, *Confirmation and First Communion*, p. 193.

3. Ibid., p. 203.

March 14, 1969: "Some Psychological and Educational Considerations," first questioned age ten as the "fitting moment" of first communion; secondly, faulted the Commission for conducting no psychological research on the matter (only "educational" research was used); and called for a cautious program of research and experimentation before implementing the Commission's recommendation. Perhaps for this reason, the 1970 LCA Convention approved a motion "that in the next biennium the LCA study the practice of communing all baptized persons regardless of age and report to the next convention of the church."

But when the Committee to Study the Practice of Communing All Baptized Persons Regardless of Age had completed its work, it recommended the continuation of the existing practice "of admitting children to participation in Holy Communion when they have some knowledge and understanding of the gospel and the Lord's Supper." Though conceding the "possibility" of infant communion in New Testament times (and sketching the history of the practice in the Church until ca. 1200 A.D.), the committee did not recommend communing infants, "in the light of the biblical confessional understanding of Baptism and the Lord's Supper, together with the church's experiences through the centuries and the conceptual development of the infant."[4] Although this recommendation was based on a consultation of the Lutheran Confessions, First Corinthians 11:17-34, it became "a crucial passage" for rejecting infant communion:

> Biblical scholars point out that there are two
> dimensions to Paul's idea of discernment. One

4. LCA Minutes, 1972, p. 196; pp. 203-204.

is the discerning of the body of Christ in the distributed elements of bread and wine. The other dimension is the discerning of the body of Christ in the fellowship of believers gathered around the Lord's Table. Infants are not yet capable of discerning the body of Christ in either dimension of its meaning.[5]

The 1964 LCA Statement on Communion Practices continued to be the basic guide defining "preparation (confession)" as "self-examination" in the context of the liturgical Order for Public Confession: "When a baptized Christian has thus examined himself and responds in faith and obedience, he may receive the sacrament. Only those under the discipline of the church are to be excluded."[6] This rubric of "self-examination" then became one of the three "objectives for instruction for first communion" in the 1970 Statement, which separated first communion from confirmation: 1) to understand and appreciate the nature of the sacrament of Holy Communion; 2) to accept his place as a communicant in the fellowship of believers; and 3) to examine himself, to make confession of sin and to receive the absolution for Christ's sake."[7]

Although many Lutherans seemed to agree that confirmation be regarded as a catechetical rite linked to baptism rather than to the Lord's Supper, questions of communion practices still needed to be addressed. So the 1974 LCA Convention decided "that the 1964 LCA Statement on Communion Practices be re-examined and possibly

---

5. Ibid., p. 203.

6. Section D of the Statement, LCA Minutes, 1966, pp. 668-670.

7. Klos, op. cit., p. 206.

revised in the light of contemporary biblical, theological, liturgical and ecumenical insights."[8] This reexamination was conducted by the ALC and LCA Committee to Study Communion Practices, and a report was submitted to the 1976 LCA Convention. The report made no reference to infant communion, and recommended that "participation need not be tied to intellectual attainment."[9]

As a result of considerable discussion, the 1976 LCA Convention adopted a motion to review the submitted report in order to clarify several problem areas: "real presence," the role of ordained Lutheran and non-Lutheran ministers in the celebration, the "reserved sacrament" and "intercommunion." The convention recommended that a "task force" continue to work between 1976 and 1978 on the Statement, "with special consideration given to suggestions/amendments forwarded from the LCA and ALC Conventions." Infant communion had not been discussed, and appeared not to have been one of the problem areas.[10]

But during the reviewing process, and by the time the final draft of the Statement appeared at the 1978 LCA and ALC Conventions, one sentence had been deleted and another sentence had been added. Deleted was the notion that "participation need not be tied to intellectual attainment"; added was the sentence, "Thus infant communion is precluded." Thus the Statement defines "admission" in the following manner (Section A,2):

---

8. LCA Minutes, 1976, p. 386. The LCA Division of Parish Services and the LCA Conference of Synodical Presidents had urged such a study.

9. Section 2, "Admission," ibid., p. 387.

10. LCA Minutes, 1976, pp. 392-395; 409-412.

Admission to the Sacrament is by invitation of the Lord, presented through the Church to those who are baptized. It is the practice of the Church to admit to Holy Communion those who, in its judgment, are ready to participate. The decision regarding readiness should be informed by the following guidelines, which are consistent with our confessions:

a. That there be *a simple trust* that the Crucified and Risen Lord is here truly present, giving himself to his people, as his words declare;

b. That there be *a basic understanding; and appreciation of the gifts* God gives through the sacrament;

c. That there be *an acceptance of one's place as a communicant* in the fellowship of believers; and

d. That there be *self-examination* in a manner appropriate to the level of maturity and recognition of the need for forgiveness.

There may be a special concern for the admission of children. The findings of the Joint Commission on Theology and Practice of Confirmation indicate that readiness to participate normally occurs at age ten or the level of the fifth grade, but it may occur earlier or later. The responsibility for deciding when to admit a child is shared by the pastor, the child, the family or sponsoring persons, and the congregation. "Thus infant communion is precluded."[11]

---

11. Quoted from the Statement as distributed in the church. Italics mine.

It is difficult to see how such a definition of "admission" fulfilled the 1974 LCA Convention's mandate to re-examine the 1964 Statement "in the light of contemporary biblical, theological, liturgical and ecumenical insights." The 1978 Statement simply used the 1964 definition of "preparation" as "self-examination" as the basis for constructing an "admission" procedure which defends sixteenth century practice, rather than reexamining this practice in the light of contemporary "insights." Thus the Statement appears anachronistic rather than contemporary. Moreover, both the language and the logic of this particular section raise so many questions, from almost any point of view, that pastors and congregations may be tempted to ignore it altogether.

A few "for-instances" may suffice to indicate the problems created by the Statement's definition of "admission" to the Lord"s Supper:

The LCA Constitution makes the distinction between "Church" ("the historic continuity of the communion of saints," in Article 4) and "this church" (the LCA).[12] Why does this Statement claim to speak for the "Church"?

The Statement speaks of four "guidelines which are consistent with our confessions": "simple trust" in the true presence of Christ; "a basic understanding and appreciation" of the sacrament; "acceptance of one's place as a communicant" in the Church (and/or the LCA?); and "self-examination." Luther and the Lutheran Confessions, however, (unlike "pure doctrine" Orthodoxy and moralistic Pietism) carefully guarded the sacraments

---

12. LCA, Constitution and Bylaws, IV, 2.

from human conditions which smell of self-righteousness. Who knows when these norms have been fulfilled?

Pastoral relationships vary. Some create strong and very faithful Christians; others do not. Rational-cognitive norms (age ten) are but one aspect of pastoral relationships. Why should they become so decisive for admission to Holy Communion, which is a means of God's unconditional grace?

Lutheran and other churches have disciplinary provisions to exclude some "sinners" from the sacrament ("excommunication" according to Luther's *Smalcald Articles*; the *Augsburg Confession* contains no such article).[13] Why "preclude" some baptized Christians on the basis of biological age? Who is an "infant"? Is it a "babe in arms," thus making "walking" a norm for admission? Or "infantile persons" such as the mentally retarded Or anyone under 21 years of age, (as is the case in some jurisdictions?)

Since the term "preclude" means "to close in front, to shut up, to make inaccessible" (from the Latin *praecludere*), the Statement clearly prohibits baptized infants from participating in the Lord's Supper. This prohibition raises serious questions in light of a historical tradition of infant communion and the ecumenical thrust of the Lutheran Confessions. Historically, Lutheran and other churches preferred to issue guidelines for communion practices without prohibition clauses. Matters like infant communion usually remained within the confines of pastoral practice in the local congregation. It is the health and intensity of pastoral relationships that determines the strength and weakness of the life of the gospel in

---

13. Smalcald Articles, 1537, III, 9. BC, p. 314.

word and sacrament. But what seems to have been a "non-issue," when compared with other issues debated at church conventions, has now become an issue because of a controversial prohibition clause; for whenever the sacrament of the altar is made inaccessible to baptized Christians, the integrity of the ministry of word and sacrament is at stake.

THE DEFENSE OF PRECLUSION BY AN LCA PRESIDENT/BISHOP

I nfant communion has been a persistent issue since the 1978 decision to preclude the practice.[14] [The largest synod of the LCA, the Central Pennsylvania Synod, memorialized the 1980 Convention of the LCA on June 15, 1980, "to delete the clause 'Thus infant communion is precluded' from Section II A, 2 of the 1978

---

14. See Eric W. Gritsch, "Infant Communion: Old Bone in New Contention," *Lutheran Forum*, XIII , no. 1 (Lent 1979), 6-7. By the same author with Charles Anderson, "An Exchange of Letters on Communing Infants," ibid., no. 2 (Pentecost 1979), 8-10. The commentaries in the *Forum Letter*, VIII , no. 1 (January 26, 1979); no. 2 (March 2, 1979); no. 4 (April 27, 1979); no. 5 (May 30, 1979); no. 9 (September 28, 1979); EC, no. 3 (March 21, 1980). *News Bureau* (Lutheran Council in the USA, December 28, 1978, and February 9, 1979). Editorial in *The Lutheran* (February 7, 1979). LCA President Crumley in his circulatory letter "Dear Partners," March 15, 1979. Gerald Christianson, "A Little Child Shall Lead Them," Swope Lecture at the Lutheran Theological Seminary at Gettysburg, Seminary *Bulletin* LVIII, no. 3 (August 1978), 12-20. Frank C. Senn, "Infant Communion and Church Statements," *dialog*, XVIII (Spring 1979), 86-87. H. George Anderson, "Infant Communion and the LCA," *Partners* (The Magazine for Professional Church Leaders of the LCA), I, no. 6 (December 1979), 11-16, 22.

Statement of Communion Practices," because the clause "represents a negativism which is not consistent with confessional statements" and "with the affirmative tone of the rest of the statement."] In 1979, when the author of this paper distributed a "study paper" on infant communion throughout the LCA, Edward K. Perry, President of the Upper New York Synod of the LCA, responded with an essay defending the preclusion of infants from communion.[15]

Perry argues that the real issue is not infant communion, but rather the question, "Is it appropriate and proper to admit any baptized person, regardless of age, to the Lord's Table, with no pre-condition or requirement other than that person's baptism in the Christian faith?"[16] To answer this question, he reviews "the study and action of the Church" (that is, of the LCA); he describes "the theology and practice of other churches" (Orthodox, Roman Catholic, Episcopal, United Methodist, and United Presbyterian, USA); he then attempts to refute "the Gritsch paper"; and he concludes his lengthy essay (61 pages) with answers to two questions: 1) "What is really going on here?" and 2) "Is there a hidden agenda?"

It is praiseworthy when a synodical president provides his pastors and congregations with his views on controversial matters. Yet, since Perry not only presents helpful information but also advances controversial views of his own, a sketch of his position is necessary for a critical review of his essay.

1. Perry's review of "the study and action of the Church (LCA)" identifies concerns for "precondition," the

---

15. See above, n. 2.

16. Perry, p. 1.

priority of the "spoken and heard word," and the "sin-confession motif" as the major strands which have dominated LCA theology and convention actions on the matter of communion practices.[17] He defends the medieval practice — initiated in the thirteenth century and maintained in the Lutheran Confessions — of requiring "both cognitive and affective preparation for participation in the Lord's Supper."[18] Although Perry detects in LCA convention actions since 1970 a shift of language from an emphasis on penitence to a stress on celebration, such a "fundamental change in the traditional Lutheran piety and practice" does not warrant a move towards the communion of all baptized persons regardless of age. Rather, the priority of the spoken and heard Word of God requires the preclusion of anyone who cannot hear and understand the Word.[19] All this leads him "to surmise that many persons will tend to take positions on the present issue depending on which bundle of liturgical practice, piety, and vocabulary they personally feel comfortable with."[20]

2. Perry's description of "the theology and practice in other churches," though sketchy, provides helpful ecumenical information to Lutherans. Although he says little about the Orthodox inclusion of infants in the Eucharistic fellowship or the Roman Catholic exclusion of them before the "age of reason,"[21] his descriptions of the ac-

---

17. Ibid., pp. 3-11.

18. Ibid., p. 3.

19. Ibid., p. 11.

20. Ibid.

21. Ibid., p. 12. For Roman Catholic discussions of infant communion, see Crawford, pp. 524-525. Above, n. 24.

---

tions of the Episcopal, United Methodist and United Presbyterian churches disclose the fact that infant communion is an open question to them, since these churches refuse to debate the relationship between age and admission to the sacrament. It would have been helpful if Perry had advanced some kind of answer to the question (which his description begs) why these Reformation churches leave the question of infant communion open and why the ALC and LCA do not. Why, for example, did the Review Committee add the sentence "Thus infant communion is precluded" to the 1978 Statement on Communion Practices, when "it is difficult to understand how the deletion of that one sentence would have changed anything"?[22] Did the delegates to the ALC and LCA Conventions need the preclusion clause because without it the Statement might have permitted infant communion?

3. Perry's attempt to refute "the Gritsch paper," which he labels "one of the more curious deposits of the recent discussion,"[23] identifies five major points which, to this author's surprise, stimulated his curiosity:[24] 1) "The issue has been clouded" (Perry's choice of words); 2) "The 1978 statement is 'anachronistic' defending 16th century practice"; 3) "The question of 'infant' communion is an 'adiaphoron'"; 4) "Matters such as infant communion 'usually remain within the confines of pastoral ambiguities' in the local congregation"; and 5) "Ecumenical rapprochement presses the LCA to permit 'infant communion'." Although the Gritsch paper may be cloudy, it attempted to show that the LCA's insistence on "readiness" for the

---

22. Perry's judgment, p. 9.
23. Ibid., p. 22.
24. Ibid.

Lord's Supper is based upon an "anachronistic" acceptance of sixteenth-century confessional norms. Neither the Lutheran Confessions nor the LCA Constitution regard Lutheranism as a new "denomination." Whereas the former are normative documents of a reform movement within the church catholic,[25] the latter adheres to a hierarchy of truths according to which the risen Lord, the gospel, Holy Scripture and the Creeds have more authority than the Lutheran Confessions.[26]

Although Perry concedes that earlier Lutheran *practice* is not "normative" but "instructive," he defends the *theology*, if not the sociology, which undergirds the Western churches' practice of admission to the Lord's Supper in the last eight centuries. Perry's readiness to deal with the issue of doctrinal and past oral anachronisms does not lead to a clear understanding of why, according to Lutheran Confessional norms, infant communion is a genuine "adiaphoron" — something neither commanded nor prohibited.[27] Yet a careful discernment of the "pastoral ambiguities" and "ecumenical rapprochement" in our time could lead Lutheran churches to struggle with the issue of infant communion — whether, in the celebration of the Lord's Supper, either the preclusion or the inclusion of infants discloses the most faithful Lutheran witness to other churches and to the world.

Instead of exercising such discernment, Perry asserts that the Gritsch paper is only a document representing the views of a small cadre of Lutherans who use "polemical rhetoric" to advance the "hidden agenda"

---

25. See Gritsch and Jenson, *Lutheranism*, p. 207.

26. LCA Constitution and Bylaws, II, "Confession of Faith."

27. Perry, pp. 28-31.

---

for a "fourth-century Utopian model of the church."[28] Perry's own reading of the "signs of the times" leads him to pose a series of questions, climaxing in a restatement of the enduring dilemma in the Western churches.

> The issue is not, as I see it, whether or not there should be "preconditions" for admission to the Supper; but who are to fulfill the preconditions and when: children, youth, adult, parents, sponsors, congregations, et. al. *The real problem, then, is not with the admission to the Supper, but admission to Baptism,* which is the only necessary prerequisite for admission to the Supper. But the original definition of Baptism, as the sole prerequisite for admission to Baptism [*sic*] assumed prior catechesis. *Whether some may like it or not, God's free grace invites a meaningful response in decision and commitment.*[29]

And there is the rub.

And that is the underlying issue.

---

28. Ibid., pp. 51-56.
29. Ibid., p. 56. Italics mine.

PROLEGOMENON

At what age should baptized Christians be admitted to the Lord's Supper? While answers to this question vary within and among the churches of the world, recent denominational and ecumenical consultations have begun to deal with the relationship between age and the Lord's Supper in theological depth, with pastoral care and with ecumenical sensitivity. A telling example is the ecumenical consultation on the theme "children and the Lord's Supper" held at the Evangelical Academy of Bad Segeberg in Germany on April 13-20, 1980, and sponsored by the World Council of Churches' Commission on Faith and Order and the Office of Education. A summary by the German Lutheran churchman Jürgen Jeziorowsky highlights the consultation's findings:

> There is no reasonable theological argument to exclude children from the Lord's Supper. The excommunication of children under fourteen from the center of worship has been judged theologically and pastorally irresponsible. A new and comprehensive vision of the "family of God" and of the Eucharistic community calls for the inclusion of children. Children are more able to enjoy community than adults. They despise being alone and

they are more able to celebrate. Adults can also learn from children in the church. The rule "Unless you become adult" has already been turned around in the New Testament. **The consultation went so far as to reject any age limit as a condition to admission for first communion.**[30]

The refusal to recommend an age limit for admission to first communion has already become policy in some churches which are neither Roman Catholic (with its condition of private confession at the age of discretion) nor Orthodox (with its practice of infant communion at baptism). In 1970, the Episcopal Church of the United States established the policy that infant communion at baptism is to be preferred, while regular communion of infants and young children is left to pastoral discretion.[31] The United Methodist Church and the United Presbyterian Church-USA leave the decision of the relationship between age and first communion open, thus allowing the communion of baptized persons regardless of age.[32] [While the United Methodist Church has not raised the issues of "admission" or age for first communion, the United Presbyterian Church-USA did

---

30. *Lutherische Welt, Information* (Press Release of the Lutheran World Federation, Geneva, 17/80, May 8, 1980), p. 8, italics mine

31. *Prayer Book Studies* 18, 1970, pp. 21 and 24 and 26, 1973, pp. 3-4. For a summary of liturgical practice, see Edward K. Perry (President, Upper New York Synod, Lutheran Church in America), *What Is Really Going on Here?* An Essay on the Rhetoric, Process, and "Doing Theology," "About the So Called Infant Communion" Issue (Syracuse, NY: Synod Office Publication, 1979), pp. 12-16.

32. For a summary of communion practices in both churches, see Perry, pp. 17-21.

---

so several times between 1970 and 1978 without, however, explicitly precluding infant communion.]

Lutheran churches have had sporadic discussions about the relationship between age and first communion, as well as about the proper distinction between baptism and the Lord's Supper. Recent decisions and discussions about infant or family communion in the Lutheran Church in America (LCA) and the American Lutheran Church (ALC) disclose a struggle with what it means to belong to the church. While there is no consensus among Lutheran churches in the world on such principal issues as scriptural authority, the ministry of word and sacrament and other matters of faith and practice, the LCA and ALC have attempted to resolve the question of admission to the Lord's Supper. They recommend age ten, or the fifth grade level, as conditions for first communion, and "preclude" infant communion.[33] While the question of communing all baptized Christians regardless of age had been considered, the 1972 LCA Convention rejected such a practice "in the light of the biblical-confessional understanding of baptism and the Lord's Supper, together with the church's experience through the centuries and the conceptual development of the infant."[34] Yet there is a growing awareness in Lutheran churches that the question of admission to the Lord's Supper is a neuralgic issue demanding careful attention to the norms of Scripture and tradition, as well as to pastoral care and Christian unity. Moreover, a study of the Western churches' historical practices regarding the Lord's Supper yields two essential findings which need

---

33. 1978 *Statement on Communion Practices*, II, A, 2, d.

34. LCA Minutes, 1972 Convention, pp. 203-204.

to be considered in any argument about admission to Eucharistic fellowship:

> 1. Infants were baptized and communed in the Western churches for almost a millennium (from about 200 to 1200 A.D.) and still enjoy this way of Christian initiation in the Eastern churches (albeit for different theological/ liturgical reasons.)

> 2. The preclusion of infants from communion in the last eight centuries in the Western churches has been, and still is, associated with an individualistic anthropology focused on preconditions for distributing and receiving communion.

I take a critical look at the traditional Lutheran barriers of age to the admission to the Lord's Supper in the light of findings within three areas:

> 1. Scriptural authority, especially the arguments deduced from St. Paul's treatment of the Lord's Supper in First Corinthians 11.

> 2. Historic tradition concerning admission to communion in the Western church, especially the role of Lutheran confessional norms established in the sixteenth century.

> 3. The proper distinction between baptism and the Lord's Supper, especially in Lutheran sacramentology and liturgical practice.

I conclude with some observations concerning the proper integration of all baptized persons into the eucharistic fellowship of the church.

[17]Now in the following instructions I do not commend you, because when you come together it is not for the better but for the worse. [18]For, to begin with, when you come together as a church, I hear that there are divisions among you; and to some extent I believe it. [19]Indeed, there have to be factions among you, for only so will it become clear who among you are genuine. [20]When you come together, it is not really to eat the Lord's supper. [21]For when the time comes to eat, each of you goes ahead with your own supper, and one goes hungry and another becomes drunk. [22]What! Do you not have homes to eat and drink in? Or do you show contempt for the church of God and humiliate those who have nothing? What should I say to you? Should I commend you? In this matter I do not commend you!

[23]For I received from the Lord what I also handed on to you, that the Lord Jesus on the night when he was betrayed took a loaf of bread, [24]and when he had given thanks, he broke it and said, "This is my body that is for you. Do this in remembrance of me." [25]In the same way he took the cup also, after supper, saying, "This cup is the new covenant in my blood. Do this, as often as you drink it, in remembrance of me." [26]For as often as you eat this bread and drink the cup, you proclaim the Lord's death until he comes.

[27]Whoever, therefore, eats the bread or drinks the cup of the Lord in an unworthy manner will be answerable for the body and blood of the Lord. [28]Examine yourselves, and only then eat of the bread

and drink of the cup. [29]For all who eat and drink without discerning the body, eat and drink judgment against themselves. [30]For this reason many of you are weak and ill, and some have died. [31]But if we judged ourselves, we would not be judged. [32]But when we are judged by the Lord, we are disciplined so that we may not be condemned along with the world.

[33]So then, my brothers and sisters, when you come together to eat, wait for one another. [34]If you are hungry, eat at home, so that when you come together, it will not be for your condemnation. About the other things I will give instructions when I come.

SCRIPTURE: WHO IS PREPARED AND WORTHY?

The authority of Scripture; the understanding of baptism and the Lord's Supper in the New Testment; the precise meaning of Jesus' last meal with his disciples; the nature and meaning of the earliest Eucharistic meals; the different interpretations suggested by the first three gospels, the Pauline letters and the Johannine writings; and especially the norms for admission to the Lord's Supper in First Corinthians 11:27-34 — all these issues have been and still are debated in the context of specific problems which confront churches in particular places and at particular times. The 1972 LCA Convention, for example, used the Pauline phrase "discerning the body" (First Corinthians 11:29) as the "crucial passage" to prohibit the practice of communing all baptized persons regardless of age, especially infants:

> Biblical scholars point out that there are two dimensions to Paul's idea of discernment. One is the discerning of the body of Christ in the distributed elements of bread and wine. The other dimension is the discerning of the body of Christ in the fellowship of believers gath-

ered around the Lord's Table. Infants are not yet capable of discerning the body of Christ in either dimension of its meaning.[35]

Although one could quarrel about the number of biblical scholars who still agree with this interpretation, it is a fact that Martin Luther and his movement understood it that way. On the other hand, the constant search for the best interpretation of Scripture, in the light of the church's mission in the world, has greater significance than the preservation of sixteenth century Lutheran norms. The Lutheran Confessions, after all, pledge the Lutheran movement first to "the prophetic and apostolic writings of the Old and New Testaments'" then to "the three ecumenical creeds" (Apostles', Nicene and Athanasian), and only in the third place to the Augsburg Confession of 1530 and its interpretation in the Book of Concord of 1580.[36] Since the prophetic and apostolic writings of Scripture are "the only true norm according to which all teachers and teachings are to be judged and evaluated,"[37] the best possible hearing, with the best possible hermeneutical methods, is to be given to such crucial passages as First Corinthians 11:27-34. To what extent, then, is this passage crucial to the practice of many churches, including Lutheran churches, when they require some "discernment" as an essential precondition to participation in the Lord's Supper — be it a profession of faith,

---

35. Ibid., p. 203.

36. *Formula of Concord*, Solid Declaration, Rule and Norm, 3-5. See Theodore G. Tappert (ed. and tr.), *The Book of Concord* (Philadelphia: Fortress Press 1959), pp. 503-504. Hereafter cited BC.

37. Ibid. p. 504.

---

confirmation, a basic understanding, or any other qualification associated with post- infant and non-pagan existence? Does one have to be prepared in some fashion in order to be a worthy participant in the Lord's Supper? New Testament scholars present some major clues. [For an informative summary of scholarship on First Corinthians 11:27-34 and a detailed analysis of the various hermeneutical arguments see Norman M. Pritchard, "Profession of Faith and Admission to Communion in the Light of First Corinthians 11 and Other Passages," the *Scottish Journal of Theology*, XXXIII (1980), pp. 55-70.]

First, the thrust of the entire passage is determined by the context Paul had in mind: the Corinthian abuse of confusing the Lord's Supper with an ordinary meal in which the hungry are satisfied, or with a feast during which people ate and drank too much (11:21). The Lord's Supper proclaims the death of the Lord as embodied in bread and wine and as the visible elements of fellowship with him (10:16-17 "The cup of blessing that we bless, is it not a sharing in the blood of Christ? The bread that we break, is it not a sharing in the body of Christ? Because there is one bread, we who are many are one body, for we all partake of the one bread."). Eating and drinking without regard to such fellowship means "not discerning the body," that is, not discerning the relationship between the resurrected Lord and the assembly of believers. Thus Paul related church and sacrament closely. As Günther Bornkamm put it:

> The body of Christ, which we receive in the
> bread, implies for Paul directly "the body of
> Christ" in which we are bound together in
> the sacrament. In it we receive the body of

Christ and, by receiving it, are and show ourselves to be the body of Christ.[38]

Paul's concern, therefore, is that the fellowship which
was created by the death of Jesus should not be abused
by confusing the Lord's Supper with other meals, be they
ordinary or extraordinary (such as a pagan meal involv-
ing the worship of idols [10:14]). When Paul speaks of
"eating unworthily" (11:27), "he is thinking of the moral
failings of factiousness and greed which marked the
Corinthian community."[39] The adverb "unworthily" is
thus to be interpreted as "a particular reference to the
abuses prevailing at Corinth, and should not be given a
wider, more moralizing interpretation than that."[40]

Second, although "self-examination" may mean the
testing of an adult's life and faith (11:28; Second
Corinthians 13:5 "It does not insist on its own way; it is
not irritable or resentful") in Paul's thinking. He intended
"nothing more than to encourage self-appraisal in the
hope that this would lead to a change in behavior and
the ending of abuses which were vitiating the celebration of communion."[41] The specific context in which Paul
uses the verb "to examine oneself" does not permit the
interpretation that he requires some sort of "profession
of faith" as a condition for participating in the Lord's
Supper. Such an interpretation is derived from situations
which differ from that in Corinth: a general self-examination of the individual member of the church (First

---

38. Quoted ibid., p. 59.

39. C. K. Barrett, quoted ibid., p. 59.

40. Ibid., p. 59.

41. Ibid., p. 60.

Corinthians 13:5) and a special examination of deacons who are to be blameless in their office (First Timothy 3:10 "And let them first be tested; then, if they prove themselves blameless, let them serve as deacons"). It is improper exegesis to apply one situation to another. Paul appears not to have limited participation in the Lord's Supper to those who had examined themselves, even though he links lack of self-examination with God's judgment (11:29): those who neither love the Lord nor each other should be excluded from the celebration. There are no other criteria, such as baptism or belonging to the church, for participation. In the words of a standard modern interpreter:

> There is nothing in the limitation, "If anyone does not love the Lord" that could exclude "unbelieving outsiders" who, through prophecy, have been led to the confession "God is truly among you," and prevent them, even though unbaptized, from continuing in the Christian fellowship in the Supper.[42]

The stipulation that only baptized members of the church be allowed to participate in the Supper first appears in the writings of the second century apologist Justin Martyr.[43]

Third, whether or not infants or children were admitted to the Lord's Supper in Corinth and elsewhere is difficult to determine on the basis of the specific situation which Paul addressed in First Corinthians 11:27-34:

---

42. Barrett, quoted ibid., p. 68.

43. *Apology* I, 66:1: "None is allowed to partake except he who believes our teaching is true." Quoted in Pritchard, p. 69.

The point may be made, however, that the requirement of self-examination applies only to adults; it does not necessarily follow from this that no children were present and participating. The *"argumentum e silentio"* (argument from silence) that the households whose baptisms are recorded in Acts 16:15 contained children should logically apply in relation to communion also.[44]

Research into the question of whether or not children and/or infants had been communed at the time of the New Testament is inconclusive.[45] Luke 18:15 "People were bringing even infants to him that he might touch them; and when the disciples saw it, they sternly ordered them not to do it" clearly speaks of "babies" to whom is promised the kingdom of God without, however, explaining why this should be so. Is it because Jesus directed his Sermon on the Mount to the poor and the lowly symbolized by a helpless baby? Such an interpretation appears possible in the light of Mark 9:37 "Whoever welcomes one such child in my name welcomes me, and whoever welcomes me welcomes not me but the one who sent me." and 10:14 "But when Jesus saw this, he was indignant and said to them, 'Let the little children come to me; do not stop them; for it is to such as these that the kingdom of God belongs" where Jesus stresses the motif of substitution: whoever receives a child receives him. "If seen in the light of the situation after Easter, it means

---

44. Ibid. P. 57, n. 1.

45. Günter Haufe, "Das Kind im Neuen Testament," *Theologische Literaturzeitung*, 104. Jahrgang, Nr. 9 (September 1979), pp. 625-638.

---

that the helpless child substitutes for the earthly Jesus. Thus the child joins the least among the brothers of Jesus (Matt.25:40 "And the king will answer them, 'Truly I tell you, just as you did it to one of the least of these who are members of my family, you did it to me';" and loving acceptance of the child is distinguished from mere humanitarian welfare.[46] The catechizing of children or adults prior to communion, leading to a profession of faith, cannot be based on First Corinthians 11:27-34, even though churches have done so,

> There can be no doubt that the practice *of catechizing before first communion* cannot be claimed to be based on the New Testament **as we now read and understand it**. The implications of this finding impinge upon several areas of church life, including the matter of the relation of children to Holy Communion.[47]

Fourth, it is extremely doubtful that Paul's words to the Corinthians should be normative beyond the situation to which they are addressed, namely the lack of love and unity in the Corinthian congregation. Sixteenth century Lutherans regarded First Corinthians 11:27-34 as crucial because it is the earliest documented reference to Eucharistic practice, but this position needs to be reexamined.[48]

---

46. Ibid., p. 628.

47. Pritchard, pp. 69-70.

48. The position is defended in the 1972 LCA Minutes, See above, n. 6. A reexamination needs to take into account the theological assumptions employed in the exegesis of the passage. If "the situational orientation of Scripture" is accepted, then the traditional Lutheran exegesis of the passage is unacceptable as Pritchard has shown (p. 70).

Moreover, the injunction to "discern the body of Christ" (11:29) did not prevent infant communion for ten centuries and still does not prevent it in the Orthodox churches.[49] A universal application of First Corinthians 11:27-34 could, for example, be balanced against the injunction of the Johannine Jesus, "If you do not eat the flesh of the Son of Man and drink his blood, you will not have life in yourselves" (John 6:53 "So Jesus said to them, 'Very truly, I tell you, unless you eat the flesh of the Son of Man and drink his blood, you have no life in you' "). Therefore, when Lutherans invoke the norm of the "prophetic and apostolic writings of Holy Scripture," they face the enduring problem of the "canon within the canon" — a problem Luther had to face in his controversies with the "sacramentarians" who, like Zwingli, used Johannine arguments in their defense of a "spiritual" over against "real" presence of Christ in the doctrine of the Lord's Supper.[50] Contemporary Lutherans need to take a hard look at their use of First Corinthians 11:27-34. As one concerned pastor put it:

> Paul's words, struggling for unity and for building up the whole body of believers, have been used to divide and to exclude. His words have a legitimate use only when they are applied to situations in the church today that approximate those of the Corinthian church.

---

49. See Eugene L. Brand, "Baptism and the Communion of Infants: A Lutheran View," *Worship L* (1976), p. 41.

50. See Luther's most extensive literary encounter with Zwingli, "Confession Concerning Christ's Supper," 1528. Vol. 37 of *Luther's Works*, American Edition (Philadelphia: Fortress Press, 1961), pp. 236-252.

They cannot be rightly applied to a cognitive understanding of the "real presence," which a child must be able to express before being admitted to Communion. Rather, we might better ask whether this text applies to our congregations' continual disregard for the weak and the poor.[51]

---

51. David L. Pearcy, "Infant Communion. Part II: Present Barriers to the Practice," *Currents in Theology and Mission*, VII, no. 2 (1980), p. 168.

Tradition:
Historical Practice
and Lutheran Norms

R esearch on Christian initiation in the history of the church has clearly demonstrated that for one millennium (ca. 206-1200 A.D.) there was a well-established practice of admitting persons to the Lord's Supper regardless of age. Such initiation consisted of baptism, confirmation or "chrismation" (anointing with holy oil), and communion — usually during the public worship conducted during the Easter Vigil or at Pentecost. While the church normally initiated only adults in this manner during the first two centuries, children and/or infants were so initiated when infant baptism became standard procedure in ca. 250 A.D. Although the first generations of Christians, in the face of persecution, seem to have received only adults into the fellowship of the church, infant baptism led without apparent difficulty to infant communion when the Roman Empire embraced Christianity as a state religion. If, then, infant communion was so well established for a millennium, why did the practice cease after the twelfth century in the Western churches?[52]

---

52. The most informative historical study is J.D.C. Fisher, *Christian Initiation* (2 vols., London: SPCK, 1965). A Roman Catholic argument for infant communion with an excellent bibliography is

Infant communion practices varied, depending on the age of the infant or young child. Sometimes priests dipped a finger in consecrated wine and let the baby suck it; at times wine alone would be offered; at other times intinction was used besides the regular distribution in both kinds. Baptism by immersion into carefully prepared water and confirmation with holy oil applied to head, chest and feet preceded communion. According to a typical seventh-century order of initiation in Rome, after the baptism and confirmation all the infants receive communion.

> Care is to be taken lest after they have been baptized they receive any food or suckling before they commune. Afterwards let them come to Mass every day for the whole week of the Pascha and let their parents make oblations for them.... Infants are held in the right arm of their sponsors, while adult candidates, of whom there can have been very few in Rome at this time, each place their foot upon the foot of their sponsor — a requirement obviously arising from the fact that they cannot be held in their sponsor's arms. Evidently past history has so far been forgotten that the initiation of infants is regarded as the norm to which the initiation of adults must be made to conform as far as possible.[53]

In 675 A.D., the first Council of Toledo ruled that anyone who refused to consume sacramental bread and wine should be expelled from the church as a sacrile-

---

Charles Crawford, "Infant Communion: Past Tradition and Present Practice," *Theological Studies* XXXI (1970), pp. 523-536.

53. Fisher, I, pp. 20 and 26.

---

gious person. Infants, mentally retarded, and sick persons were absolved from blame when they involuntarily vomited the "elements." Such rulings clearly show that infant communion was certainly not an offensive practice, in Spain or elsewhere, until the twelfth century.[54]

The practice of infant communion decreased between the eleventh and thirteenth centuries when increasing attention was given to the care and protection of the "elements" of bread and wine as "consecrated substances." Already in ca. 250 A.D. the North African bishop Cyprian had worried about the relationship between consecrated elements in the Lord's Supper and holy food in pagan festivals. He warned parents not to defect from the Christian faith and join pagan rites under pressure of Roman persecution. For such defection would destroy the solidarity of the Christian family, which, through the Holy Communion of all its members, is bound to the world as a witness of a new world to come.[55]

Metaphysical theories about consecration, the steadily increasing power of the priest as the consecrator of the elements in the Mass, and the theological battles over the precise relationship between human nature and divine grace (known as "Pelagian" controversies since the fifth century) led to the termination of infant communion in the Western Church by action of the Fourth Lateran Council in 1215 A.D. Although the Council did not prohibit infant communion, it stipulated that

---

54. Ibid., p. 95.

55. Cyprian, "On the Lapsed," 25. See the *Ante-Nicene Fathers*, eds. Alexander Roberts and James Donaldson (Buffalo and New York, 1885-1896, American reprint of the Edinburgh Edition), V, p. 444.

all Christians go to confession before holy communion at least once a year (known as "Easter Duty"). Since the confession was tied to the "age of discretion," it became difficult, if not impossible, to admit young children to holy communion. It is significant that the reasons for terminating infant communion are linked to the sacraments of ordination and penance rather than just to the sacrament of the altar. The conciliar decisions of 1215 A.D. safeguard the power of the priest through the doctrines of transubstantiation and of penance, which demands priestly absolution in public and private confession. The already existing doctrine of concomitance clinched the case against infant communion by asserting that the distribution of bread alone constitutes a valid Eucharist. Thus once all baptized Christians were obliged to confess individual sins to the priests and were not permitted to drink from the chalice (because of the fear of spilling holy substance), holy communion was essentially tied to rational-cognitive factors. A communing Christian was now someone who had to be able to enumerate sins and to chew the transubstantiated host.

Yet, even though infants were now excluded from communion, they were permitted to be carried to the altar and receive "blessed bread" during the Mass after baptism. Some church synods denounced this practice while others, like the Synod of Bordeaux in 1255 A.D., permitted it.[56] But infant baptisms still took place during the Easter Vigil in many churches and were followed by the Mass at which infants were present. "In this way and to this extent the Church still gave

---

56. Fisher, I, p. 105.

visible expression to the corporate and social aspect of baptism, and the rite still retained some of its primitive solemnity."[57]

Although the practice of infant communion continued sporadically, even in the West, for quite a while (still documented in 1609 A.D.),[58] Western churches in general discontinued it. Luther and other reformers, by and large, adhered to the medieval tradition which excluded infants from holy communion. Luther himself, however, did not share later Lutheran anxieties about doctrinal orthodoxy or inner moral certainty as conditions for admission. Although he did not change the medieval practice of linking the Lord's Supper with confession ("self-examination"), he clearly instructed new Lutheran parishes to see this sacrament in the context of God's unconditional grace rather than within a framework of burdening "policy." Instruction and exhortation should occur with the understanding that:

> No one is to be compelled to believe or receive the sacrament, no law is to be made concerning it, and no time or place should be appointed for it. We should so preach that, of their own accord and without any law, the people will desire the sacrament and, as it were, compel us pastors to administer it to them.[59]

---

57. Ibid., p. 108.

58. Frank W. Klos, *Confirmation and First Communion. A Study Book* (Minneapolis: Augsburg Publication House; Philadelphia: LCA Board of Publication; St. Louis: Concordia Publishing House, 1968), Leader's Guide, p. 28 (bottom note).

59. Luther's Preface to the *Small Catechism*, 1529. BC, pp. 340-341.

Would Luther have communed baptized infants if parents had attempted to "compel" pastors to administer it? Perhaps not. Luther did not address the issue of infant communion, because no one seemed to have been concerned about it. He simply admonished families to teach children "the things they ought to know. Since they are baptized and received into the Christian church, they should enjoy this fellowship of the sacrament so that they may serve us and be useful. For they must all help us to believe, to love, to pray, and to fight the devil."[60]

Most sixteenth-century Lutheran churches appeared to have communed children between the ages of six and fifteen, using confirmation as the condition for first communion. Reformed and Anglican churches followed similar practices. The Roman Catholic Council of Trent 1545-1563 A.D.) reaffirmed the decision of 1215 A.D. to withhold communion from infants. But the Council did not expressly "preclude" or forbid it:

---

60. *Large Catechism* V (Lord's Supper), 87. BC, pp. 456-457. In sermons on Matthew (1537-1540) Luther preached on Matthew 19:13-15 defending infant baptism against Anabaptists who only baptize adults. He argued that 1) the "little children (*Kindlein*)" were babes in arms less than two years old, and 2) being like these little children is the appropriate way to receive both baptism and the Lord's Supper. "Reason cannot comprehend the articles of faith, also not the doctrine of the sacraments of baptism and the Lord's Supper. Therefore it is written, 'You shall become a little child'." In what appears to be a casual reference to the Lord's Supper in the context of Lather's well-known arguments in defense of infant baptism, he comes close to the issue of infant communion without, however, discussing it. See Dr. Martin Luther's *Sämmtliche Werks* (Erlangen Edition, 1826-1857), 44, pp. 155-158.

Little children who have not attained the use of reason are not by any necessity bound to the sacramental communion of the Eucharist; for having been regenerated by the layer of baptism and thereby incorporated with Christ, they cannot at that age lose the grace of the son of God already acquired. Antiquity is not therefore to be condemned, however, if in some place it at one time observed that custom.[61]

Although this Council condemned much which the sixteenth century reformers asserted, its decision not to condemn infant communion exemplifies a deep respect for infant communion as part of a long ecumenical tradition both in the West and in the East. Seventeenth-century Lutheran orthodoxy, with its insistence on "pure doctrine," and eighteenth-century Lutheran Pietism, with its stress on psychological evidence for moral "rebirth," did not exhibit such ecumenical wisdom. Lutheran communion practices have been shaped, more often than not, by a stronger concern for the religious disposition of the communicant than for the integrity of the Lord's Supper as a means of God's unconditional grace.

The Lutheran Confessions do not derive their views of baptism and the Lord's Supper from a systematically argued doctrine of the sacraments. They only speak of the sacraments' "use" (Article 13 of the *Augsburg Confession* is deliberately placed after Articles 9 and 10 on Baptism and the Lord's Supper). Luther and Melanchthon

---

61. H. J. Schroeder (tr.), Canons and Decrees of the Council of Trent (St. Louis and London: Herder, 1941), Session 21, ch. 4, p. 134.

are concerned that the "gospel" be embodied in a variety of ways.

> For God is surpassingly rich in his grace: First, through the spoken word, by which the forgiveness of sin (the peculiar [better expressed as "proper," from the German *eigentlich* and the Latin *proprius*] function of the gospel) is preached to the whole world; second, through baptism; third, through the holy sacrament of the Altar; fourth, through the mutual conversation and consolation of brethren.[62]

Although the proclaimed word is the "proper function" of the gospel, it does not have superiority over the sacraments. (This runs counter to the favorite argument of Lutherans who have difficulties with "rites" and "ceremonies.") Why word *and* sacrament (as Article 5 of the *Augsburg Confession* stipulates for the office of ministry)? According to Edmund Schlink,

> The only answer is, "Because God commands both and because Christ instituted both — the preaching of the Gospel and the sacraments." We are forbidden to eliminate or even to overlook this divine institution. This prohibition is confirmed by the statements which say *the sacraments are necessary for salvation.... This is true (not only of baptism) but also of the Lord's Supper:* "Let it be understood that people who abstain and absent themselves from the sacrament [of the altar] over a long

---

62. Luther's *Smalcald Articles,* 1537, Part III, 4. BC, p. 310.

period of time are not to be considered Christians" (*Large Catechism*, V, 42, 49).[63]

It was very significant for the Lutheran movement to reject the medieval *materialistic* understanding of the sacraments (as "holy substances") as well as the "left wing" (*Schwärmer*) *spiritualistic* notion of the subordination of sacraments to preaching (sacraments as merely "ceremonies"). But when the movement shifted the argument from polemics to edification, the significance of sacraments as "visible words" was asserted. What a sacrament *says* and what it *does* is not two things but one! That is why Melanchthon defined the sacraments as "signs and testimonies of God's will towards us for the purpose of awakening and strengthening our faith." (In the Latin version of Article 13, it states, "sacraments should be so used that faith, which believes the promises that are set forth and offered, is added.") Melanchthon seemed especially concerned to avoid the medieval rivalry between word and sacrament by using the Augustinian definition of sacrament as "visible word":

> Through the Word and the rite God *simultaneously* moves the heart to believe and take

---

63. Edmund Schlink, *The Theology of the Lutheran Confessions*, tr. Paul F. Koehnke and Herbert J. Bouman (Philadelphia: Muhlenberg Press, 1961), pp. 184–185. Italics mine. See also BC, pp. 451-452. The view that both baptism and the Lord's Supper are "necessary for salvation" was rejected by Charles Anderson at the 1978 LCA Convention (Minutes of July 17). For an interpretation of "necessary" in the Lutheran Confessions, see Eric W. Gritsch and Robert W. Jenson, *Lutheranism: The Theological Movement and Its Confessional Writings* (Philadelphia: Fortress Press, 1976), pp. 200-206.

hold of faith, as Paul says (Romans 10:17), "faith comes from what is heard." As the Word enters through the ears to strike the heart, so the rite itself enters through the eyes to move the heart ... for the rite is received by the eyes and is a sort of picture of the Word, signifying the same thing as the Word. *Therefore both have the same effect.*[64]

Does this mean, for example, that Melanchthon did not make any distinction between baptism and communion *as far as their effect is concerned?* If so, would he have allowed infant communion if some Lutherans had urged it? The conjecture that this is an open question is warranted, in light of the Lutheran Confessions' polemical as well as non-polemical assertions.

Based upon what the Lutheran Confessions teach, and what traditional Lutheran dogmaticians assert, the question of admission and the matter of infant communion appear to be genuine "adiaphora": things neither forbidden nor commanded (even though some dogmaticians, for example Gustaf Aulèn, argue that the church cannot exclude infants from baptism.)[65] Sixteenth century Lutherans asserted that there is nothing which the Christian must do to be right with God. God has set him/her right with himself in Christ, and he continues to pro-

---

64. *Apology of the Augsburg Confession,* 1530. 13, 5. BC pp. 211-212. Italics mine.

65. Gustaf Aulèn, *The Faith of the Christian Church,* tr. Eric H. Wahlstrom and G. Everett Arden (Philadelphia: Muhlenberg Press, 1948), pp. 381-382. See also Bernard J. Verkamp, "The Limits Upon Adiaphorist Freedom: Luther and Melanchthon," *Theological Studies* XXXVI (1975), pp. 52-76.

vide for him/her through word and sacraments. Why, then, are certain things — such as the communication of the gospel and the administration of the sacraments — necessary? What is the proper distinction between "necessary for salvation" and "necessary for the mission of the church in the world"?

The Lutheran adiaphorist controversy, in the sixteenth century (over Melanchthon's liturgical concessions to Roman Catholics during the Leipzig Interim of 1548 A.D.), discloses both the strength and the weakness of the Lutheran notion of adiaphorist freedom.[66] On the one hand,

> the community of God, in every place and at every time, has the right, authority, and power to change, to reduce, or to increase ceremonies according to its circumstances, as long as it does so without frivolity and offense, and in an orderly and appropriate way, as at any time may seem to be most profitable, beneficial, and salutary for good order, Christian discipline, evangelical decorum, and the edification of the church.[67]

On the other hand,

> at a time of confession (*in statu confessionis*), as when enemies of the Word of God desire to suppress the pure doctrine of the holy Gospel, the entire community of God, yes, every individual Christian, and especially the

---

66. See Gritsch, Jenson, *Lutheranism*, pp. 194-197.

67. *Formula of Concord*, Solid Declaration, 10:9. BC, p. 612.

---

ministers of the Word as the leaders of the community of God, are obliged to confess openly, not only by words but also through their deeds and actions, the true doctrine and all that pertains to it, according to the Word of God. In such a case we should not yield to adversaries even in matters of indifference (adiaphora).[68]

Lutheranism's strength is to call for careful discernment of those matters which are integral to the commission to proclaim and to enact the gospel, that is, what is integral to the communication of the word and the administration of the sacraments. Thus sheer biblicism and spiritualism are both avoided — for example, the notion that one must keep the Sabbath because Scripture demands it, or the assertion that the word alone, without sacraments, is the gospel. Lutheranism's weakness is to assume that the adiaphora concept is a comprehensive expression of Christian liberty, that is, to use the concept without discerning a specific historical situation to be an opportunity for mission — for example, the frequently uttered message, "Only believe, and, as for the rest, it does not matter what you do." Such an interpretation of adiaphorist freedom frequently resulted in a disregard for liturgical practices. Yet the Lutheran Confessions clearly assert that some liturgical practices — such as the celebration of the Lord's Supper — are never adiaphora. Liturgical "use" and "action" in communion

> ...does not primarily mean faith, nor the oral eating alone, but rather the entire external

---

68. Ibid., 10:10. BC, p. 612.

and visible action of the Supper as ordained by Christ: the consecration and words of institution, the distribution and reception, the oral eating of the blessed bread and wine, the body and blood of Christ. Apart from this use it is not deemed a sacrament.[69]

In other words: *the whole event* is the "holy element" which constitutes the Lord's Supper, not just the bread and wine are the "holy things." That is why Lutherans oppose the concept of materialistic consecration, which leads to the adoration of consecrated bread and wine and to abusive "reservations" of them long after the Eucharistic event has ended. The interpretation of the Lord's Supper as the meal of the church in which Christ is truly present "in, with, and under" the bread and wine should be sufficient reason not to link the preclusion of infant communion with the care and protection of the "elements" of bread and wine as "consecrated substances" — as the Fourth Lateran did in 1215 A.D. when it prohibited infant communion. The adiaphorist question concerning infant communion might be, "What do Lutherans, as defenders of the gospel's freedom, want to say to the world when they either preclude infants from the Lord's Supper or include them?"

Recent theological discussions of infant communion have been prompted by the awareness of its historic practice (especially in the Eastern churches), as well as by the ancient ecumenical concern for the relationship among baptism, confirmation and the Lord's Supper. A 1961 International Seminar of the Lutheran World Fed-

---

69. Ibid., 7:86-87. BC, pp. 584-585.

eration, for example, agreed that admission to the Lord's Supper is an act of pastoral care unrelated to confirmation. On the whole, European Lutheran (and non-Lutheran discussions) focus on the problem of infant baptism rather than on infant communion, since Karl Barth and other theologians questioned the origins and practice of infant baptism.[70] However, the basic issue in all these discussions is the relation of the infant to the sacrament as it is celebrated in the liturgy.

Several attempts have been made to deal with this question, especially with reference to infant communion.[71] Most recently, Eugene L. Brand has made a solid Lutheran case for infant communion in a study of the relationship between baptism and first communion.[72]

---

70. For the pros and cons of the origins of infant baptism, see Kurt Aland, *Did the Early Church Baptize Infants?* (Philadelphia: Westminster Press, 1963) and Joachim Heremias, *The Origins of Infant Baptism* (London: SCM Press, 1963). Barth's arguments against infant baptism are similar to arguments against infant communion: infants cannot make a "cognitive" response to God's offer of grace in Christ. See Karl Barth, *Kirchliche Dogmatik* (Zollikon-Zrich: Evangelischer Verlag, 1932-1970), VI /2, pp. 193ff.

71. Brand, op. cit., above n. 21. Paul Bretscher, "First things First: The Question of Infant Communion," *Una Sancta* XX, no. 4 (1963), pp. 34-40. Berthold von Schenk, "First Communion and Confirmation," *Concordia Theological Monthly* XLII (1971), pp. 353-360. William Streng, "Age for First Communion," *The Lutheran Quarterly* XV (1963), pp. 291-307). For a summary of views see Eric W. Gritsch, "Infant Communion: What Shape Tradition?" *Academy* (The Lutheran Academy for Scholarship), XXXVI, no. 3 (October 1979), pp. 85-108. For a systematic analysis of pro and con arguments see Robert W. Jenson, "The Eucharist: For Infants?" *Living Worship* (The Liturgical Conference) XV, no. 6 (June-July 1979).

72. See above n. 6.

Starting with the premise that contemporary Lutheran (and ecumenical) theology needs to move from a defense of the "objectivity of grace" to the contemporary Christian's quest for "identity in terms of the relationships in Christ rather than as subjects of a hierarchical or theological system."

Brand makes these salient points:

1. Infant baptism, though nowhere clearly reflected in the New Testament, is ritual action which must result in a relationship of faith; and faith, according to Luther and many Lutheran fathers of the seventeenth-century like John Gerhard and Martin Chemnitz, is life in the Holy Spirit, signaled by chrismation with the laying-on of hands during the rite of baptism.

2. The separation of infant baptism and chrismation (later called confirmation) came to mean that real membership in the church is conditioned by an "age of discretion" — the capability of the baptized to examine themselves.

3. Infant communion produces the same theological problems as does infant baptism, namely that a sacrament is beneficial only when received in faith; if Luther and the Lutheran fathers got around the problem of infant baptism and faith "by virtually equating faith with the gift of the Holy Spirit ... could not the same theological gymnastics be applied to Holy Communion for the newly baptized infants?"

4. First Corinthians 11:28-29 ("discerning the body and blood of Christ") can mean, if applied to children, that they are to be perceived as interrelated with a community such as the family; and the passage has never been used to prevent infant communion when it was practiced.

5. Whether or not to practice infant communion is a question of pastoral strategy, not of doctrine and/or

theology; a "mediating compromise" would be to commune the newly baptized infants, thus clearly demonstrating their right of access to the altar, but then delaying the next communion for "very few" years.

Although standard Lutheran systematic theologies — written by theologians like Gustav Aulèn, Werner Elert and Francis Pieper — deal with infant baptism, they do not treat the question of infant communion. A standard German Lutheran encyclopedia suggests that infant and/or children communion (*Kinderkommunion*) was not a problem in the Reformation; if it had come up, the writer suggests, Lutherans would have to discuss the question of how infants and/or children can believe and accept "the kerygma about Christ" (Rom. 10:14-17, "Faith comes through hearing").[73] This approach to the problem, of course, has made infant baptism a persistent issue since the Reformation.

Martin J. Heineken has opposed infant communion on similar grounds.[74] He interpreted participation in the Lord's Supper as an "I-Thou" encounter, which precludes non-verbal communication, since such communication would be "sub-personal." The Lord's Supper, like sexual relations, requires a maturity which children do not have. Thus they are to be excluded; and he attributed the resurgence of interest in infant communion to an unhealthy Lutheran occupation with "ceremonies."

---

73. K. Dienst, "Kinderkommunion," *Die Religion in Geschichte und Gegenwart* (3rd ed. rev., Kurt Galling, Tübingen: JCB Mohr, 1959), III, 1285.

74. Martin J. Heineken, "Confirmation in Relation to the Lord's Supper," *The Lutheran Quarterly* XV (1963), pp. 22-28. See also by the same/author, "A Reply to 'Communion Malpractice'," *dialog* XVIII (Autumn 1979), pp. 291-292.

Robert W. Jenson has tried to avoid the perennial temptation of Lutheran dogmaticians to regard either word and sacrament or baptism and the Lord's Supper as rivals contending for priority as did some "neo-protestant" theologians with their "word theology" and some spokesmen of "neoliturgical" movements with their "substantialist sacramentology." His recent work on the interpretation and practice of the sacraments tries to avoid also the "disastrous mistake to distinguish analysis of Christian sacraments as *communication* from analysis of them as events of God's real presence and action."[75] Once that distinction is overcome, it is possible to appreciate the power of the Lutheran confessional insistence that the gospel is embodied in the "audible" and "visible" word; and that any attempt to derive the one from the other either leads to the "magic" of medieval sacramental materialism or to the "charismatic" spiritualism of the left-wing radicals (*Schwärmer*). Infant communion can be justified or rejected on the basis of either of these two versions of a disembodied gospel. But it can also be a powerful witness in the church to the world that, not only the washing of infants through baptism, but also their feeding at the Lord's Supper by faithful parents, congregations and pastors embodies the loving (albeit at times offensive) presence of the triune God. The "integrity" of the sacrament rests upon the mandate, "Do this..." rather than upon the question of "validity," or "What must I do to receive the blessing?"[76] Thus,

Whatever arguments could disqualify persons of such-and-such age or attainments from the Supper would

---

75. See Robert Jenson, *Visible Words. The Interpretation and Practice of Christian Sacraments* (Philadelphia: Fortress Press, 1978), p. 5.

76. Ibid., p. 8.

disqualify them also from baptism. Moreover, there can be no such arguments; for while there are indeed considerations that tell directly against infant baptism, in the nature of the case there can be nothing against infant communion. For one thing we do well at any age, is to participate in fellowship by accepting nourishment.[77]

---

77. Ibid., p. 164

Baptism and the Lord's Supper: Proper Distinctions

My faith does not make the baptism but rather receives the baptism, no matter whether the person being baptized believes or not; for baptism is not dependent upon my faith but upon God's Word.... Likewise, if I administer the sacrament to someone who cherishes anger or the like, he nevertheless receives the true body [and true blood of Christ]. Therefore it is false to say that infants do not believe and therefore should not be baptized. You have already heard that they do believe, because the fruits follow, namely, the gifts of the Holy Spirit. The sacrament [of the Lord's Supper] does not rest upon faith but upon the Word of God, who instituted it , and so it is with baptism also.[78]

---

78. Luther, "Ten Sermons on the Catechism," 1528. *Luther's Works* (American Edition), op. cit., vol. 51, p. 186. Similar statements in the *Large Catechism* on "Infant Baptism," BC, pp. 442-446. See also "Concerning Rebaptism," 1528. *Luther's Works*, vol. 40, pp. 229-262.

Thee words disclose how Luther argued for a sacramentology grounded in the unconditional promise of God's "visible words": the bodily enactment of the gospel in baptism and the Lord's Supper. At the same time, Luther's frequent insistence upon the priority of the "audible word" as the "live word" (*viva vox*) between hearer and speaker has often been used to propagate the separation of word from sacrament as well as of baptism from the Lord's Supper. In reference to what is "necessary for salvation," statements like these are often made:

> Baptism is complete ... it alone is necessary for salvation.... Holy Communion is not.... Baptism is the sacrament of God's prevenient grace, creating full fellowship with God ... the Lord's Supper is the sustaining sacrament ... it is not the central community-constituting event in the community of believers.[79]

The Lutheran Confessions have a hard time maintaining proper distinctions — be it between the "audible" and the "visible" words (in Article 13 of the *Augsburg Confession*)[80] or between baptism as "necessary for salvation" (only in the Latin, not in the German text of Ar-

---

79. In the 1972 LCA Convention, Minutes, p. 195. Charles Anderson, 1978 LCA Convention, Minutes of July 17. Usually the young Luther is quoted from "Concerning the Ministry," 1523. *Luther's Works*, vol. 40, p. 9: "the Eucharist is not so necessary that salvation depends on it." On the other hand, see the statement in the *Large Catechism*, 42, BC, p. 451: "people who abstain and absent themselves from the sacrament over a long period of time are not to be considered Christians."

80. BC, p. 35 and *Apology*, ibid., pp. 211-214.

---

ticle 9 of the *Augsburg Confession*)[81] and the Lord's Supper, which must be attended by church members who want to be "considered Christians" (according to Luther's *Large Catechism*).[82] Melanchthon only increased the tension, when he listed penance among the genuine Lutheran sacraments.[83] What, then, are the proper distinctions between baptism and the Lord's Supper, in light of the controversial issue of admission to the Lord's Supper regardless of age? Why are infants baptized but not communed? Why does the ALC and LCA *Lutheran Book of Worship*, Ministers' Desk Edition, 1978, remind pastors that "the gift of Communion is the birthright of the baptized"?[84] To what extent does liturgical practice reflect doctrine? Since proponents of infant communion have been accused of making no distinction at all between baptism and the Lord's Supper, some clarifying points need to be made about the proper distinction between the two sacraments.[85]

The sixteenth-century Lutheran understanding of sacraments battled the notion that word and sacraments are rivals. Medieval sacramentology had stressed the priority of sacraments, especially the Lord's Supper, thus tending towards a sacramental materialism — sacraments were holy substances to be "infused" into the sinful human life which was thus redeemed. Non-Lutheran

81. Ibid., p. 33.

82. Ibid., p. 451

83. *Apology of the Augsburg Confession*, Article 13:4. BC, p. 211.

84. p. 31 on "first communion."

85. For the accusation, see Walter A. Kortrey, "The Way We Commune," *The Lutheran* (February 20, 1980), p. 6.

Reformation sacramentology, especially Zwinglian, stressed the priority of the word, thus tending towards a non-sacramental spiritualism — sacraments are merely celebrations of a faith nourished by the cognitive word which alone is a "means of grace." According to normative Lutheran understanding, the word of God is external: that is, it addresses me from the outside, for anything which emerges from the inside is basically sinful and self-righteous. As an external word, be it audible in preaching or visible in the sacraments, it has a "body" — an externality embodied in a word both heard and spoken and seen and tasted. Therefore, ministry, or "gospelling," is the communication and enactment of the "means of grace," namely the word and sacraments to which God has attached his unconditional promise of salvation. "For through the Word and the sacraments, as through instruments, the Holy Spirit is given; and the Holy Spirit produces faith, where and when it pleases God, in those who hear the gospel" (Article 5 of the *Augsburg Confession*).[86] The Holy Spirit is given through both word and sacraments which "awaken and confirm faith in those who use them" (Article 13).[87]

Lutherans insist upon a christocentric doctrine of the Holy Spirit: it is linked to the word and sacraments as the embodiment of the gospel about the risen Lord. One is baptized into the death of Christ, by which comes forgiveness; one speaks and hears the story of the Jesus of Israel as salvific good news; and one participates in the real presence of Christ in the Lord's Supper. The Holy Spirit grants faith when the gospel is so enacted.

---

86. BC, p. 31.
87. Ibid., p. 35.

There has always been a Lutheran debate about sacramental gospel-communication. What needs to be done so that the gospel is really enacted? How is verbalization related to such enactment? The history of Lutheranism discloses a preference for preaching and a denigration of sacramental celebration. Especially since the philosophical Enlightenment and the eighteenth century theological Pietism, Lutheran liturgy has tended to stress the word more than the sacraments, the individual more than the community. Eucharistic liturgy has suffered from reductions to bare minimum, while the services of the word have enjoyed expansion. Verbal utterances must, no doubt, retain a certain primacy in sacramental enactments, since the sacraments must also say something specific about the gospel. Washing a baby in silence, or sharing a meal without words, are not enactments of the gospel at all. "The word comes to the element; and so there is a sacrament, that is, a visible word" (Augustine).[88] Baptism and the Lord's Supper consist of specific words and actions to which God's promise of salvation are attached. Lutherans insist they must be performed as "instituted" by the historical Jesus; to be faithful means to be obedient to the instituted mandates. But here is the rub. Why preach a particular version of the gospel when there are others — for example, Paul's justification by faith, or James' justification by works? Why baptize infants, when there is no explicit mandate to do so in the New Testament? What are the precise features of the eucharistic meal, when New Testament scholars are unable to agree on them? Who is to be admitted to the Lord's Supper? Only those who have a basic understand-

---

88. Ibid., p. 212, n. 5.

ing? The mentally retarded? Persons who doubt the resurrection of Jesus, or even betray him, like Judas, who was at the Last Supper? When is the gospel communicated "purely" and when are the sacraments administered "rightly," as mandated by Article 7 of the *Augsburg Confession*?[89]

Although these are enduring questions demanding constant discernment of what is pure and right in the ministry of word and sacraments, the answers to them depend more upon practice than on doctrine, for the liturgy of sacraments communicates more by what is done than by what is said — even though verbalization is an integral part of the liturgy.

Lutheran liturgical renewal in recent years has attempted "to restore to Holy Baptism the liturgical rank and dignity implied by Lutheran theology," according to which a new and never-ending life in Christ is begun through the power of the Holy Spirit in the fellowship of the church.[90] Recent theological discussions of baptism, especially of infant baptism, have centered on the questions of origins and of contemporary meaning in a culture which is no longer Christian. Jürgen Moltmann goes as far as to call for a moratorium on infant baptism, in view of the gross misunderstandings of Christian life in German and other state churches.[91] If baptism is to

---

89. Ibid., p. 32.

90. See *Lutheran Book of Worship*, 1978, Introduction, p. 8 and pp. 124, 125: the baptized is told, "You have been sealed by the Holy Spirit" and "We receive you as fellow member of the body of Christ." Luther's *Small Catechism* calls baptism "a washing of regeneration in the Holy Spirit." BC, p. 349:10.

91. Jürgen Moltmann, *The Church in the Power of the Spirit*, tr. Margaret Kohl (New York: Harper & Row, 1977), pp. 240-241.

be the liberating event proclaimed and celebrated in the liturgical washing, much careful catechetical instruction is needed in contemporary Lutheran churches which are increasingly threatened by an illiteracy regarding faith. If there is a similarity between the bloody persecution of early Christians and the bloodless illiteracy of contemporary churches, then the rite of infant baptism may have to be tied to rigorous catechetical instruction to parents who, as baptized "common priests," are to exercise their vocation as Christian teachers to their children.[92] Baptism, in contrast to the Lord's Supper, is the initiation of a person into the Christian assembly which promises to love, nurture and protect the new member. If the new member is an infant, then nurture is one of the most important tasks, since it should lead to the adult reaffirmation of baptism on the part of the nurtured member. Thus the mandate to baptize is linked to the promise of life in Christ through the power of the Holy Spirit, whose instruments are word and sacraments. The practice of infant baptism, therefore, raises the question of infant communion — whether a baptized infant should be nurtured by both the "audible," and "visible" words in the ecclesiastical family as well as in the biological one.

The Lord's Supper differs from baptism in that it is the center of the Christian *communal* life. It is "given as a daily food and sustenance so that our faith may refresh and strengthen itself and not weaken in the struggle, but grow continually stronger."[93] The Lord's Supper is the meal of the baptized, who recall Christ's Last Supper, receive strength from his presence in the celebra-

---

92. This is a proposal by Jenson, *Visible Words*, p. 168.

93. Luther in the *Large Catechism* V, 24 BC, p. 449.

tion of the meal, and look forward to Christ's final return. Memorial, support for the struggles with the world, and joyful anticipation are the basic eucharistic features expressed in the liturgy. Should some of the baptized be excluded from the Lord's Supper? Jürgen Moltmann sketches the dilemma caused by "open" versus "closed" communion:

> The question of "admission" to the meal becomes burdensome. Confession and absolution often precede the Lord's Supper, so that the open prevenient invitation of Christ is linked to legalistic injunctions and moral conditions for "admission." Christ's original feast of joy is then unfortunately transformed into a meal of repentance where people beat their breasts and gnash their teeth.
>
> It is therefore no wonder that many people excommunicate themselves from this meal; and even serious Christians experience an unholy dread before the Lord's Supper. This moral legalism spoils the evangelical character of the meal just as much as dogmatic legalism does. *We should therefore start from the Lord's Supper as something done together and openly, and try to explain the moral questions on the basis of this action and fellowship.*[94]

When Lutheran theologians speak of baptism as "the sacrament of prevenient grace" and of the Lord's Supper as "the sustaining sacrament,"[95] they need to rethink

---

94. Op. cit., p. 245. Italics mine.
95. 1972 LCA Convention, Minutes, p. 195.

the relationship between initiation and sustenance. How are the initiated to be sustained? If baptism grants whatever the church is and has, as Lutheran sacramentology asserts, why should baptized members be excluded from the Lord's Supper? This is not a question of "sacramental magic" or of a rivalry between word and sacrament regressing to a notion of "infused grace." Rather, it is a question of the proper distinction between baptism and the Lord's Supper within the context of Christian nurture — the nurture through word *and* sacrament.[96]

---

96. Consideration could be given to the move from "natural to sacramental pedagogy," that is, to a more balanced relationship between catechetics and worship in family life in the church. For a more detailed argument in favor of such a move see Robert W. Jenson, "The Return to Baptism," *The Martin Luther Colloquium 1978*, Institute for Luther Studies, Lutheran Theological Seminary at Gettysburg, *Bulletin* LIX (Winter 1979), pp. 31-39.

Conclusion

Reflection about the way in which admission to the Lord's Supper regardless of age has emerged as an issue in Lutheran churches warrants the conjecture that there is a real need to clarify the relationship between past Lutheran practices and present ecumenical challenges. When we encounter the basic thrust of the Lutheran reform movement in the sixteenth century, we become well aware of the fact that it was a movement geared to the reform of the church catholic rather than to self-preservation. In the Preface to the *Augsburg Confession*, Melanchthon declared, "We on our part shall not omit doing anything, insofar as God and conscience allow, that may serve the cause of Christian unity."[97] Although Luther had a healthy respect for medieval anthropology (in the form of scholastic research of the vicissitudes of the human soul), he was never really bound to a tradition which viewed the sacraments from the viewpoint of human disposition. When he did adhere to existing folk-piety, he did so with the confidence that faithful pastoral work, under the freedom of

---

97. *Augsburg Confession,* Preface, 13. BC, p. 26.

the gospel, would yield an openness to the universality of the Christian faith.

Standard Lutheran theological reasons for excluding anyone from the Lord's Supper on the basis of age are often burdened by folk-piety, entrenched anti-ecumenical school opinions, and a lack of pastoral concern. One can always argue that infant baptism is "complete," and does not need an additional "initiation process," but one should not therefore conclude that "infant communion is precluded." Such a conclusion creates the impression that the practice is an abuse rather than an appropriate method of gospelling. Biblical, theological, liturgical and ecumenical insights support the thesis that infant baptism and infant communion are both "adiaphora," the witnessing powers of which are to be determined by Christian gatherings in particular places and at particular times.

It would be wise to leave the question of infant or family communion open. Let the decision concerning first communion be a communal, congregational decision — including the decision to have or not to have infant communion. Pastors, congregations and parents can make decisions and provisions for infants to be baptized and communed in order to bear witness to the fact that new members of the church are full participants in the public celebration of word and sacraments. After all, local congregations are still the frontiers of the gospel in our time, and delicate decisions concerning the life of the gospel on the frontier of the church are better made there. In our time, the cost of discipleship may be more important than the price of uniformity. Infant communion could be liturgically initiated at the time of baptism, which may take place in the context of the service of word and sacrament. When the smaller gathering of parents and sponsors moves from the font to the altar, the pastor may commune the infant/child (using a spoon for intincted elements or another method) either alone or together with parents and/or sponsors ("family communion"). This procedure would clearly indicate that the newest member of the congregation has been received into full membership in the church, with the clear promise, made by pastor, parents and congregation, that the nurture through sacrament and word will lead to the public "reaffirmation of baptism" at the member's appropriate adult cognitive level. Although first communion at the time of baptism is the most prevalent ecumenical tradition in the church, some pastoral reasons may dictate a minimal separation between baptism and communion; yet God's unconditional grace in baptism and the congregation's caring initiation of the new member into the Eucharistic fellowship should not be unduly separated. It is the "visible" words of baptism and the Lord's Supper together with the "audible" word that constitutes the church as Christ's body on earth.

Biography

Eric W. Gritsch was born April 19, 1931, in Neuhaus, Austria, in the southern Burgenland near the Hungarian border. His father came from an old German Saxon family settled in Harkau in western Hungary at the Austrian border. Before 1918, both regions were united in the Hapsburg Empire. His father spoke German and was graduated from the Lutheran Theological Faculty in nearby Sopron, Hungary. His mother came from Neckenmarkt, Austria (a town in northeastern Burgenland near Sopron). One year later, the family moved north to Bernstein in the center of the Burgenland. A majority of the inhabitants were Lutherans, the rest were Roman Catholics who dominate Austria (94%). There was a gypsy camp of about a hundred families outside the town. The town and the camp became Eric's playground, enjoying the privileges of a PK ("pastor's kid"). Educated in the local elementary school and in the neighboring well-known Oberschützen "Gymnasium" (high school-college), he graduated in 1950 with the "Matura" certificate (B.A. equivalent). In 1944/45 the school was closed because of the war. At age ten Eric was drafted into the Hitler Youth. In the same year, 1941, his father, who refused to support the new regime in Austria (annexation to Nazi Germany in 1938), was drafted into the army. He never returned home and died in 1945 as a prisoner of war in Russia.

In the final years of the war, Eric was drafted into an army unit known as "Werewolves" because they were to become a guerilla force behind enemy lines. In April of 1945, Eric escaped from his unit at the front, not far away from Bernstein, before the Russian army attacked. He was captured by Russian soldiers, posed as a gypsy and stayed with a Russian tank crew until law and order was restored in the fall of 1945. In 1948, Eric's mother married the new pastor in Bernstein. Her only other child, Günther, seven years younger stayed home while Eric branched out on his own, earning enough money to survive as a student with free tuition. Until Austria was declared neutral in 1955, Russian, French, British and American armed forces occupied the country. Bernstein was in the Russian zone.

Eric continued his education at the Lutheran/Reformed Theological Faculty of Vienna in 1950 concluding with the Cand. Theol. Degree (B.D. equivalent) in 1956. He spent the time of school vacations hitch-hiking to various parts in Europe, including work camps sponsored by American Quakers and other religious groups who assisted in rebuilding post-war Germany. He received scholarships for study at the universities of Zurich(1952), Basel (1952/53) and Yale (1954/55, Fulbright-Smith-Mundt Scholarship, STM 1955, MA 1958, Ph.D. 1960). His "doctor father" was Roland H. Bainton who shepherded him through a dissertation, "The Authority of the Inner Word. A Theological Study of Major German Radical Reformers of the Sixteenth Century."

Eric served as a "Vicar" in a large congregation of Bruck/Mur in central Austria near Graz (1956/57). In 1962 he became an American citizen and was ordained in the United Lutheran Church of America (ULCA). He taught at Wellesley College (1959-61); Gettysburg Lutheran Seminary (1961-94) where he also directed its Institute for Luther Studies (1970-1994); the Melanchthon Institute, Houston, TX (1995-2005, with interruptions) where he was honored with the Dr. Eric W. Gritsch Chair of Theology; the Catholic University of America (1997); California Lutheran University (1998); the Ecumenical Institute of St. Mary's Seminary and University in Baltimore (part-time faculty, 1995-2005). He spent a sabbatical leave as Interim Pastor in Fairfield, PA (1990-91) and in Baltimore (1999-2000).

He was married to Ruth Sandman (1954-1994) and then Bonnie Brobst (1995-) and had three foster daughters (ages 15-18) in the 1970s. He was a delegated participant in the North American Lutheran-Catholic Dialogue (1971-92) and principal lecturer at the International Congress for Luther Research in Lund (1977), Oslo (1988). He gave many lectures and workshops in parishes, synods and in the church at large. He served as board member at the Ecumenical Institute, Strasbourg, France (1992-2004), at the Ordass Foundation in Oslo and Budapest (1986-98) and at the Ecumenical Institute, Baltimore (2005-).

Eric had an "open house" every Monday evening in his large faculty home on Seminary Ridge. He was active in the civil rights and anti-Vietnam war movements of the 1960s and 70s. He was an opera fan, enjoyed cooking Hungarian Goulash and directed the Forum for German Culture in his home congregation, the German/American Zion (ELCA Lutheran) Church of the city of Baltimore.

HONORS

Fulbright-Smith-Mundt Scholar (Yale University, 1954-55). Director, Institute for Luther Studies, Gettysburg Lutheran Seminary (1970-1994). Principal Lecturer at the International Congress for Luther Research (Lund, Sweden, 1977; Oslo Norway, 1988; Seminar Leader, Heidelberg, 1997). Lecturer (with Marc H. Tanenbaum) on Jewish-Lutheran Relations (New York, 1983). First Bainton Lecturer (Yale Divinity School, 1988). Lecturer at Catholic University, Lutheran Theological Faculty, Luther Society (Budapest, 1999), University of Copenhagen (2002). Delegated Participant in the US Lutheran-Catholic Dialogue (1971-92). National Catholic Workshop on Christians and Jews (Seminar Leader, Houston, 1999). Board of Directors, Ecumenical Institute of the Lutheran World Federation (Strasbourg, France, 1992-2004); and on Ordass Foundation (Oslo, Budapest, 1986-98). Dr. Eric W. Gritsch Chair of Theology (Melanchthon Institute, Houston, 2000).

PUBLICATIONS

24 books: authored 10, co-authored 1, edited 9, translated 4. Popular: *Lutheranism* (with Robert Jenson), 1976. *Martin: God's Court Jester*, 1983. *Fortress Introduction to Lutheranism*, 1994 (Hungarian edition, 2000). *A History of Lutheranism*, 2002. *A Handbook for Christian Life in the 21st Century*, 2005. *The Wit of Martin Luther*, 2006. *The Boy from the Burgenland: From Hitler Youth to Seminary Professor* (I: A Memoir. II: Literary Legacy), 2006. As well as numerous essays, reviews and audio-visuals in professional journals and church centers.

About the Editor

Lawrence R. Recla, STS

Pr. Recla serves as the Dean of the Florida Chapter of the Society of the Holy Trinity *(Societas Trinitatis Sanctae)*. He began his relationship with Dr. Gritsch as a first year student at Gettysburg Seminary in 1965. Dr. Gritsch did a presentation at every parish Pr. Recla served: Columbia, PA, Harrisburg, PA, Colorado Springs, CO, Brigham City, UT, Queens, NY and as teaching theologian at an STS Chapter Retreat in Florida. Eric was also the celebrant at Larry and Sherry's Nuptial Mass.

51015037R00043

Made in the USA
Charleston, SC
12 January 2016

THE
RUGGED
ROAD TO
FREEDOM

A Prayer Process for Change

JOY BREWSTER

CLEMENTS PUBLISHING
Toronto, Ontario

Published 2006 by Clements Publishing
6021 Yonge St., Box 213, Toronto, ON M2M 3W2 Canada
Website: www.clementspublishing.com
E-mail: info@clementspublishing.com

Unless otherwise noted, Scripture quotations are taken from
the New Internation Version of the Bible,
copyright © 1973, 1978 by the International Bible Society.
Used by permission of Zondervan Publishers

Quotations from Oswald Chambers are taken from *My Utmost
for His Highest* by Oswald Chambers, ©1935 by Dodd Mead &
Co., renewed © 1963 by Oswald Chambers Publications Assn.,
Ltd. Used by permission of Discovery House Publishers,
Grand Rapids, MI 49501. All rights reserved.

Cover design and layout by Greg Devitt Design
<www.gdevitt.com>

Library and Archives Canada Cataloguing in Publication

Brewster, Joy, 1932-
The rugged road to freedom : a prayer process for change
/ Joy Brewster.

Includes bibliographical references.
ISBN 1-894667-72-7

1. Christian life. 2. Habit breaking—Religious aspects—
Christianity. 3. Prayer—Christianity. I. Title.

BV4501.3.B748 2006   248.4   C2006-902229-1

Do not conform any longer to the pattern of this world, but be transformed by the renewing of your mind. Then you will be able to test and approve what God's will is--his good, pleasing, and perfect will.

(Romans 12:2)

Now the Lord is the Spirit, and where the Spirit of the Lord is, there is freedom. And we, who with unveiled faces all reflect the Lord's glory, are being transformed into his likeness with ever-increasing glory, which comes from the Lord who is the Spirit.

(2 Corinthians 3:17,18)

We demolish arguments and every pretension that sets itself up against the knowledge of God, and we take every thought captive to make it obedient to Christ.

(2 Corinthians 10:5)

CONTENTS

ACKNOWLEDGEMENTS AND DEDICATION

I am hard pressed to remember all those who have been so helpful to me in the writing of this book. I first wish to thank all those clients I worked with as a counselor who helped me by being there so that I developed and utilized this process. I do also thank all those in my church, New Life Community Baptist Church of Duncan, British Columbia, who took the course based on this book, and who responded to its contents and thereby furnished me with many of the examples I subsequently added, as well as encouraged me.

My pastor's wife, Cheryl Buchanan, encouraged me tremendously in her response and utilization of the concepts this book develops. The same is true for another pastor in our church, Carol Boschma. Thanks also to those who have studied and employed these concepts in their lay counseling and prayer mentoring, especially Laura Miller and Colleen Sumner. Their excitement in using this prayer process was very encouraging to me. These four as well as many others must be thanked as well for their sustaining prayers in my behalf.

Special thanks to Ann Anderson who read and edited my early efforts and made splendid suggestions. I cannot fully express my gratitude to Anna Beketov who not only took the course offered, but offered to edit the manuscript, and combed over it with me time and time again to make necessary corrections and refinements. Bless you a hundredfold, Anna! Thanks again to the Prayer Counseling Team for the final work on editing and revisions. I especially thank Rob Filgate for great advice and wonderful editing, and Allan Kinnee for all his computer wizardry and ready help.

It is also impossible to sufficiently thank my pastor, Mark Buchanan, for all his encouragement, and especially for his efforts in my behalf in finding ways to give this manuscript an opportunity to be published. He is, after all, my favorite author. Mark, you are my champion.

To our church secretary, Loni Searl—you are a jewel. Your assistance in the preparation of the manuals that the classes used and your help in getting the book in manuscript form were invaluable.

A huge thank you, my dear husband George, for all the hours you spent reading and praising and encouraging me. Thank you for fielding without complaint the sound-boarding I did from time to time. It was more helpful than I can say.

More than all, thank you, Lord God, for all the ways in which you moved in me to actually get the words on paper. It was your assignment from first to last, and I felt your joy as I engaged in it. I praise you.

I dedicate this book to all those who have already responded to this prayer process and are employing it in their daily walk with the Lord.

PART I

BEGINNINGS

Through the Valley of the Shadow

ALL MY ADULT LIFE, I have loved mountains. I couldn't say why, having been brought up on the plains of Texas near Dallas. But when I first saw the mountains in my teens in Colorado and hiked in them, a love affair began. I desired to hike in every mountain range in the United States. Only one or two are left; my knees refuse.

When I was in my fifties, I went on an extended hike out of Sequoia National Park in the Sierras of California with three other avid and younger women. I trained for the hike for weeks. When the day of departure arrived, I was ready.

We checked in with the ranger, shouldered our packs, took our pictures, and moved out through those giant trees. Our steps were vigorous and sure. Then what a mixture of arduous effort and extravagant delight we experienced. What blue skies, what awesome trees, how fresh the mountain streams and waterfalls, what flowers, what bends in the trail that promised and delivered magnificent views and vistas.

As we went we had to put aside again and again our desire to just quit and be spared the trials. We weren't used to this entirely different way of living. Our muscles ached as we scrambled over rocks, sank in mud pools, avoided the tangle of obstructing branches and fallen limbs. Our lungs begged for breaks as we pressed forward and upward. Our minds questioned the pay-off for all this effort.

We did stop from time to time to drink from the pure water that gushed over rocks and into our waiting cups. Treasures of the trail insisted we stop to admire—to relish flowers, to admire views, to rest into overwhelming beauty.

Back to the hard work of climbing. Our destination was a peak that towered over ten thousand feet and gave us a panoramic view of range upon range, as far as the eye could see. I personally had to take it very slowly on the last stretch because of my tendency to altitude sickness. But I made it! To be sure, the climb each day was arduous. Each produced exhaustion, sore muscles, mosquito bites, dry skin, sweat and strain. Was it worth it? A thousand-fold! My memories flood my mind at this moment, filled with delights.

I believe the Christian life is like my hike in the mountains, a step by step adventure with our great God, an arduous rugged road that is filled with challenges and with delights. But many changes will need to be made in your life and mine before we are truly effective climbers. You, as a Christian, are on a new trail. You will need to throw off old habits of living, and learn from the Holy Spirit, your guide, teacher, and your encourager, the new ways of climbing. Both the climb and the destination will be sources of great delight. The greatest delight, though, will be the One who is your constant companion, Jesus Christ Himself.

I believe the daily life of the Christian is of immense importance to God, and that He intends to use every day of my life to teach me how to become more and more conformed to the image of Jesus Christ. This is true of you too if you are a Christian. We have entered this climb by His invitation and now as we climb with Him, we will be learning continual changes from our old way of life to God's way.

I'd like to present a prayer process I believe the Lord gave me. I came to use it in my own life and in my counseling practice with clients (I was a professional counselor for eighteen years, and still counsel on a volunteer basis). It has proved to be very effective in learning to change. It has brought me into this growth and increasing freedom in my Christian life and most importantly into a much closer walk with Jesus Christ. I think it has brought others into the same fellowship.

How did this come to be?

Let me begin by telling you a true story. It's about a young woman named Jodi. She was a freshman in a Christian college, struggling to stay focused on her studies and at the same time to deal with her yearnings to have fun, to be noticed, to be asked for a date. And she was. As the year progressed one of the young men who most attracted her was the lab assistant in her geology class. He was helpful but with a flair—the clever quip, the charming smile, the sheer affability, and his obvious interest in her were magnetic. He was a junior, a member of the varsity football team, captain of the wrestling team, a big dog on campus. What would a popular guy like Greg see in a Podunk Center girl like her, she wondered.

But there was surely something he liked; he asked her for a date—and kept asking. They had great fun together, and talked freely about anything and everything, especially hopes and dreams. By the end of the year, they were not only deeply in love but talking marriage. That summer he visited her at her home, met her family, and bought her an engagement ring. It would be a long engagement, for he planned to go to seminary after graduation and believed they should wait to marry until she finished college.

They almost made it. But the separation proved too much to bear, so she transferred to a university near his seminary, and they married at the end of her junior year. The first year might have been difficult (both were still hard at it with studies). But it wasn't. They carved out time to laugh and play and decorate their dismal dwellings with thrift store finds, bricks and boards and paint, and prints of great art. They listened to music, enjoyed outings with friends, found a good church, and grew together in their faith and worship.

Each summer Greg worked long hours painting houses while Jodi took any summer clerk's job she could get. When she graduated, she was hired by the city school system to teach junior high English. Money worries eased a bit. Life was good, the future clear.

Their second summer changed everything. Greg woke her one hot night to announce that he was being led by God to be a medical missionary! Jodi was astounded. She could only listen in wonder, and then hold in herself her disappointment that this would mean so much more time for Greg in school, and according to his wishes, the delay of starting a family. Following seminary, he would have to return to get pre-medical courses before he could enter medical school. Then four years of medical school, internship, and possibly residency as well. It boggled the mind.

But she diligently sought the Lord, and accepted that this was His will, and adjusted her thinking accordingly. She continued teaching in one school or another the entire time Greg took pre-med and then medical school courses. They had moved to Cleveland, Ohio, so that Greg could take all his course work at Western Reserve University, and the first three years had been a difficult but stimulating adventure. Christian friendships and church fellowship sustained them. Then the summer following his sophomore year at med school, Greg began to be strangely distant. He was cordial, but would not draw close; he showed little interest in their intimate relationship. He dropped church and Christian friends. Jodi was hurt and puzzled and, as was her way, rendered silent and afraid.

An entire series of traumas began as well. Jodi was accosted one evening as she walked the long block home from the bus to their apartment on the edge of a very rough neighborhood. Her assailant dragged her behind a dark apartment building and began to tear off his clothes and hers. He squeezed her throat. Then he stopped when he heard a noise. Jodi made an immense effort to scream, first mere whimpering, but finally a terrified shriek. Her attacker didn't return. Inhabitants of the apartment building appeared. She was rescued. But now her continuing fears and nightmares began.

A short time later she noticed the lump on her throat. She immediately began to assume she had cancer. Biopsies were not yet a possibility. She could have exploratory surgery or undergo months of testing to see if the tumor enlarged. Greg chose the latter, explaining it would be more convenient to him if she waited until summer to have the surgery. Her fears ran rampant.

A few months later, their apartment was robbed, their few items of value and a small store of cash gone. Her terror mounted; she was glad each day to flee to her job and forget the horrors of a dying love, a fear-filled home, a dread of the future. She was encased in anxiety, paralyzed, a zombie except at work. God seemed far away and silent. She felt completely alone and vulnerable.

Then came that balmy spring night of his announcement, "I have to tell you I have completely lost my Christian faith. I am now an agnostic. This won't change anything for you, because I'm sure you'll choose to keep on believing all the myths. But you need to know it will change a lot for me. I intend now to exercise my freedom to do a lot of the things I've always wanted to do, but Christian rules held me back. They won't now. You don't talk to anyone about this or I'll make you sorry you did." With that he walked out the door. Torrents of grief swept her, for she *KNEW* this was the beginning of the end, as indeed it was. Yet she was immobilized; she needed her tumor to be removed, so she pledged to stay until the end of the school year. The operation was scheduled for June.

Though they moved to what Greg considered a safer location, she felt no safer.

He left her with a gun, while he went his way, doing as he pleased, often being out the entire night without a word of explanation. He hardly spoke to her, and she was afraid to speak to him, for when she did he often derided her, sarcastically lampooning her weak intellect. "But don't even think of leaving me. We'll divorce after I finish medical school. I can't afford to now—it would hurt my reputation. So keep your mouth SHUT!" Scathing words.

He never touched her with affection. He never touched her at all.

Now her depression grew in measure along with her fear. She felt incredibly desperate. Finally, she asked her mother to come to be with her when the surgery was performed. She asked too that she might then spend the summer at her parents' home. Greg offered no comment. His indifference was all too clear.

June finally came and the long awaited surgery on her throat. The tumor was removed and pronounced benign, but a different cancer was draining her life. She went to her parents' home.

Greg wrote one small note to her the entire summer, claiming incredible busyness. No phone calls—nothing. Her loving parents were there for her but asked few questions, sensing her distressed condition.

Jodi rested and prayed and resolved to seek courage to confront him. At the end of the summer she returned to the apartment. But on entering it, she found every evidence of her had been removed, and she *knew* he had been living there with another woman. It was the absolute breaking point. Her anger finally rose. She unleashed a torrent of rage, pouring out accusations, questions, recriminations and demanding he leave or she would. He admitted nothing, but agreed to go. He again threatened her, telling her to say nothing to anyone, gathered a few things, and strode out the door, slamming it harshly. She sank to the sofa and began the deep crying she thought would never stop. She lapsed into deep depression, stunned and alone, and remained that way for a month.

She returned to teaching. October came, but its beauty did not lift her despair.

In desperation she dared calling another young woman, Maggie, who attended her church. She was also a microbiology graduate student, attending many classes with the medical students, so she knew Greg fairly well. When Jodi asked for her help and poured out her story, Maggie listened, empathized, and began to befriend her and check on her almost daily.

A few days later Jodi walked into the teacher's lounge. It was buzzing as she entered, but then grew incredibly quiet. A fellow teacher walked toward her, took her arm and led her outside. "You haven't seen the morning papers, have you? It's all over the front pages of all three. Greg took a nurse out sailing last night. He says they went for a swim, went out too far, and she just disappeared. He says he called and called, dove and dove, trying to find her, but couldn't. He swears it was an accident, and no charges have been filed."

In shock, Jodi went to her principal and he sent her home. She cried all day, called Maggie, and went to special services at church with her that night. There she poured out her heart in agony to God and begged Him to salvage the situation, to bring Greg to his senses and to restore him to faith and fidelity. After the service she asked Maggie to take her to the house where Greg was living.

Maggie hesitated. Then she told Jodi the scuttlebutt around the med school: that Greg had gotten the nurse pregnant and had deliberately arranged the drowning to deal with the problem. Jodi was aghast, sincerely believing Greg incapable of such actions.

Greg was standing out on the sidewalk as they drove up. Tears streaming down her face, Jodi jumped out and ran to him, "Oh Greg, I'm so sorry about what has happened to you. I've been praying—"

Greg interrupted her curtly saying, "Jodi, I insist you get a divorce immediately. I have no grounds. You do. Everyone must know we've been separated. I've got to salvage my reputation, or my future is shot." This was a complete opposite of his previous demand for her silence. The irony of it smote her, adding incredible pain.

Although Jodi listened to Maggie's appeal to move in with her, she continued to pray and agonize over Greg, begging God to bring him back to faith and to their marriage. Yet she despaired and could muster little hope. One day in January, Greg appeared and again insisted she get the divorce or somehow he would. She realized the end had come. All hope died. She found a lawyer.

Divorce. For one who had promised, "Until death do us part." But surely death had, the death of a marriage. For Jodi it seemed worse than death, for she somehow had to go on living beyond it.

And she did—in torrents of grief, in the rise of incredible anger, in loss of faith in God, into bitter agnosticism and fruitless search for truth apart from Christianity. Into libertine ways and deep depression to the point of suicide. Into intense distrust of men, yet into relationship addiction, clinging to any one of them that offered a modicum of care for her. Into further failed relationships.

Into the valley of the shadow of death.

What could ever heal this severe wounding and self flagellation? It took many long years for her to find the complete answer. Her return to God was gradual, her understanding of His forgiveness slow and incomplete, her eventual shame completely overwhelming. And even when she was able to accept His love and a new beginning, *horrible patterns and habits of behavior remained to trouble her.*

I know. This is my story.

There were layers and layers of hurt, anger, and guilt. There was my inability to forgive others and myself. It took several years of further hurt and pain and alienation from God, before I returned to Him, finally in full commitment, and with more filling of the Spirit than I had ever known.

I learned to walk in intimacy with Him. He challenged me to forgive. I describe this process more fully in the chapter on Release. As I tell there, this process took years. But at length, I had poured out my woe to Him, released it to the cross, and forgiven every single offender and transgressor every single thing the Lord brought to my mind. The hardest to forgive was myself in that I had so misunderstood and accused God, and thus betrayed Him and wounded myself so badly. But I persisted until all had been removed.

But I didn't go far enough. I didn't realize that I had not dealt with all the habits and patterns of underlying thought and behavior that had led to my relationship addiction. They were still there. They had not been addressed nor removed, nor the true way learned to *replace* them. I did not sufficiently invite the Lord's scrutiny day by day as Psalm 139:23 and 24 reveals. In my pride I thought I knew enough and had done enough. I did not give God the opportunity to do a thorough cleaning of all my sinful habits and patterns. What a different story I would be telling if I had allowed Him to continue His Put Off/Put On process with me.

Instead, after having drawn so close to God again, I became disappointed in Him because all my following after Him had not removed the trials and struggles of my life. I had thought that was *the deal*; I'd be the good girl and He would produce happiness ever after. He didn't. My faith again weakened by degrees.

At length I wandered away again and began to look in other directions for help. My pride blocked my seeing four incredibly important facts about God:

1. He *never* barters or makes deals.
2. He does not leave a *vacuum*. When He takes away a sinful habit, thought, attitude, behavior, He replaces it with Himself and His ways. I walk out of the old and into the new. When I Put Off I must also then Put On.
3. There is *no other way* to become healed and whole than by complete and continual surrender to Jesus Christ and by inviting the Holy Spirit to cleanse, to teach, guide, and to empower in accordance with the Scriptures He has written. And this must continue day by day for a lifetime!
4. All God does to this end is for His own glory, as well as, with His compassionate heart, for the well being and increasing holiness of His children. Therefore the motivation for change must be for the glory of God.

These four truths cannot be applied without the filling and enabling of the Holy Spirit. I have found no lasting and sufficient change from adherence to any other teaching, technique, philosophy, or set of principles. I personally had to learn to let the Trinity love me until my old ways died before I found the way of full life.

I have met many, many Christians with wrong thinking similar to what I had whose faith in God has been greatly weakened or has disappeared. They are living in great pain. For them the Christian life is anything *but* abundant life. Many have troubled marriages, relationship difficulties, and severely incomplete joy and freedom in Christ. Is there hope for insight, repentance and healing? Both from Scripture and my own experience I say yes. And I sincerely feel the call of God both to warn and to enlighten in these respects.

Let me enlarge a bit on my story after my second departure from God. In my own search for answers, I personally turned to psychology, believing there was something I had surely missed in my master's level studies in the field of guidance and counseling in the early sixties. Then in the eighties (and I in my fifties), I entered a program of studies and internship leading to obtaining certification as a Marriage, Family, Child Counselor for the State of California. I learned a great deal in those years. I came to understand far more fully how very many ways human nature can go wrong in relationships and why. I learned much in classes and through wide and extensive reading, and I found the knowledge indeed helpful to an understanding of myself and others. But I found little to help me in my own efforts to set things right in the way I lived out my life. Effective ways to change were presented, but the *power* to change was missing.

I was able to identify clearly my relationship addictions and the patterns involved. That was very helpful to me to see and understand. I grasped the poisoned thinking that had betrayed me again and again into the same patterns and behaviors. I exerted great effort with these insights to make changes. I really tried. Yet the secular thinking and techniques I tried gave only minimal help and not permanent change. I slipped again and again back into the same bondage. Was I just a weak person? Was there no hope, no help anywhere? Was there no power strong enough to enable the changes I needed? In my desperation I prayed to God to rescue me. I was again in a pit of despair and faced the truth that only He could draw me out.

Finally, I had an amazing insight, and I do not remember how or why it came. This question came to my mind: who related to people better than anyone who ever walked the earth? The answer came swiftly—Jesus Christ. Surely He could show me the way out.

Jesus, of course. How fully my pride had obstructed me. But now fear came to replace pride.

Had I, after all my failures and sinfulness, the right to pray? I now felt abjectly overwhelmed by shame and guilt. I prostrated myself before God and sought His forgiveness afresh. The Holy Spirit speaking through the Scriptures instructed me that God gives total and full forgiveness to the *repentant* heart.

I was still afraid. *Was I fully repentant?* Would I fall again? I also felt immense sorrow, and I almost drowned in an ocean of tears and regret. How greatly I lamented that I could never be one of the staunchly righteous followers of Christ. My record was forever tainted. I would never be one of the many who had never strayed for an entire lifetime, one of the stalwart faithful, well known or not, who had been utterly true to the Master, never a pure daughter of the King. My sins were manifold, my past years were forever marred. Was I disqualified permanently? Was I shelved? Held back from all further service to the Lord? Probably, I thought. So what's the use?

The Scriptures gave answers. I heard *Jesus* say clearly, as He had to Simon the Pharisee about the woman who had washed His feet with her tears, "...her many sins have been forgiven—for she loved much. But he who has been forgiven little loves little." And to her, "Your sins are forgiven" (Luke 8:47,48).

I realized that it delights Jesus, having purged all sin on His cross, to forgive the repentant. And at long last I was truly and fully that.

Short years were now left to me. I saw they must be years of total devotion, not trying to atone for my wrong, but because the Lord God was worthy of such righteous living. There simply and clearly was no other way. And so I began again to move with Him along the rugged road to reclamation and restoration.

On that road this is what the Spirit taught me: He would expose the stronghold patterns of my sin if I would acknowledge them and fully open myself to the truth about them that He would reveal to me. With each exposure I was to fully repent, let go, and then lay hold of the *replacement* for each one. This meant *every* thought, *every* emotion, *every* attitude, and *every* action, as He presented them to me, one by one. I was to listen to the mildest whisper of the Holy Spirit; I was to tune myself to His slightest prompting; I was to be acutely aware of His gentle nudge. I came to see then clearly that this was a long process He would bring me through. I knew I would be in this Put Off/Put On school for the rest of my life.

First I learned to become aware of the tempting thought or urge whenever it first occurred. I could depend on the Holy Spirit to show me this if I was open and not blocking Him, nor rationalizing when I wanted to follow the thought or urge. I learned instead to immediately seek God in prayer, to again surrender my life and all I am to Him, *to set my motivation to please His heart above all things.*

I further learned to release all my thought and feeling on the subject to Him so that He could give me insights regarding it. I could not hurry at this; I must do it fully as He enabled me. He would clearly show me what was true and what was not true. I could then immediately repent of the pattern of behavior I was contemplating (i.e., the sin), or in some cases had already engaged in, if only in thought.

I could fully release *all* into His cross, accept His forgiveness, and allow His fresh love to be poured out on me. I could stay in that place of intimacy and love with Him until I was filled with His love, filled with His Spirit, and ready to be instructed.

Next I found He led me to stay and listen very closely to His teaching and instruction. He would offer me the *replacement* in this put off/put on process. He would tell me quite specifically what to do instead of what I had previously been contemplating or had done.

He would not *make* me obey these instructions, but He would certainly be grieved and blocked if I did not.

When I did obey, how greatly we then, He and I, rejoiced together.

Every day, every hour, moment by moment, as I was willing, I learned to walk out my Christian life frequently engaging in this prayer process of putting off and putting on as He directed. There were small daily issues to deal with; there were also very deeply rooted habits that took long sessions with Him. I found I often needed to linger in one step of the process or another. I learned not to hurry Him, or second guess Him, but to walk it out in His pace until the full process was complete.

At this point in my life I had been counseling for several years, with limited success in my view, I might add, though I had a waiting list of clients. Now I began to use this same prayer process with all clients who were willing to engage in it. I saw a distinct difference for those willing to pray in this way. I offered them the insights the Lord gave me into their defeating patterns and habits and then led them to Him in prayer into the process that He had established with me. Session after session, as we spent our time in this way, I came to know the joy of watching Him bring each one into realms of freedom and joy and change that lasted.

I now *know* without a doubt that His love can forgive and heal you too. Whether your wounds, sins, and hurtful habits spring from childhood, from young adult years, from marriage strains, from parenting, from trials of the elderly—He can forgive and heal them all. And He will, if you will embrace *His* process and engage in it with Him. Let Him lead you. It may not be the process I am presenting. He guides each individually. And for some, there may be instantaneous deliverance. For most it is a process, and He will lead you through it.

In regard to child hurts, there is no love great enough to reach back in time and heal these wounds of omission and commission except the love of the Father God. This reparenting love alone can heal the heart of the child. The process I was taught brings the hurt one to the Father heart of God for healing. If you present yourself to Him, praying with the psalmist, "Search me, Oh God, and know my heart; test me and know my anxious thoughts. See if there is any offensive way in me, and lead me in the way everlasting" (Psalm 139:23, 24), He will. He will recall to you those moments when pain was inflicted, or when fear ran rampant, and He will come at that moment as you open to Him, to rescue, to heal with His love. He will then *reparent* you with His estimate of your worth and value to Him. He will express this to you in His words and ways of love. For you are His creation and ultimately belong to Him, the perfect parent. I will describe this process in greater detail later, but I would like to give hope at this point to those most severely hurt, by neglect, by abuse, and by devaluation.

When habits and the wounds are many, the process must continue for some time, as I have previously noted. If you find you are too distracted or busy to engage in the process in the moments of your days, I would invite you to set up a "Wonderful Counselor" session with Him every day, if possible, carving out the time and putting it as an appointment in your daytimer. Day by day, invite Him to search your heart, one habit at a time, one memory at a time. Move through the healing process with that one habit or memory, as described in these pages. Allow Him to begin where He will. If you trust Him, He will clearly bring to your thoughts the memory He chooses to begin healing.

Join with one or two others in praying, helping each other as you engage in this process. This serving one another in love is very dear to the heart of Jesus; three times during His last supper with His disciples He exhorted,

"Love one another." What better way to love one another than to join each other at God's throne for His work of transformation.

Seek Him also individually and with each other to remove and replace *any and all habits* formed by sin. It is the same process whatever the source of the habit. Yes, this takes time. This takes walking it out daily. This takes the rest of your life.

This process I believe He revealed to me and took me through (and still does). Is it really in line with Scripture? Let me ask you in answer to examine and meditate on the following:

> *You were taught with regard to your former way of life, to put off your old self, which is being corrupted by its deceitful desires; to be made new in the attitude of your minds; and to put on the new self, created to be like God in true righteousness and holiness.*

> *Therefore each of you must put off falsehood and speak truthfully to his neighbor, for we are members of one body.... He who has been stealing must steal no longer, but must work, doing something useful with his own hands, that he may have something to share with those in need.*

> *Do not let any unwholesome talk come out of your mouths, but only what is helpful for building others up according to their needs, that it may benefit those who listen....Get rid of all bitterness, rage and anger, brawling and slander, along with every form of malice. Be kind and compassionate to one another, forgiving each other, just as in Christ God forgave you.*

> *(Ephesians 4:22-32)*

> *Do not lie to each other, since you have **taken off** your old self with its practices and have **put on** the new self, which is being renewed in knowledge in the image of its Creator.*

> *(Colossians 3:9, 10, emphasis mine)*

14

Note the Put Off/Put On found in these verses.

Let me give you a fuller outline of the stages or steps He took me through in the prayer process. I want them to be as clear as possible. But this is no lock-step technique, no formula that I am describing. It is the way the Lord led me and still leads me, as I have said, and the way He has effectively worked with many of my counseling clients. So I offer it as a way to walk out the sanctification process in prayer. For "he who began a good work in you will carry it on to completion until the day of Christ Jesus" (Philippians 1:6). The most wonderful dividend is *fellowship* with this wonderful Lord, far more wonderful than the freedom itself.

PART II

OVERVIEW

*Surely you desire truth in the inner parts; you
teach me wisdom in the inmost place.*

Psalm 51:6

W HEN I ENGAGE in the kind of prayer I have just described, I usually experience six stages of praying with the Lord that accomplish the changes needed. The first three are on the *Put Off* side; the last three are on the *Put On* side. Each of the six is a way of meeting with the Lord, of receiving the work of the Holy Spirit in me, of knowing Him and loving Him. Also each fosters freedom in its own right, and a great deal has been written about each of them. I do not hope to explore these states or stages individually in book length depths. My desire is to see all six actually brought into the *daily* prayer life of the believer whenever an issue needs to be dealt with.

How the Lord uses these stages to bring us into His Put Off/Put On process is His own doing. Let me say again that He will not *always* proceed in the way I am describing. I am saying that I have found most of the people I have counseled by using the prayer process do move through these stages. But how long each lasts, how the Lord applies it, which He may skip—these are for Him to direct. Again I am not seeking to dictate a technique. I am looking at six realms of *prayer* for *believers*. I look at the process that *the Lord* takes us through in removing habits and adding His life in us.

Here, then, is a summary of the entire process, an overview. In the remaining chapters I will examine each stage separately to give a fuller explanation, field questions I've been asked, and illustrate application.

For my use I decided to label the six stages with words beginning with R. That may not be helpful to you, so feel free of course to label any way that fits for you, remembering that there are two halves—Put Off/Put On—and that there are three steps or stages for each of the halves.

REACH

The first stage I labeled *Reach*. Whatever my problem, I need first to realize my helplessness to do anything in my own strength, with my own wisdom, or with my own natural gifts or skills that will be *pleasing* to God. I will likely be only marginally successful as well. If *I* am successful, I will probably give all the credit and glory to *me*. But those who have given their lives over completely to Jesus Christ must live in His *Spirit* if they are to be pleasing to God. "Without me you can do nothing," Jesus said. Of course, I may do *something*, but what will it avail me, and how will it impress or please God? It will not. When I realize I am thinking, feeling, or living in such a way that does not draw on the Spirit, I must move into the realm of the spiritual. I must move into prayer. I must seek my God. I must set my motivation again to please Him and only Him. I must seek His solution to my problem for *His glory*. I must join Him in His life and not dictate how He must help me in mine.

To do this I think of the safest, most peaceful place I know. I go there if I can, although I may of course pray at any time and in any place. A safe and silent place will help you to focus on the Lord, so you may choose a favorite easy chair, your bed, your sofa, your backyard, or a place you can easily go to—the beach, a favorite spot by a river, a meadow overlooking the sea. You may even have a place in your imagination that you go to. That is, you "see" a favorite place that makes you feel safe and peaceful. I have a favorite chair; this is my "closet." Jesus has instructed us, when we pray, to enter our "closet" (Matthew 6:6, KJV) and shut the door. Choose for yourself a place of peace where there are no distractions, i.e. "closet". You may eventually have several as I do now, for prayer increases as the day unfolds. But begin with one place. In that haven realize that the Lord who is always with you is right there, now. Ask the Holy Spirit that you may sense His presence strongly.

RELEASE

The second stage is what I have termed *Release.* In this stage, I pour out to God all that is in my emotions/mind, choosing as I do so to let it all be turned over to Him so that He can give me His discernment. This is what David did so clearly in Psalm 142. I do as he did, I tell it out. As I do I begin to see the truth; if I do not, I ask the Lord to show me the truth as I review what I have told Him or journaled to Him.

I then see where sin lies in myself so that I can quickly confess it, put it on the cross, repent of it, and release it fully to God.

Emotions are given to us by God, and we are wise not to repress them. We need to allow them to be expressed fully, so that we *may* release them. When we do, we can then think clearly, and hear what God is saying in regard to their content and cause. Emotions are often mixed, and need sorting. They are often incredibly changeable, as we all know well; they are fickle and as unreliable in reporting truth as an imaginative five year old. But when a child is hurt or frightened or puffed up with pride, who can penetrate, understand, absorb, and comfort? Who can sort truth from exaggeration? Who can curtail hurtful vengeance? Parents are best. Therefore we as children of God must go to Him. To Him then we must practice releasing emotion lest we act as led by the feelings and do irreparable damage to ourselves and others.

What do I deal with in this Release stage? Worry, anger, fear, discouragement, depression, hopelessness, frustration, confusion, ineptness, failure, accusations of others, hurt and woundedness incurred from others, blame, wrong thinking, choices, temptations—the list goes on and on. Each aspect of each one I release to God. Whether it takes a moment or days and days, I pour out everything on the subject at hand to Him. If the sin is also in another, I see clearly where I must move into the hurt, pain, anger of having been sinned against, then release it to Jesus fully, and move into forgiving.

How very important it is to forgive. I release the sinner from the outcome of sin against me. I come to experience forgiveness of sin against myself. I release even what I consider unfair treatment by God. If I do not do so, I will become embittered and resentful, and often I will be consumed by the desire for revenge. Forgive I must. The Lord has commanded it. I must release the entire case into the hands of my advocate, Jesus Christ. I must release to Him all my feelings and thoughts in regard to it. He listens with complete understanding, assuring me that justice will be done. He will "try the case" and I will be content to let Him. I let go and leave it with Him. I may not forget, but I choose not to allow disrupting and revengeful feelings and thoughts to return. If they threaten, I remember I have released all into His hands, for He is advocate, judge, and jury and it is His to handle this case, not mine. It is His and because of His work on the cross He is the only One who can. I trust Him to do so, and do not question how He will proceed. Then I will listen clearly to His instructions as to how to bring about reconciliation if possible.

I find much in the Release stage that indicts me as well. I linger with Him to deal with confession of sin, repentance, cleansing, as well as my shame, guilt, and need of restoration.

For the Release stage, many find it helpful to journal their process. For simple issues this may not be necessary. I may need to engage in prayer processing many times a day. But for complex issues I often journal out my thoughts and feelings, not hurrying to get through, allowing the Spirit to fully examine all that is involved. However I proceed, I must proceed knowing that I intend to release *in order to* let go.

REST

Now I can enter *Rest.* That is the third stage. If I have released to the cross all that is involved, I must now stop. Period. It is done. If I sought to repent, I have done so. If I sought forgiveness, it has been administered. I must see God in a fresh way as the great, infinite, all-powerful, all-knowing God that He is, realizing He is the one who desires relationship with me. He has done all that was necessary to have it. Will I come? I must return to renewed fellowship with the great loving heart of my Father. I must renew intimate fellowship with my Jesus and His Spirit.

I must allow the Holy Spirit to bring me into the rest and peace that is required before I can *hear* what the Lord wants to tell me. What would He have me now think, believe, do? Before I am able to hear it, there is a big stop sign I need to read and heed: *stop* considering my solutions, my plan of action, my haste to solve the problem. Do I sincerely want God's will to be done? If so, I will need to get into this restful state in order to become aware of it. Ask it I may, but I must not pull on God or twist His arm. I must not insist He speak immediately. I must rest down with Him until all that is in me is still, at peace, and utterly receptive of His love and wisdom. Otherwise I will try to get Him to do my will. It will simply not work. He won't.

God's heart is delighted when His child comes to Him just for the loving. I need this loving more than I can possibly realize. Why do I deny Him that pleasure? And why do I deny myself that which is my deepest need? This resting down together is vital for Christian life. I will never thrive without it. There I will come to realize that He is more eager to show me "right paths for His name sake" than I am to know them. I must be at an end of my anxiety, my push and rush, my prideful sound reasoning, and my demands—in order to *listen.*

This rest brings me to the end of the *Put Off.* After the Rest stage, I am able to listen and hear what He would have me *Put On.* In this part of the process I again found three stages helpful.

RECEIVE

The next stage I have called *Receive*. I believe in the faithfulness of God to lead every seeker into right paths. Why would He who longs for us to put on right ways hesitate at all to tell us what they are? He doesn't. If I listen, longing to hear His heart, He will speak. What comes to mind as I listen? A verse of Scripture, a song, a line from a sermon, a picture, a word from a friend, a vision, an impression, a definite thought or thoughts—in these and others ways He speaks. All the ways in which He speaks are *ALWAYS* in accord with the Scriptures He has written, and with His character and nature. The outcome of what He asks is *always* godly.

He may tell me something very surprising, so I must not presume to think I already know what He will say. Sometimes He does not answer when I call because I am not ready to hear. If I have fully entered into the *Rest* stage and am now fully yielded and waiting, *He will speak.*

Now lest my enemy try to deceive me with his own messages (since Satan, we are told in Scripture, parades as an angel of light), it is obvious that I had better know my Lord and His words very well. This means I must remain diligent in taking in Scripture on a daily basis, so that when the Lord wishes to give me a message I will *know* it is from Him because it is marked indelibly with *His* character, *His* words, and *His* desired outcome. If I doubt the leading I receive is from the Lord, I ask trusted mentors and Christian friends to pray with me in regard to it, and to listen together with me for God's answer.

RESPOND

When I have heard clearly the Lord's instructions, I am ready for the next stage—*Respond*. How will I respond to what He has told me to do? Will I obey? This is crucial. I have learned not to respond with just a "yes, Lord," but to do exactly as He has instructed as soon as I possibly can. Sometimes I simply do not want to. It is hard, or humiliating, or seemingly beyond my skill. No matter. My motivation remains the pleasing of my God. Therefore, quick obedience is my only option. Sometimes His instructions seem to be going against common sense. Naturally. His instructions are for the realm of the spirit, and I will need to draw on all the power of the Holy Spirit to fulfill them. When I believe it is impossible, I ask Him to enable me to begin. Then I do.

Three mistakes present themselves to me every time: "I can't!" (never true since He never requests I do anything without giving me the power and know-how to do it if I will draw on the Holy Spirit). Or "Oh sure I can!" This is equally amiss, since the effort of my merely trying in my own strength will never please Him. Unity with Himself is always what does delight Him. The Apostle Paul has it right: "I can do all things through Christ who strengthens me"(Philippians 4:13). A third mistake is procrastination. This is usually a cover-up for simply not wanting to do what He has asked. Though I may have to forego obedience for a short time, I do as He has instructed as soon as I possibly can.

REJOICE

When I have obeyed, I need to take time to *Rejoice* with Him in having done so. That is the last stage in the prayer process of Put Off/Put On. How important it is to thank Him! How glad He is to celebrate and rejoice *with me* in my obedience.

A word of caution here: do not make the mistake of waiting to see what the outcome will be before you rejoice with Him. Leave the outcome to Him. You can rejoice and give thanks *again* if all goes well. The flip side is that sometimes it doesn't; He has given people free will and they may not respond as we would desire. Your joy is that you did as He asked. He wants to rejoice with you about that.

My tendency is to say, "O.K., that's done. What's next?" and to hurry on to the next thing without realizing the moments of celebration with Him that I am missing. When I realize my habit of hurry, I go back to the beginning of my Put Off/ Put On process. That hurried pace is definitely not His will for me.

Of course I may certainly have many moments of rejoicing throughout my day, and I do, not just at the end of a time of obedience. There is no curtailment on rejoicing. But that moment of completed obedience is certainly a prime occasion for it.

This overview has been just that, so I hope you will continue reading as I explore each stage of the process for deeper understanding. I end this section with some reminders.

As much as I desire freedom from hurtful and sinful habits, I know I must not make freedom alone my aim. If it is, no matter how much liberty from encumbering habits I obtain, it will not satisfy. My aim must be *to know the God of freedom*. The quality of relationship with Him is at stake.

If I am blocked from realizing the wonder and comfort of my Father God as His child, if I am unable to know and enjoy the intimacy and fellowship of Jesus, the Bridegroom, on my pilgrimage with Him, if I am unable to hear the voice and know the power of the Holy Spirit at work within me, guiding, quickening, instructing, correcting, restoring, enabling, manifesting the glory of the glorious God, I am indeed impoverished, regardless of my experience of freedom.

Our motive for seeking God needs first to be purified. It seems to me that we Christians today have adopted the habit of non-believers in focusing on the self. "I insist I have to be relieved of what is irritating or bothering me. It's my right. I shouldn't have to suffer. God should come and take this away. He says He loves me. Then let Him show me that love." This "God must serve me" mentality must be changed.

God indeed loves us and does want to relieve our pain. But *ease* is not the birthright of the children of God, for we see that all of the Lord's disciples, as well as Paul and many others, suffered greatly as His servants. *His life in us* is His desire, and that life is strengthened as He relieves us of habits and hurts that weaken and curtail. As He removes each one, He replaces it with His own life and character to be lived out through us.

It is this very freedom to enter in fully to the relationship with the triune God that we need desperately. Man craves nothing as much as genuine intimacy, and yet he fears it. How many have known even deep soul intimacy? How many have known true spiritual intimacy? How shall I know the fulfillment of Christ's words, "Now this is eternal life: that they may know you, the only true God, and Jesus Christ, whom you have sent" (John 17:3)? To have freedom to know *Him* in ever increasing measure is the prize.

PART III

PUT OFF

Reach, Release, Rest

CHAPTER ONE

REACH

Let us then approach the throne of grace with confidence, so that we may receive mercy and find grace to help in our time of need.

Hebrews 4:16

W E KNOW THAT the God who has come to indwell the believer delights in fellowship and communication. When I am in that continual state of at-oneness with Him, I delight in it too. But I'm often out of that state because of one old habit or another.

As I have previously stated, I have found I lack sufficient power to remove effectively almost any habit.

In the natural way of exerting myself, I seem to merely exchange one habit for another. No amount of self effort suffices. Will power doesn't persist. I may succeed for awhile, only to find I drift back into the same habit, or exchange it for a similar one. I may have stopped lashing out in anger toward my irritating son, only to find I now resort to sarcasm instead to punish him.

This is true in regard to the serious issues that are deeper and often hidden to me and on the spiritual scene as well. For instance, what do I do with my devious heart that longs so greatly for praise and commendation? I may congratulate myself that I no longer commend myself for all the Bible reading I have been doing; yet I now find I'm proclaiming how diligently I have prayed for that needy neighbor.

I read, "Do not be overcome by evil, but overcome evil with good" (Romans 12:21). I try, but don't often succeed, although I sincerely want to.

Also again, "You were taught, with regard to your former way of life, to put off your old self, which is being corrupted by its deceitful desires; to be made new in the attitude of your minds; and to put on the new self, created to be like God in true righteousness and holiness" (Ephesians 4:22-24). Good, good! I want to do that, but how can it be done?

Jesus provides the way: "I am the vine, you are the branches...apart from me you can do nothing" (John 15:5). Very obviously, the first step in the Put Off/Put On process is to reach to Him Who alone has the power to change me. It isn't just a step toward freedom, however. It is the life-blood of the Christian life. It is that which opens the powerful flow of the Vine through the branch.

Probably the most practical verse in the Bible for a Christian is I Thessalonians 5:17: "Pray without ceasing" (KJV). The NIV translates this verse: "pray continually." It is then a never ceasing reaching to God, calling on Him, talking with Him. But why the necessity to *reach* to Him? Isn't He always there? Of course He is. It is our *awareness* of His presence that is missing. I use the word *reach* to indicate that it is my responsibility to reconnect. I broke the connection; I must come back.

Jesus said that a man must be truly born again into a spiritual realm. It is not the realm we are used to, as we are the natural realm where we react continually to soul and body. It is beyond the realm of our intellect; it is not led by our emotions. It is a new dimension; it is *spiritual.* It is that place within me where my spirit is *inhabited* by His Spirit.

As I have previously told, I finally understood that God wasn't going to work through my natural life. He was bringing me into a *spiritual* realm. He wasn't going to come and *help me.* He had put *His life* in me and would draw on that. What did this mean?

After being broken of rebellion and agnosticism, after repentance and then restoration of my faith in God, I began to study the gospels afresh. I read them as if I were a member of Jesus' band of followers. I became, in my mind and imagination, a young disciple too, and watched Him, entered into the reactions of the disciples and the crowds, listened to Him teach, rode in the boat and nearly drowned until He stilled the water, watched Lazarus come forth—all of it, including His trial and crucifixion, His resurrection and ascension. Day after day, month after month I continued the pilgrimage with Jesus, until I *knew* Him. It was incredibly exciting, arduous, magnificent, and humbling to behold Him, to know His glory. One day I also realized that *He knew me*! It was the beginning of the most intimate, most satisfying love relationship of my life.

Scriptures began to come alive for me, to be full of meaning and excitement. I began to sense His presence in my daily life. I began to receive the amazing awareness of Him personally as I entered into worship, truly adoring Him in song and prayer I heard brothers and sisters in Christ speak of Him in a way that brought Him to life before my very eyes. I began to see with Him the work of His hands, to marvel at sunsets and exult with Him, to gaze at flowers and share His delight in their beauty, to have my heart stirred by the look of wonder in a child's eyes and to know that stirring was Him. Slowly I *grew* in the *spiritual* dimension. I learned to stop asking God to change my natural domain rather than entering into the spiritual with Him.

I was also taught how to become attentive to the sound of His voice as He spoke within me: "...the sheep listen to his voice. He calls his own sheep by name and leads them out....His sheep follow him because they know his voice" (John 10:3, 4b). As sheep train the lambs to listen for the sound of the shepherd, so my Christian teachers trained me to become quiet within and to listen for His voice. I did. And I began to hear Him in my spirit, to sense His presence, to know His speaking. And as I practiced listening, I became more and more clear as to whose voice I was hearing—my own, the world's (devil inspired), or His. I heard Him more and more. And I began to long to stay in this new realm, to "abide" there, to relish His constant presence and His fellowship. It was no duty; it was *joy.*

I came to realize He didn't take me out of the natural realm, but rather the spiritual *invaded* the natural. Everything came under the dominion of His Spirit. I was living in *two* realms at once: a seen one and an *unseen* one. I came across Colossians 3:2: "Set your minds on things above, not on earthly things. For you have died, and your life is now hidden with Christ in God." Died? I hadn't died physically. But in a sense my old life had truly died, for my way of living without Him just wasn't sufficient anymore, and could never be again. I now viewed everything through the life of His Spirit in my spirit, and did not want to go back to natural life only.

We read Paul's explanation in I Corinthians 2:10-16:

The Spirit searches all things, even the deep things of God. For who among men knows the thoughts of a man except the man's Spirit within him? In the same way no one knows the thoughts of God except the Spirit of God. We have not received the spirit of the world but the Spirit who is from God, that we may understand what God has freely given us. This is what we speak, not in words taught by human wisdom but in words taught by the Spirit, expressing spiritual truths in spiritual words. The man without the Spirit does not accept the things that come from the Spirit of God, for they are foolishness to him, and he cannot understand them, because they are spiritually discerned. The spiritual man makes judgments about all things, but he himself is not subject to any man's judgment:

"For who has known the mind of the Lord that he may instruct him?" But we have the mind of Christ.

It may take awhile for the new believer to be at home with his new country, the spiritual kingdom of God, and with his ever-present, indwelling Lord. He *may* still travel much of the time alone and apart from the Lord, still loving and engaging in the old way of life. But hopefully he will learn the meaning of the Lord's call to *abide in Him*, the most joyous place of all to be. In many respects life is the same as always; but in the mind set, it is becoming totally different.

But here's the sad part: even after I have learned to be at home in the spiritual realm and to hear the Lord's voice, I may still *choose* to go back, to be apart from Him, to walk in the natural alone. Another voice within me—my own selfish longing for having what *I* want—leads me back. And I have often gone, to my detriment and shame, especially if I have taken a lengthy detour. Also, being in the natural alone and on my own may occur many times in a day, in a back and forth fashion. Old habits leap up to take over, and I allow it without a moment's notice.

I have said the Christian walk is like being on a rugged road mountain hike with Jesus; with that image in mind you will understand when I say I often run ahead of Him, lag behind, or wander off onto a side path, not paying attention to His guidance. Often I'm not even aware I've strayed until I feel entangled in these old way brambles. That's when I cry out to the Lord to come rescue me. I reach imploringly to Him.

Sometimes I just begin feeling lost and lonely, homesick for God. *I* left *Him* somehow. Time to go back.

I reach to God. He's there. He is waiting. If I would be free from the tyranny of the old natural habits, if I would return to the pleasure of His company, I must turn to Him, tune to Him, and confess to Him my leaving. In a word, pray. And having prayed, having confessed my wandering away, that at-homeness with Him washes over me and I sense freedom from the entanglements with the old. I'm delighted.

Until I forget again, and slip away again.

Perhaps you are still not clear on this difference in living the natural life the way you always have and now being in the spiritual life. How can I further illustrate the difference between the natural life alone and the spiritual one that dominates the natural? I recalled the way we lit our home when I was a child. We had kerosene lanterns. They were smoky and smelly and gave off dim and limited light. But they were all we had. Then came the advent of electricity in those rural areas of Texas. Our house got wired for it, and lights installed. What a difference! Not only could we now see clearly, but we had a source of power that could be used in ways we hadn't dreamed. We could now get a refrigerator. No more ice box. In years to come we would add an electric toaster, iron, freezer, and many other wonderful appliances that used this great power source.

Imagine how natural it was for my mother to walk into the kitchen and begin to light the kerosene lamp, only to suddenly realize she had only to reach to a light switch to have all the light she could want. It was a whole new way of living, though the house and furnishings and activities were still the same.

Am I trying to walk in the light of my feeble "natural" lamp, or have I plugged into the Great Light of God that not only illuminates my life, but shows up all that needs attention, and also provides the power and means to clean it out?

Put another way, why do I reach to God? Do I want him to do my bidding so all will go well for me? Or do I come because I realize I am helpless to diagnose, fix, and change without seeking His will for me? I need a change of focus.

One of the ways we most easily slip into the merely natural is our tendency to care what others think about us, and to be ruled by their opinions. We want to please them. We want them to like us. We always have. It's natural. Yet one of the most tremendous aspects of the freedom of belonging totally to Christ is that we now have only *One* to please. We need look at only one face, listen to only one voice. What liberty! If we believe this we must now risk displeasing all the others in order to please Him. That's not an easy habit to form. Pleasing others is not an easy habit to break. Criticism is never pleasant to hear, whether first hand or second.

I must ask myself: when am I trying to impress? Wearing a mask? Where am I false to my truest self, thus displeasing to God? I know that I need to be naked before Him gladly, unashamed, redeemed. I need to be fully arrayed with His inner light, now able to be my true self, unadorned and uncovered.

Well then, let's say I've done it again—"left" Him to impress them. Now I feel ashamed. That too will keep me from reaching to Him, confessing my leaving, restoring the fellowship. All too naturally shame and guilt do not bring us to God; they send us running away. Naturally. That's not the spiritual life though. And it is the spiritual life we are called to lead. In fact, how shall I be rid of the shame and guilt if I *don't* reach to Him? I won't. When is the time to return? As soon as I am aware I've departed.

I find I also run away into innumerable distractions. Little things—you know. Captured afresh by small thorns of worry, fret over irritations, moments of pure vanity. Or being snared by a vapid TV commercial, humming along to the indecent lyrics coming over the radio waves, glancing at a lurid picture in the grocery store. You know.

Perhaps the most frequent return to the natural comes about through our assuming that our *daily* ways of approaching life, our daily habits, are just as they should be, never dreaming that they need reviewing with God. Are these the ways *He* has chosen for us? Is there any change He would like to make? If the hairs of my head are numbered as I am told they are in Matthew 10:30 (incredible!), then is not God interested in every facet of my life? And if He knows my thoughts before I think them (see Psalm 139), is He not aware of the very motives that established those habits in the first place? Should these not be reviewed with Him?

Oswald Chambers says, in *My Utmost for His Highest*:

> The golden rule for your life and mine is this concentrated keeping of the life open towards God. Let everything else—work, clothes, food, every-thing on earth—go by the board, saving that one thing. The rush of other things always tends to obscure this concentration on God. We have to maintain ourselves in the place of beholding, keeping the life absolutely spiritual all through. Let other things come and go as they may, let other people criticize as they will, but never allow anything to obscure the life

34

that is hid with Christ in God. Never be hurried out of the relationship of abiding in Him.[1]

I taught a class in the spring of 2003 on this prayer process. It was always a delight to me to see Colin come in. He could be such a clown, but most nights he came quietly to his usual spot, giving me his sly grin. This very aware, bright, and savvy young man had come from a totally secular lifestyle into full belief in Jesus Christ about three years earlier. Since then, his spiritual growth and knowledge had been abundant to the delight of his teachers and fellow believers. He shared that his desire to know the Lord better was his sole motive for joining the class. At the end of the twelve weeks when the group shared their final experiences with the prayer process, Colin offered, "My problem has been cockiness. I really do think I can handle it all by myself. I know I have a brain and I know how to use it." We ummmed and laughed lightly, knowing he spoke truth. His fake-humble lop-sided grin ended and he said, "Now I'm learning to reach to God and that's the most important place for me to walk—in the spiritual, not in the natural. The rest of the process just follows this. I really am learning to want to please Him by seeking His wisdom. O.K., I know I need it. It's great. I like being in His company."

What breaks your fellowship with Him? What turns you back to the natural? To being on your own again? Many more things could be named, but suffice it to say, we all know that we break away from Him over and over each day. How significant it is then to form the *habit* of reaching to God repeatedly, continually, and without a moment's hesitation. The stronger *this* habit the sooner we are free from the tyranny of the natural.

I am reminded of Jesus' words in John 7:38, 39: "'If anyone is thirsty, let him come to me and drink. Whoever believes in me, as the Scripture has said, streams of living water will flow from within him.' By this he meant the Spirit, whom those who believed in him were later to receive."

Do I thirst? Do I drink? Do those living waters of the Spirit life flow in me and out from me? Here is life abundant. I reach to God.

CHAPTER TWO

RELEASE

I cry aloud to the Lord;
I lift up my voice to the Lord for mercy.
I pour out my complaint before him;
before him I tell my trouble.

Psalm 142:1,2

T HE RAIN FELL steadily for two weeks. Lake Cachuma in the Santa Ynez Valley of California, filled from the run-off of nearby hills and mountains, rose steadily. The massive dam on the west end contained the waters and protected the valleys below. Yet a current of anxiety lingered in those who lived there. What if the waters rose until they spilled over the top?

And spill they did, first in small flows that sent the river below running with fresh vigor.

Then, as massive downpours pelted the lake and land, the spill grew to a thunderous torrent. Now the river ran wild, spilling its banks, flooding the fields, tearing out fences, washing out bridges, submerging streets and filling basements and ground floors. Damage was estimated in the millions.

Have you ever witnessed scenes of such flooding on your TV news? But what of those experiencing it, finding their homes and lands caught in the path of it? During the Lake Cachuma flood their moans and cries ascended and their accusations were flung angrily at officials. "Why was the flood allowed? It could have been prevented! Why wasn't the dam opened to gradually spill the pent up waters as they gathered? Why wasn't there daily release of water over the danger mark as soon as it was reached? The river would never have rampaged if this had been done."

I wonder how often dangerous build-up has actually been the case, as it truly was when I witnessed it decades ago in Santa Ynez and nearby Lompoc. It occurs to me that the same is true of each of us personally. When I sense the waters of strife, of depression, or discontent, of anxiety rising in me, do I run to the only One who can manage the release? Release—that's the key word. Not hiding, not ignoring, not stuffing. Sensing the danger, I must go to the Lord.

CLOGGED

In such release lies incredible freedom to experience God fully. If I seek to come into true intimacy with Him without the willingness to release all to Him, I merely deceive myself. I think I can come and praise Him and worship Him and experience His love for me but it is often only form and lacking in fullness. I am not able to love Him with all my heart, soul, mind, and strength because I am blocked. Like a fountain whose pipes are clogged so that free flowing water from a pure source can not flow, so I can not, when clogged, experience fully what Christ promised I would know: "'If anyone is thirsty, let him come to me and drink. Whoever believes in me, as the Scripture has said, streams of living water will flow from within him.' By this he meant the Spirit..." (John 7:37-39).

My experience tells me that our most frequent clogging is emotion. Worry, anger, fear, depression, frustration, anxiety, doubt, vacillation—is any one of these clogging you now? Emotions are struck by our perceptions, and are followed instantly with thoughts, many of which occur over and over, in haunting fashion. Sometimes my own thoughts are hidden from me, and until I begin to speak of my feelings I do not even know the thoughts that lurk behind them. We cannot deal directly with emotions themselves, but we can certainly deal with the thoughts that accompany them. What is necessary is that you hear these thoughts fully, review them with God, and hear the truth in regard to them. Then you can know what to put off.

Do you ever realize that God wants to fellowship with you in your emotions? Even the unpleasant ones? Do you realize that He, as the perfect parent He is, wants you to come to Him so that He can parent you?

I have asked clients repeatedly down through the years to fully recount experiences, to describe emotions, and to track the thoughts that accompany these experiences and emotions. This proves hard because they do not want to encounter their pain, fear, terror, or anger again. Yet when the emotion and the accompanying thoughts are released to Christ, He can then touch the wound and heal with truth and spiritual ministering. Emotions stand first on the list of what we need to release.

Sometimes, however, I think I am doing just fine in handling my issues. My *own* thoughts seem quite sufficient, and I neither seek nor welcome God; I feel no need. I am now clogged by my pride.

Sometimes I am clogged by my own goals, or my own efforts, even though I may believe, as I press on in my own physical energy, that I am in the Spirit and doing His will.

Whatever the clog, I'll not receive the necessary release until I realize my need and seek Him.

Certainly, as previously stated, my approach to God needs always to be one of grateful praise for Who He is and for my access to Him. First, indeed, "Our Father...Hallowed be thy name...." Yet even as I come to Him I often realize I am seeking to avoid being real with Him. I avoid being transparent, lest He discover in me and reveal to me my *own* efforts to flow. Avoiding discovery, I may seek formula praying rather than real intimacy.

Yet, it is genuine intimacy which we yearn for and which we may have. Why do we hesitate to release our feelings and thoughts to Him when we realize we are clogged? Why do we postpone? Run away? Ignore? Get distracted?

We may not realize it, but beyond conscious choice there is our innate *habit* of maintaining *control*. We want to feel proud of ourselves, and confident; we want to go far beyond the mere realizing our value, potential and giftedness before Him. If we have a problem and if we hold it in, solve it, or handle it, we feel strong, able, and self-satisfied. We don't want to be like children running to mother, blubbering and whimpering, weak and undone, with every little trial of life. We really needn't bother God with this.

39

It is definitely true that human effort to get unstuck, unclogged, past the problem can help and often does. But how much deeper the Holy Spirit goes in tracing out the root causes and asking us to address them, He who discerns the "thoughts and intents of the heart." When He points out our motivations, when He reveals our reaction patterns, then we can begin to experience true and lasting change of mind and heart, and not merely the surface change of behavioral habit.

RELEASING EMOTIONS

Consider what happens when you suppress your emotions. What happens if you do not go and pour out these pent-up feelings to God? What happens is that you stuff them until they rise up above the danger mark, spill out in all directions, and do all kinds of damage, much of which is incredibly hard to remedy. Consider what happened the last time you stuffed your anger, and then, without warning, became a volcano. Who felt the molten lava?

Obvious wisdom is to hide nothing from the Lord and from ourselves. We need to spill emotions immediately so that harmful build up does not occur. David knew the power of fear, danger, anger, discouragement, despair, the powerful emotional accompaniments of thought, that had to be given over to God, lest sin build and overflow. We read his cry in Psalm 142:

I cry aloud to the Lord;
I lift up my voice to the Lord for mercy.
I pour out my complaint before him,
before him I tell my trouble.
When my spirit grows faint within me,
it is you who know my way.

(Psalm 142:1-3)

We know David was no weakling. This is a mighty warrior speaking. No false pride prevented him from crying out to God. Releasing his soul unclogged the channels through which he would hear from God, and he knew it.

How do I go about this release? I do not monitor, modify, or tone it down. I simply pour it out as it comes, with all the bitterness or self-pity or blaming another that accompanies the emotion. I vent it utterly. God is not surprised.

He already knows what those feelings and thoughts are there. As I pour these out to God without editing them, especially if I put them down on paper, I can then begin to realize how God is sifting them for me. I begin to see fully the sin involved, whether mine or another's or both, and in what measure. This is the first thing that release gives me.

When I have clearly discerned these thoughts as led by the Spirit, I can then go into much deeper release. Now I can confess thoroughly and completely. Now I can place all sin on the cross of Jesus Christ. Now I can release forgiveness to the one who has sinned against me. Now I can accept God's forgiveness of me. Now I can truly let it all go, end it, and refuse to re-ignite the feelings I began with. I have truly "cast my burden on the Lord." Now I genuinely repent and go on to the other steps in the process.

I've often heard the excuse, "I don't think it is right to dump all I'm feeling on anyone! Certainly not on God. It is too awful and He is too holy." Yet David said clearly, "I pour out my complaint before him, before him I tell my trouble...." Surely if Psalm 139 is to be believed, God already knows:

> ...*you perceive my thoughts from afar*
> ...*you are familiar with all my ways.*
> *Before a word is on my tongue you know it completely, O Lord.*

> *(Psalm 139:2-4)*

So why hide my thoughts, or even try to clean them up before telling them out to Him? I am the one who needs to know fully what is resident within me. If I am not clean when I come to the Lord, I must *be* cleaned by Him. The true confession is the complete one.

I remember a lady who told me she couldn't pour out her feelings about her estranged husband to God because they were too vile and too sinful. I asked her if she wanted to keep carrying them. She said she didn't because they were so painful, prevalent, and persistent. I asked her what she thought she could do about it. She shrugged. I turned her to Psalm 142 and showed her what David did: scream to God. She said she literally wanted to scream, but where could she do this? She hadn't enough privacy at home. I said I thought her car, with windows rolled up, made a good prayer closet. She expressed fear that people would see her and wonder. I said it would be dangerous to engage in this prayer process when driving, but in the privacy of her driveway or garage there would be no onlookers. I asked her to limit her pouring out to ten minutes with the understanding that she was *releasing* them. She was not to voice them to build them or to defend herself but to be rid of them.

I asked her to picture Jesus on the cross, and to see a stream of vileness pouring out of her mouth and into Him, for He bore *all* our sins there, and also "Surely He hath borne our griefs and carried our sorrows..." (Isaiah 53:4 KJV). Therefore, at the end of the release session, she was to pray the prayer of relinquishment: "Lord, I release all this to you. You took it into yourself on the cross, and it died there. I thank you and I leave it there." She was then to accept His cleansing, and to receive His love and rest in it. She was to repeat these steps daily—scheduling a daily appointment with God—until she had released all to the cross.

"How long does it take?" she asked.

"As long as it takes," I said. "Some reservoirs are so full, it takes a long time to spill it all. A session daily will help."

A few weeks later, I encountered her again. "Guess what," she said, brightly. "I know I doubted what you suggested I do, but I needed relief, so I tried it. Screamed everyday. Said every nasty thing I was feeling about Joe. I got rid of the screaming after awhile. But I could tell I was still angry, so I just kept pouring it out. Some of it was me, of course, and I could see how sinful I'd been. It was hard to realize I had to ask the Lord to *forgive me.* I think that's when I realized I wanted to forgive Joe so I could let it all go. I think I finally managed that and now I feel free of it. I can't believe how good that feels."

Another lady came to counseling with resentment towards her mother that she had held for over twenty years. She said she'd admitted it many times, and confessed it to God, but couldn't get past it. I suggested that she was trying to dump it all in one load without going into the feelings that were entangled in it. I asked her to journal out her accusations by going back to the time she'd felt hurt and bereft. I asked her to be specific and to say exactly how she felt. I asked her to tell the Lord all about it in detail on paper.

I asked her further to let the Lord come in and heal the hurt of each incident as she remembered it. I asked her to envision Him walking right into the day she'd experienced the hurt she was dealing with, for in truth and Spirit, He was always there. I asked that she receive Him and record what she believed were His thoughts on the subject.

She accepted the assignment and journaled diligently every day. I saw her each week, and each time she read to me what she had written. It took her eight weeks to finish the assignment. Then I asked her to relinquish all to Jesus on the cross, to forgive her mother completely, and to ask the Lord to forgive *her* for holding on to her bitterness. It was a time of tears, to be sure. When she finished all this, she felt immeasurably free, joyful and thankful.

But what if it is God Himself with whom you feel offended? Has He allowed something in your life that you find appalling? Do you think He will defend himself, and accuse you if you challenge Him? If you truly come into His presence, not just to rail at Him but to encounter Him truly, I believe you will find He will certainly hear you out. Then let Him examine your accusation with you, until *you* understand—or at least trust Him again even when He gives no explanation. He will hear and sort it through with you until you are able to fully release all to His heart and leave it there.

Have you ever seen a little child angry toward a parent? Hitting out? Furious and trying to hurt the parent? It is slightly above freezing outside, but Susie insists, "I want to wear my pink shorts! You want me to look ugly! You're soooo mean! I hate you!" If Mama is patient, holding Susie at arm's length as she flails away, Susie begins to wear herself out. Perhaps there's more yelling. Maybe a little foot stomping. Usually, she then begins her crying session, loud and impressive, tapering off into piteous whimpering. After that, since she needs her mother desperately, she's ready to let Mama love and comfort her, condescendingly of course. Susie's little heart is healed even though she still may not understand Mama's decision that so angered her.

I am certainly Susie with God now and then. I need to release my pent up feelings towards Him until I can trust again. I need Him desperately. "Lord, to whom shall we go?"

Or Susie may accuse, strike out, run away and stay alienated, afraid, and alone. Choices exist—even for the young. And the same is true for God's "little children" in the spiritual realm. "For your thoughts are not my thoughts, neither are your ways my ways, saith the Lord. For as the heavens are higher than the earth, so are my ways higher than your ways, and my thoughts than your thoughts" (Isaiah 55: 8, 9, KJV). Therefore, God will not always explain Himself. But He doesn't withdraw when I wail, "Why?" I am assured He will not change Himself to suit me. But He will keep on loving me and making Himself available. I choose to repent and trust again.

THE POWER OF ANGER

Sometimes I don't want to be free of my feelings when I think I've been wronged, whether by others or as I perceive God has wronged me. I actually enjoy my anger. It makes me feel powerful. It fuels me: I look for ways to retaliate; I focus on ways to sabotage; I think about the cutting remarks I'll make; I strategize to even the score. I may even experience self-righteous feelings. I enjoy them when I am *accusing God* of being unfair. If I decide to hold onto my anger, I pay a price. I lose my deep and abiding joy of intimacy with the Lord.

Shall I hold onto my feelings, or release them to God? I must choose. One thing is certain: He is the only one who will fully understand. We are assured and instructed in Hebrews:

> *For we do not have a high priest who is unable to sympathize*
> *with our weaknesses, but we have one who has been tempted*
> *in every way, just as we are—yet was without sin. Let us*
> *approach the throne of grace with confidence, so that we may*
> *obtain mercy and find grace to help us in our time of need.*

> *(Hebrews 4:15, 16)*

Such an amazing invitation and appeal from God!

"Yes, O.K., but what about the person who has offended me? Why don't I just tell the person involved how I feel and be done with it? Why hold back on expressing my anger or disapproval or hurt? Why not release directly and immediately to that person instead of to God?" These are good questions I have often been asked. Here is what I answer: "You certainly may, and it is healthy for the relationship to do that if you can do it with maturity and wisdom. Consider the last time something or someone aroused strong feelings in you. Were you at that point tempted to say or to do something in an impulsive way? In a cruel and destructive way? Most of us are. If you were to release your emotional thinking immediately to the person, what harm would come of it? Consider the repercusions. If instead you were to release your feelings and the thoughts created by them to the Lord, telling him just how you feel about it and what you'd like to do, what would happen?"

I remember the time my four year old son Glen came running into the house furious with his visiting playmate. "I hate that Billy," he declared loudly.

"I'm going to kill him!" With that he grabbed a knife from the kitchen counter and was making for the door when I caught him. "Whoa there, son. Come here and tell me about it. What happened?" I sat down with him, confining him to my lap even though he struggled to get loose. He began to yell and scream about all Billy's kicking and scratching him, and his vows to do in Billy once for all. I held on and let him spew. After a few minutes, his anger turned into sobbing, and then into crying, while I listened and absorbed his pain. Gradually, he quieted and then calmed down totally. I rested him against me, just holding him, saying nothing. After several more minutes of silently and gently rocking him, I was able to speak to him softly and assure him I'd take care of the problem. It took a lot longer for both of us to do that than to take impulsive and angry action, but think of the problems avoided because we did.

We may protest we are not children; we are adults. We have responsibilities. True. But we, like children, need to recognize that we need God's direction in *every* facet of our lives. We also need to pour out hurt, anger, confusion, fear to God. Then we need to rest with Him until we are quiet enough to hear how *He* is directing *us* to handle the problem wisely. He will voice again the wisdom of His Scriptures if we listen. He will remind us of the ways Jesus dealt with such issues on earth. He will lead us "in right paths for His name's sake." For men especially, battles must be fought and won, not by violence but by strength, by boldness, by cunning as the Lord directs. Women too must hear and understand the instructions of God lest they resort to nagging, fretting, and sabotage.

First, however, the release. I think God is like I was as a mother that day in my story of my four year old. In fact, David, again, tells us that He is:

> *...I have stilled and quieted my soul;*
> *like a weaned child with its mother,*
> *like a weaned child is my soul within me.*

> *(Psalm 131:2)*

A weaned child does not seek his mother for nursing, but for the peace and love that come from drawing on her nurture and wisdom. Do we, weak as we are in sin, not need to go to our "Abba" for release, rest, love, and wisdom? If we are to act toward one another in love ("as I have loved you,"

45

Jesus said) as commanded thirteen times in the New Testament, will we not first need the release that comes from pouring all out to God?

In addition to releasing our feelings and the thoughts that accompany them to God, we need to see several other necessary aspects of release. The first of these is forgiveness. Once I have released my emotion to God, and seen where sin lies, I will need to release forgiveness to anyone who has sinned against me. Also I may need to "forgive God" so to speak. Next I will need to fully confess any sin I see in myself and be willing to repent of it. Then I must be certain to receive God's forgiveness and to acknowledge that I have. Lastly, I will need to relinquish the entire issue to God and let go of it. I would like to examine each of these in turn.

FORGIVE

"I say I forgive. And I mean it. But I can't seem to give up the bitterness and resentment I feel." Or the anger, or the desire for retaliation. How often I have heard such statements. What then is forgiveness? Why does Jesus warn: "For if you forgive men when they sin against you, your heavenly Father will also forgive you. But if you do not forgive men their sins, your Father will not forgive you your sins"? Scary stuff. How then do I know if I have forgiven?

First, clearly you don't forgive by spreading a big blanket covering every item, nor by making a mere declaration of intent. Each act of the sinning against you requires examination. In Mark 11:25 Jesus instructs: "And when you stand praying, if you hold *anything* against *anyone*, forgive him, so that your Father in heaven may forgive you your sins" (emphasis mine). Item by item, act by act, along with the emotions each arouses, must be brought before the Lord until all the sin and hurt involved is fully released into the Body of Christ on the cross.

Jesus said, "And whenever you stand praying, forgive if you have anything against anyone, so that your Father also who is in heaven may forgive you your transgressions" (Mark 11:25, NASB). In that verse I believe we have a clear definition of unforgiveness: I hold something against someone. Forgiveness then means I no longer hold that one thing against that someone who sinned against me. As I release and forgive the items, one by one, one day I will hold not *one* thing against that *one*.

Jesus has won the right by His death to be your advocate, having Himself already paid the penalty for every sin that will ever be committed. He will try your case in God's courtroom. In regard to each offense, pour out to Him

46

every detail of the wrong done against you. Then leave the case to Him. He will present it for you before the Father who is judge and jury and who gives the verdict and assigns the sentence. Hear your advocate clearly when He instructs you to trust Him. It is not yours to try the case nor seek your own vengeance. If you trust Him, leave it to Him.

"Do not take revenge, my friends, but leave room for God's wrath, for it is written: 'It is mine to avenge; I will repay,' says the Lord" (Romans 12:19).

At the end of our twelve week spring class, Ronna, pulling back her long dark hair, sending sparks with her flashing brown eyes, shared her story:

> I have had a long-term issue with lack of justice and discrimination in the workplace. I've been filled with indignation over incidents—it lasts for days as anger and then goes underground and becomes bitterness. Now I have learned to pray for grace in regard to each incident—not that I would fail to be moved by injustice, but that I would pray over each issue and then leave it to God to settle in His courts. I've been *releasing* each incident as it arises, and I am dealing with incidents from my own past as well. The Lord is enabling me to see behind each one and to understand the motivations in those involved. This is poured out grace! Then if He wants me to take any action, I know He will guide me into it, and I will be able to do it in His way and strength, and without my indignation.

But what about your own personal feelings? What about all the pain caused you? For these you come to your Father and begin the process: you pour out your emotions to God until you can release the hurt and anger. Then you *leave* it with Him. You rest with Him as your loving parent who comforts you until you choose to let the hurt and anger die. You forgive the sin against you, as you confess your own desires for vengeance. If you have truly forgiven the wrong-doer, you can now remember the incident with sorrow over the sin, but no longer with personal emotions of anger, hurt, or bitterness because of yourself.

FORGIVING MY DADDY

I recall when I first learned all this. I knew I had stuffed my inner closet with unforgiveness, because the least little thing would rekindle all my tamped down anger. It would flare out instantaneously. I'd always lash out with far more of it than the situation called for.

I realized that my father would be at the top of my list of people to forgive. His fierce temper scared me mightily when I was a child. I could remember many episodes that left scars.

When I realized how greatly it pleased the Lord for me to forgive each and all, I asked the Lord to begin this cleaning of the closet (process of forgiveness) in me, and I chose to set aside time each day for it. In my time with Him I prayed that He would recall to me any one thing I held against anyone who had ever sinned against me. I was led to deal with one person at a time. Dad was the person I began with. In regard to him, I reviewed my life year by year so I wouldn't miss anything.

The first memory that came to mind was of my October evening with him at the Texas State Fair when I was four years old. I was mesmerized by the bright midway lights. The giant Ferris wheel turned, seats rocking and swaying, lifting into the black velvet sky. The merry-go-round's stallions and lions and tigers raced round and round to the sound of the calliope, syncopated by the whirr of the Tilt-a-Whirls and the screams of its riders. Booth-keepers barked loud invitations to throw, pitch, ring the bell to the milling crowd. Smells of frying hamburgers, grilled onions, steaming hot dogs, beer, roasting peanuts and popcorn filled the air. All around me a fine dust rose from hard-packed ground scuffed into a fine powder by strollers munching snow cones and pink cotton candy. My head swiveled; my ears rang; my mouth watered. Then I saw the monstrous roller coaster thundering up and down the heavily wooded, latticed track. Awestruck I let go of Daddy's hand.

I turned to share my wonder with him. He was gone!

"Daddy? Daddy?" He was nowhere to be seen. Panic hit me like an ocean wave. I dashed all about shrieking and screaming and shouting, "Have you seen my daddy?" No one had.

Finally I stood still, sobbing mightily, hopeless, realizing my terrible sin of losing my daddy. Resigned to the terrible peril of being lost.

The man in the booth in front of me had been frowning with concern. Suddenly he shifted and called, "Hey!" He was now grinning and pointing. I whirled to look.

Daddy! I ran to him sobbing and he caught me up. How and when did I come to realize that he had been following me, hidden, and amused by my tearing about and my mounting panic?

My father could be very wonderful, as I tell in a later episode, but he could also be very sinful and thoughtless as in this instance. A child's heart is so very needy of the absolute love and trustworthiness of a parent that each offense against that trust is usually buried, though still alive, as a hidden hurt and resentment. So it was for me in this case.

In my session with the Lord, I asked Him to restore the entire incident to my memory, so that I could submit it to him. At the point I felt most lost and afraid, I stopped and found Jesus there beside me. As the child, I saw myself come into His arms. I spiritually sensed His assurance, as He held and comforted the four year old, that He would never laugh at me, leave me, fail to protect me, hide from me. All these promises given in the Scriptures were retroactively applied (Jesus being present with us always) to the four year old's fear and pain spiritually, so that the wounds of this experience were healed.

Then as the adult I took my hidden-to-me, pent up anger at my father's sin to Jesus as my Advocate, poured out my case against my father, railing against his indifference to the child's fear and pain. At length I finished. I had expended it all. I left it with Him.

That one thing I had against my father was now gone. I could still remember it, but now I felt no animosity towards him for it, and no urge to be understood or to get revenge. I continued to willingly recall all the other times he had inflicted fear or pain or anger down the years. I re-entered each and forgave in the same way as I had the first one. It took me weeks to process them all with the Lord. One day I could say in truth that I had *nothing* against my father. Indeed, I felt much more understanding, compassion, and appreciation of him than I ever had. And I loved him far more than ever. I remembered the many good times with him with unalloyed joy.

Please believe I didn't stop there. I wanted to forgive everyone everything and be totally free. Now I began the daily process of doing so. Thus "Jodi" came to learn how to release all her pent up anger and resentment toward "Greg". Enabled by the Spirit, I put it on the cross, and I learned to let it all go and to forgive, truly and at length completely.

Then I had to deal with forgiving *me*. With each release of sin against me, the Lord also revealed to me where I had sinned as well. Again and again, I released my sin to the cross and the shame and guilt I felt as well. Now I had to accept His forgiveness. That was even harder.

After I finished with everyone I knew who had sinned against me, I asked the Lord to show me where I had sinned alone. He did. The process was the same.

Hardest of all was the case I'd had against the Lord. I admitted each time I held resentment toward God for doing nothing to prevent all my suffering down through the years. Each time He assured me that He had given free will to the person sinning against me and He did not remove that will at the time I was hurt. He did assure me that He was more grieved than I about the pain and injustice I endured. He reminded me that He was there each time, and that I was able to turn to Him and to receive comfort and healing from Him.

I admitted that I was angry toward Him for His lack of guidance. For instance, why hadn't He steered me away from marrying Greg in the first place? He assured me He had warned me, but I had failed to hear. We dealt with it—the Lord and I—I talked it through with Him until I saw my lack of trust in His character, goodness and sovereignty. My sin! Back to confessing and being forgiven. Then I was able to "forgive" Him, even though I still didn't fully understand. Did Job? With no more case against God, I had come to the end of my list. I began to feel an immense freedom and lightness.

I also sensed the Lord's delight in this entire process. After several months I could finally say truthfully, "Today I have *nothing* against *anyone.*" How we rejoiced, Jesus and I, that day! From that day on, each day I ask Him to check my heart to be certain I have nothing against anyone. If I do find a grievance, I process with Him and forgive as quickly as possible, so that I may stay in the glorious fellowship of the Lord and in the freedom forgiveness gives. If during my day I experience a hurt, an injustice, a slight, a grievance, I take it to Him as soon as possible, and release it to Him until I am able to forgive. I don't want anything to mar my walk and talk with Him. Unforgiveness does, you know.

Wait a minute. Scripture also says, "If your brother sins, rebuke him" (Luke 17:3). True, and having forgiven, we will then be able to hear how the Lord would have us do this. Will He not instruct us how to rebuke in love, even if sternly, and for the sake of the wrongdoer? How different this is from seeking to justify ourselves or flinging out punishing words.

What about when both parties have sinned? First consider yourself personally.

At this point God is not asking you to get the *other* person to release. He is dealing with *you.* Where is *my* sin? There is also the matter of repentance— where does that fit into this choice to release?

I know the instruction of the Master: "...first remove the plank out of your own eye, and then you will see clearly to remove the speck from your brother's eye" (Matthew 7:5). What will He have you do in regard to the one who has sinned against you? Confront? Draw boundaries? He will surely make this plain to you if you ask. I will deal with this aspect more fully in

Stage 4: Receive. But "first remove the plank" as He instructs. How shall I do this?

CONFESSION AND REPENTANCE

One thing new Christians are taught is the importance of confession. Certainly if I hide my sin from God and myself, it stands in the way of my fellowship with Him. I am quickly willing to admit my wrong. Does that mean I merely say, "Oh, sorry, Lord," and go on my way? If that is all I do in my time of release, I'll be committing that sin again shortly in all probability. Clearly it is not enough merely to confess to having sinned. True sorrow for the wrong done precedes genuine repentance. And my *repentance* is surely what the Lord desires. We need the work of the Holy Spirit in order to do this.

John Ortberg writes,

> We have to see our sin through new eyes. We need to see them through the eyes of those against whom we have sinned. Two questions in particular help us gain a new perception. The first one is "Why did I do what I did?"...The second question is, "What happened as a result of my sin?"[2]

When I have the answers to those questions clearly in mind, repentance means I also ask, "Lord how can I change?"

And who can reveal these things to us except the Holy Spirit as we come to the point of willingness to repent? "Oh, God, I hate my sin. I truly do. I hate the harm I've done. I *want* to change. I want to end this habit!" Until we reach this point, we go no further.

Many times I do not realize the extent of my sin until I have poured out to God *all* that I have been holding. When I am not blocked in my listening to Him, He is then able to reveal to me where sin lies in me, show me the hurt of it, reveal my motivation, and point to its outcome. Now I know how damaging it has been. Now I can fully confess and truly *repent*.

I believe repentance is also greatly motivated if, when I confess my sin, I see what happens to it. My sin flows like a stream of filth right into the body of Jesus on the cross. In fact those who help others to be healed of personal sins as well as sins against them will instruct, "Place that sin on the cross" or "Press into the cross." I think we have to be careful here to make clear that it isn't a symbol of the cross, nor the actual cross itself that receives our sin. It wasn't a piece of wood that bore the sin; it was the flesh and blood body of

Jesus Christ. His death on the cross occurred in history two thousand years ago, but in spiritual terms, that death is outside of time. He died as we know for all sins—past, present, and future. That is what the Infinite God made possible for our full salvation. So I need to apply the truth of it *now*. I need to see that sin I've just committed flowing into His body *now*.

"He hath made him to be sin for us, who knew no sin; that we might be made the righteousness of God in him" (2 Corinthians 5:21, KJV). I consider that. I picture that. That is *my* sin pouring into Him. Nothing so motivates me to repent as the Spirit-led awareness of my Savior suffering defilement for me.

Genuine repentance goes further. When I have released all my sin to Him, confessing it and receiving forgiveness, I realize I must *complete* the process—I must take up a new way to replace the old sinful one. We will deal with this in future chapters.

SHAME AND GUILT

When I realize the extent of my sin and its destruction, I am overwhelmed with shame and guilt. Shouldn't I be, so that I will not engage in such sinning again? But repentance means I must leave my shame and guilt at the cross as well. I would not take away from Christ's sacrifice for me by thinking it wasn't sufficient. That is an insult to God. Did the Savior's blood wash away my defilement? Does it *now*, at this moment as I repent?

Certainly God means me to accept that it did. "...and the blood of Jesus Christ, his Son, purifies us from all sin" (1 John 1:7). "If we confess our sins, he is faithful and just and will forgive us our sins and purify us from all unrighteousness" (1 John 1:9). "To him who loves us and has freed us from our sins by his blood..." (Revelation 1:5). Holding onto my guilt and shame means I believe I must be further punished for the sin committed. It is as if I say to God, "Ah yes, I know You forgave all on the cross, but You will need to scold me some more so I don't do it again!" That isn't God scolding me; I do it to myself. I allow Satan to inspire new feelings of guilt and shame so I will be further defeated in my Christian walk. I do not change because of scolding. Instead I feel defeated, unworthy, demoralized. And in that state it is actually easier to engage in sin again!

Jesus was never astounded by sin in a person. He was astounded by faith. Will I *believe* Him when He says, "You are forgiven"? Will I accept a fresh start? In the strength of His love, will I go a new way?

Sometimes memories haunt me though. When I remember again those words I said and those deeds I did that trigger my shame, I *choose* to remember releasing them to Jesus on the cross. Having done so, I *choose* to release the shame immediately to the Lord, knowing He has dealt with it. If I do not do so, my enemy will surely haunt me with it.

One Sunday, my pastor, Mark Buchanan, preached a sermon entitled, "Getting Past Your Past"; he ranked the biggest obstacle of human nature as just that. He explained how your enemy, Satan, loves to threaten to expose you in regard to your past. If it is exposed, he whispers as you tremble, it will surely jeopardize your mission and ministry in the present. With a past like that you can't serve! You are disqualified! That's what your enemy tells you.

Not so with the God who *redeems our past*, however tainted. I thought, as Mark spoke, that this does not apply to *just* the sins of my life as an unbeliever. I have great regrets and shame that I have sinned against the Lord *since* I became His follower. I have wandered away, or walked away, or stalked away. Having returned, confessed, and repented, God has forgiven me and shown me a new way to walk. And in His mercy and grace, He does give me a fresh beginning if I will allow it. He removes the shame and guilt if I let him. Beyond that He will even use my learning from that sin to bring good out of evil! Incredible.

Mark's major point: "Your past does not define you!" God can and is willing to break in and change everything. His attention is on your *present* in order to give you a *future.* "The only way to deal with your past is to make a future out of it." God can and will redeem everything from that past. Let Him, as Rahab did.

GRIEF AND SORROW

Now consider grief and sorrow, emotions that are certainly not sinful, but need to be released so that they do not turn to resentment and bitterness.

Recall: "Surely He has borne our griefs and carried our sorrows..." (Isaiah 53:4, KJV). On the cross He took them into Himself and there they were absorbed and ended. Retroactively we must place our griefs and sorrows into Him and let them die there. Until we rest from them we are not free of the sin that will evolve, nor can we forgive another of sin against us. This form of releasing usually requires repeated releases over a period of time as wave after wave of grief pours forth. Grieving is a process that is not helped when we try to shorten it. It is helped by our grieving *into* the Lord.

Lynda and her husband Bill agonized over their daughter, Anna. Beautiful Anna, happily married and anticipating children and a joyful home down the years, found instead that she was dying of cancer and there was nothing that could be done to prevent it, though the family's prayers and those of many others ascended day after day. For three and a half slow, pain filled years, Bill and Lynda besought God for a miraculous cure, and latched on to every turn for the better, to every good day among so many dismal ones. But the persistent decline continued and the pain increased until the day Anna faced home. Bill was with her at the time and saw the radiance on her face as she sat up at the last moment and proclaimed her joy at the scene of heaven before her and then died in his arms.

He was able to grieve and recover. Lynda was not. She buried her bitterness toward God and became increasingly busy, serving the Lord, or so she thought. Yet she knew she was not free, and she knew no true intimacy with the Lord. In her deep anger towards him, her inability to understand why he had taken Anna, why he had done no miracle healing, she was left alone in her bitterness and cried alone in it night after night.

One night two years after the burial she came to prayer ministry at our church. We in the prayer circle sat listening as she recalled the facts of Anna's death and stated her inability to forgive God. I spoke to her of relating to the Father as a hurt child, in spite of her inability to understand His choice for Anna. I told her the story of my hurt little boy, and how, as he sat in my arms, I had absorbed his pain. I asked her to picture a child in the arms of Jesus, doing the same. We then asked her to come into the arms of the Father and to release her pain to Him, screaming at Him if need be, as David had done (see Psalm 142), and allowing Him to absorb it into Himself and retroactively onto the cross. We all prayed in silence that this release would occur, and Lynda did too. Suddenly, the flood rose and the dam broke. Tears flowed down her face, the grief waves washed over her, the agonized sobs of the hurting mother sounded. After a time her pain subsided and we all sat in the marvelous silence, each in Spirit seeing her enfolded in His arms. After a time I asked her if she thought it would be possible to meet with God each day and to invite Him to reveal any grief that was still there and then to release it to Him as she had just done. She nodded, her wet eyes shining.

And in the days that followed she indeed did release her grief to Him. She told us that sense of freedom from pain was increasing as well as her joy in being intimate with God again. Then God assigned her a ministry to those who have experienced grief and loss. She and a co-leader taught a twelve week course on grieving the following fall.

No matter what troublesome emotion or combination of them I am experiencing, I now know beyond a doubt that wisdom is to release them to the One who can and already has borne them. "Cast your cares on the Lord and he will sustain you; he will never let the righteous fall" (Psalm 55:22).

Often it seems impossible for the grieving one to release fully enough alone. Trusted friends are a grace gift of God to such a one. They can listen and pray the griever into the presence of God. There the griever can cry into Him and let go of the pain. This is indeed help to the one grieving and blessing to the friends.

THOUGHT LIFE

All that we find true of emotions and accompanying thought applies to our intellectual thoughts as well. I may not recognize a mere thought as taking me out of the realm of the spiritual and into the realm of the natural. I find, however, that this often happens for me when I have a sense of my own sufficiency and self designed goals. Suddenly, I realize I have taken over control with my thought. I want things *my* way. I see how to do what I want done, and I follow after my thought. This doesn't seem like *a feeling* I need to release, but the motivation behind the thought, nevertheless, tells me whether it pleases or displeases God.

For instance, I find myself delighting in *knowing* the answer or knowing more than another person, whether I voice it or smugly keep it to myself. Is the Lord in these thoughts? Is He pleased with them? What is their source? What do they motivate in me? One moment of releasing them to Him for review will reveal instantly the motivation behind them.

Our thought life is harder to track than our emotional life. Emotions register strongly on the conscious mind. Thought is so innate that I often do not realize it is happening. For instance, I may have negative thoughts when I hear a certain person speak. I don't *feel* much about the person; I simply make some swift judgments that are negative toward him. "Dumb idea. Not the brightest guy around." One up! Or perhaps I think those thoughts in regard to myself in comparison to someone, "Goofed again! Dumb me." As soon as I check out the thought in the presence of the Lord, I know He had no part in it, and I know it needs a quick release *and replacement*.

Satan, as we know, is the father of lies, the accuser of the brethren, and master at insinuating accusing messages within us. No matter where the lies originated, he and his forces note them and perpetuate them. Think of your self thoughts. Does this sound familiar: "I'm a failure." "That's dumb!" "You're stupid!" "What will people think?" "That is simply not good enough." "You disappoint me." "You simply must do this—now!" "You're just not attractive enough"—or tall enough, thin enough, clever enough, humorous enough, doing enough, giving enough, and on and on.

We know we need to face the truth about ourselves squarely with the Lord, but frequently it isn't the Lord we are hearing with these convicting thoughts; it is our arch enemy, the one who brings despair to the soul.

We do well to take to heart Paul's admonition in 2 Corinthians 10:4 and 5: "The weapons we fight with are not the weapons of the world. On the contrary, they have divine power to demolish strongholds. We demolish arguments and every pretension that sets itself up against the knowledge of God, and we take captive every thought to make it obedient to Christ." Are my thoughts obedient to Christ? Did He speak this thought into my mind? If not, I need to see the work of Satan or the world or myself, and I need to go straight to God for the weapons of spiritual warfare that will defeat it. Single thoughts can be processed very quickly: "Oh, Lord, that's not you, is it?" When we know it is not, we need say aloud, "Satan, that's a lie!" We turn again to the Lord and ask, "What is your thought here?" That's Put Off/Put On in a very short time, and soon you find a great transformation in the way you think.

SPEAKING AND REACTIONS

Consider the enormous problem many of us have with the way we speak. In the twinkling of an eye I gush out words that hurt, maim, anger, demolish. If instead I hold them, reach to God, release and review them with Him, I realize in an instant that I must come to a full stop, and not speak until I know His words of wisdom and love instead of what I was going to say. That takes enormous discipline, but it can be learned; the Holy Spirit is willing to teach you. You *can* change your talk by engaging in this prayer process before you speak. God has the power to change your heart, your motivation, *and* your speech.

Reactions are even harder to track, for they often are so instantaneous that neither emotion nor clear thought is apparent. When I was a child I learned to protect myself from pain and put-downs by reacting in a way that became habitual. If I felt someone didn't like me or was in any way displeased with me, I learned to deal with the threat I felt in a way or ways that became habitual. These became *reactions.* I see that they can be put into four main categories for easy reference: Above, Toward, Away, Against.

If the child feels threatened by the taunts of children or the insulting remarks of family members, he may decide to go *above.* He may decide he will be better than any other person in what he does, at least in one area. He may decide he is smarter, and look down on all others as not bright enough. He may choose to be quicker, funnier, more efficient, more artistic, more informed. This is not just living up to his potential; this is being *better than* so he can feel good enough. Here is the over-achiever, the workaholic, the "I'll show them" mentality. She may decide she must be the most beautiful, have the most fashionable attire, have the best body, be the best sex partner. After awhile, the one who goes above others may say, "That's just the way that I am," not realizing it was a *learned* reaction. And the performer only scales the heights to realize it is never high enough (there are still others above me) or that the pinnacle cannot be held indefinitely. So Marilyn Monroe commits suicide.

The second reaction is to try harder to please those who could give me acceptance and love. The child goes *toward* others. "I'll just please them; I'll try harder and then they will like me." So looking for ways to please, to win favor, to make an impression, to obtain applause, to amuse, to impress with kindness and serving are the ways the child begins to practice in order to feel qualified to exchange the pain of rejection for the satisfaction of acceptance. One problem—it is never enough. The pleaser always has to be assured he/she is pleasing. Performance must have a pay-off. This gets tiresome for those chosen to be the pleased.

Third, "I'll just disappear." Or hide, avoid, escape. This one goes *away.* It hurts to be rejected, berated, scolded, put down, so much so that the child hides from the pain by getting into something that can take away the hurt or even the threat of experiencing hurt. So hide from it—get lost in a book, in an adventure, in make believe, in games, TV, videos and on into eating, drugs, alcohol, sex, gambling, work, sports, the internet. If I want not to feel pain, I can find a great variety of ways to bury it beyond awareness. At length, I do not know why I do what I do. I only know I am addicted to doing it, and I can't stop.

The fourth direction is the most frequent for nearly all of us: we go *against*; we retaliate. When I was insulted as a child, I defended myself. I hit, kicked, pounded, yelled, barked insults, planned revenge, and learned to use the wonderfully sarcastic barb, the grand put-down. Ah, sweet. My resolve: "I'll pay him for this pain. One way or another he won't get away with it." Here is the motivation for violence, war, attack, terrorism. Here is the instigator of the slap, the push, the spousal abuse, the road rage. The violence may go underground and come out in more indirect ways—the rapist, the con man, the self righteous "prophet", the harsh teacher, the punishing parent.

These reaction patterns are learned and practiced by all of us in defense of the self. Most of us learn to use all four, sometimes in a revolving way, sometimes specializing in one and then another as it serves us. These become so ingrained as feeling/thought that we become unaware of the origins. But as we are willing to invite God to search us out and to reveal to us these hurtful ways, He will do so. Over the years God has delved into me and revealed them, one by one, and spurred me to put them off, using the same steps of process I have outlined. Each reaction pattern as it arises must be stopped, taken immediately to Him (Reach) and then fully released. I must see it with His eyes for what it is—a defense from pain and hurt that I must cease to practice. It is sin, and I must acknowledge and confess it as such, and no longer *defend my defenses*.

Frequently, too, when I have already been hurt and triggered and so have moved into giving out a hurtful reaction, I need to see the benefit of replaying the whole incident with God. In my imagination then, replaying the incident, I am able to stop at the very moment of being triggered. At that moment I realize my pain *before* I engage in reaction. I practice releasing it to Him. When I do this I find when a similar incident occurs that I can move closer and closer to the exact moment of releasing to God inside myself before acting on my reaction. I begin to think differently. I quit running. I quit pleasing. I speak out or act out less and less. My reaction becomes delayed and finally disappears altogether. I can then go on to the further steps in the process.

PULLING OUT THE STOPPER

Sometimes it is very difficult to simply let go of all I may be thinking and feeling. To pull out the stopper. To stop avoiding and stop stuffing it in. In my years as a professional counselor I would often encounter those who would come admitting that they were in pain and needing release from it. I would sit with such a one, ready to listen to a full outpouring of the problem, the accompanying feelings, the various perspectives regarding it, the accusations of others involved. Sometimes none of this was forthcoming. I would begin to ask questions. Reluctantly the person before me would speak. Just answers to the questions. Sometimes only yeses or noes. I'd ask more questions. I'd make more effort to get the dam unblocked.

Sometimes the flow would begin, and when it did, then the client would give me a veritable torrent of jumbled facts, emotions, suppositions, accusations and misguided perceptions. Good. For now we could begin to discern and to sort. Very often the outpouring alone gave the hurting one great relief.

So it is with each of us. When we first come to release all to the Lord, we may find it hard going. We don't know how to begin. But we must persist in allowing Him to question us until the outflow begins. Again, meeting with trusted others, talking it out, and then praying together can help greatly to get the process underway.

In the physical realm I would liken it to throwing up offending contents of the stomach, or to having a boil lanced. It doesn't feel good to the one suffering, but when it is done, what relief!

Then we need to practice praying individually Psalm 139:23 and 24 daily to keep the process going. More and more relief will be experienced. Here is David's prayer:

> *Search me, O God, and know my heart;*
> *test me and know my anxious thoughts*
> *See if there is any offensive way in me*
> *And lead me in the way everlasting.*

It isn't just that we *need* to pray this prayer. The *Lord invites*! Let us not disappoint Him. Let us delight His heart by coming, by releasing. Recall again: "Let us therefore come boldly unto the throne of grace, that we may obtain mercy, and find grace to help in time of need" (Hebrews 4:16, KJV). The Spirit instructs through David, "Trust in him at all times, O people; pour out your hearts to him" (Psalm 62:8).

Recall the old hymn *What a Friend We Have in Jesus.* Perhaps you remember these words,

Oh what peace we often forfeit,
Oh what needless pain we bear.
All because we do not carry
Everything to God in prayer.[3]

RELINQUISHMENT

But mere letting go of feelings and thoughts without relinquishing them will not suffice. What is relinquishment? Many Christian authors have written well on the subject. I have found their ideas very valuable. Here, however, I want to stress the relinquishing to God of the very emotions and thoughts you have released to Him, and the very issue with which you are dealing. Very often we use God as a sounding board but fail to *let go* of thoughts or emotions or intentions. Indeed, our releasing to God may simply serve to *build* our anger, worry, fret, fear, sorrow, or shame unless there comes a point when we choose to relinquish all to Him and to depend on Him entirely to deal with it.

Mothers of grown children often seem to have the problem of relinquishing. They maintain that maternal sense of responsibility and need to control. Mom has been depended on to solve the problem so often she still plays that role, thus experiencing all the worry, fret, anger, and frustration that goes with it. (I'm sure lots of dads do too; maybe it's just that I keep hearing this from moms.) Several members of our spring class shared their struggles:

Rose said, "My son has long created a heaviness in my heart because of his rejection of Christ and his waywardness. I finally quit trying to reach him. I poured out my heart to the Lord and released my woe and my son to Him. I truly and finally *let go*. Shortly after I did this, my son called me and I was able to talk with him easily and freely and without bad feeling. It felt wonderful."

Ann shared, "I have long felt anger and frustration about my second son. He has many problems, and I have a history of trying to solve them. It never succeeds. He has now lost everything. That did it! I poured out to the Lord all my negatives in regard to my son."

"As I was praying the Lord broke in with these words, 'Your job is to be a good mother. *My* job is to work in his heart.' How freeing! I could release my son fully to the Lord. I could open and receive further instruction from Him on being a 'good mother.' I asked Him about it. He assigned me 'encouragement.' That's it. My heart is set to obey Him, and I am doing so. I am speaking encouragement to my son. It gladdens my heart."

Selene had a different slant. She said, "My oldest daughter really experienced the presence of the Holy Spirit when I was baptized a year ago. She then came to the Alpha group at our church. I asked her, 'Are you doing this just for me?' and she said yes. I became angry with her. I was angry with God as well.

When I asked God about it, He impressed me to release her to Him. I hadn't realized I was trying hard to control her!"

"I did release her, and then my daughter stopped coming to church altogether! I wanted to fix it, but I didn't. I stayed in my rest with Him."

"A while back my daughter began coming to church again on her own. Two weeks ago when Pastor Mark spoke, she told me the message was spoken right to her. She opened her heart to the Lord, and sought baptism, and I was amazed. Yesterday she was baptized—a glorious event of her own choosing! But how *I* too am rejoicing!"

What are the Lord's instructions concerning relinquishment? Let's review them.

Cast your cares on the Lord
and he will sustain you;
he will never let the righteous fall.

(Psalm 55:22)

"Come to me, all you who are weary and
burdened, and I will give you rest...."

(Matthew 11:28)

Cast all your anxiety on him because he cares for you.

(1 Peter 5:7)

Do you recall the story I told of my four year old son, Glen? There came the time after he had cried out his woe, that he *left it* with me. He trusted me to deal with it. Even so, if I, as the child of the Father, am to be free of the disturbance in me, I will have to trust Him with it, and relinquish it to Him. This is *not* to say, of course, that there is nothing more for me to do. But unless I truly *let go* of my urge to control the situation, I will stand in His way. I will not trust Him, and thus I will not hear His voice nor discern His will when He does tell me what to do.

In our fall class, a young man named Brad shared his experience of this:

When I was growing up, my dad put me down a lot. I developed a really low opinion of myself, so I was usually quiet and shy around people, not wanting to be rejected. I pretty much stayed that way until I met the Lord two years ago. Since then He's been bringing me out of it by giving me His opinion of me. But I'm still learning.

I was at a Missions Committee meeting to introduce myself to them as a candidate for a summer missions trip. They were all pretty much women who had known the Lord a long while, and I suddenly felt shy and afraid to say a word to them. How was I going to tell them who I am and why I think I should go? I just knew I was going to botch the whole thing.

Then I remembered the processing and began to pray. I knew I had to let go of this fear and my sense of inadequacy. I just began releasing my feelings and thoughts to Him in silence, giving them over to Him, and trusting Him to take my fear. Suddenly He broke in on me with these words: "I trust you." That was all, but peace dropped all over me in a way I can't describe. It was total. When the lady near me asked me a question, the words just flowed out of me. And what the Lord said to me then has stayed with me to continue to heal a lot of my father's wounding. God's amazing! He's great.

FEELING LOST

But suppose you have no idea what to release to Him. Perhaps you don't know where you are or even who you are. You just feel lost, alone, or afraid, or most likely all three. When I have encountered someone who came to me in that condition, I have prayed with that one in the following way:

First I prayed with Ryan, asking the Holy Spirit to fill both of us with His truth and enlightenment. Then I said, "Ryan, will you please picture yourself as a child. When you are able to do so, tell me how old you are."

Ryan was silent for a minute or two and then said, "I'm about three, I think."

"Now will you allow yourself to return to being that child for now. Tell me when you have done that."

After about a minute of silence (as I prayed for him silently), he said, "All right. I'm picturing myself as that child again."

"Now tell me what is going on in the child's heart. What is he feeling and experiencing?"

"He is afraid."

"Any other feelings?"

"He feels lonely, rejected. Isolated."

"Now Ryan do you remember the story of Jesus when He blessed little children? Do you remember what He said? 'Let the little children come to me, and do not hinder them, for the kingdom of heaven belongs to such as these.' Are you picturing that scene as I speak of it?"

"Yes, I am."

"Ryan, when you were a child, Jesus was there. Do you believe that?"

"Yes, I do."

"You are right now remembering and picturing yourself as the child you were.

What do you think Jesus wants to do in your life?"

"He wants me to come to Him and let Him bless me as He did the children."

"Are you willing for Him to?"

"Yes."

"What are you, the child, doing, now that you know He is near?"

"I'm running over to Him."

"What is He doing?"

"He is holding His arms out to me."

"How does His face look?"

"Joyful. Delighted."

"What do you do?"

"I let myself be lifted onto His lap."

"What is He doing?"

"He's hugging me and holding me close."

"Does He *cherish* you?"

"Yes."

"How do you know?"

"I see it in His face, in His eyes. How He holds me. I just feel it."

"What else do you feel? Are you safe?"

"Yes."

"Do you feel rejected in any way? Do you feel that you shouldn't be there because you somehow aren't worth it or good enough?"

"No, I know He wants me. I know He—uh, uh...."

"Thinks you are wonderful? Of course, since He created you! Does He find any fault in you?"

"No."

"What is He doing now?"

"He is just holding me close. Resting with me."

"What would you like to do?"

"Stay here. I choose to. Something I never had is being restored to me. I need to do this often, I'm sure."

"Yes, I believe you do."

Please note that I did not tell either the Lord or Ryan what to do. I only asked Ryan to return to his childhood and introduced a portion of Scripture. Beyond that point I didn't manage the encounter, but only asked what was happening to Ryan. I believe it is the work of the Holy Spirit in His ministry of "redeeming the years the locust have eaten" (Joel 2:25) in the life of a believer. I believe He acts in retrospect to heal, to restore, and to give what was omitted in the lives of needy children. I believe I need only bring the believer to Jesus for this encounter.

I do not believe the counselor or a mentor has any right to order God around. I don't believe as a counselor that I should make anyone who comes to me engage in a spiritual encounter of this sort. But I do strongly believe that I can encourage a believer to allow God to minister in the past years of his life in the way presented above. It is always the faith of the believer that opens the door to God's redemptive process.

I can't say how very many times I have had similar encounters with those for whom I have prayed. Very few failed to come into this place of rest and of being at home with Christ. Neglect, omission of love, hurt, anxiety are healed there, not in one encounter alone, but as one is repeatedly willing to come. It was true for me personally, I know.

Consider these words written by Oswald Chambers:

> If you have never used your imagination to put yourself before God, begin to do it now. It is of no use waiting for God to come; you must put your imagination away from the face of idols and look unto Him and be saved. Imagination is the greatest gift God has given us and it ought to be devoted entirely to Him. If you have been bringing every thought into captivity to the obedience of Christ, it will be one of the greatest assets to faith when the time of trial comes, because your faith and the Spirit of God will work together.[4]

Some have told me that this kind of envisioning is New Age or is manipulating God. I do not see how it is either. I personally find it impossible to read the gospels without seeing Jesus, the disciples, and the people on the screen of my mind. The vast majority of believers are not able to read Bible stories without some visualization of them. Their visualizations may differ. It is not how they enter vicariously into the story nor identify with the characters in it or imagine the size of the person, or the hair color and length, or the physique. The spiritual truth and impact come as the Holy Spirit conveys it to us *through* our imaginings, our picturing, our inner videos. These imaginings are *metaphors* to convey God's truth to us personally.

Some theologians have argued that picturing Jesus Christ in any way is breaking the second of the Ten Commandments. But man did not fashion Jesus Christ. God did. He ordained a body. And He ordained the true humanity of Christ. Carefully consider the following scriptures: 2 Corinthians 4:6; 1 John 1:1-4; John 1:14; and Hebrews, chapters 1 and 2.

Consider the story of the prodigal son. What do you see, hear, imagine as you recall this story? It is not how perfectly you can imagine this story that is significant, for who can say whose imaginings are the most exact. But if you are experiencing it spiritually, you will truly sense the prodigal's desperation and repentance, the father's overwhelming love for him and the joy he has in the son's return, as well as the jealousy and anger of the older son. This is above and beyond the story line; this is the work of the Author, the Holy Spirit.

Recall Ryan's encounter with Jesus. Did a strong, grown man feel ridiculous in entering into this kind of intimacy with God? He didn't. Neither did David, who wrote, "But I have stilled and quieted my soul like a weaned child with its mother..." (Psalm 131:2). Many other verses flood my mind:

"And he took the children in his arms, put his hands on them and blessed them" (Mark 10:16).

"He called a little child and had him stand among them. And he said: 'I tell you the truth, unless you change and become like little children, you will never enter the kingdom of heaven. Therefore, whoever humbles himself like this child is the greatest in the kingdom of heaven'" (Matthew 18:2, 3).

"For you did not receive a spirit that makes you a slave again to fear, but you received the Spirit of sonship. And by him we cry, '*Abba* (the Aramaic word for Father, a little child's designation which we might translate "Daddy"), Father. The Spirit testifies with our spirit that we are God's children" (Romans 8:15, 16).

"At this time Jesus said, 'I praise you, Father, Lord of heaven and earth, because you have hidden these things from the wise and learned, and revealed them to little children. Yes, Father, for this was your good pleasure'" (Matthew 11:25).

"O Jerusalem, Jerusalem, …how often I have longed to gather your children together, as a hen gathers her chicks under her wings, but you were not willing" (Luke 13:34).

If our need is that of a little child, and we are humble enough to admit it, will He not receive us into His healing arms of love, and minister to our needs there? Will not the envisioning be filled with His love and truth? Indeed, it will and is. And there we can rest. That leads to my next step in the process.

I don't believe I have finished with release on any given day until I can hear God say, "What do you want?" And I answer, "I want You. And I want what You want." That's when I realize it is fellowship with me that He wants, a time of abiding, a time of resting in His love.

CHAPTER THREE

REST

He makes me lie down in green pastures....

Psalm 23:2

I N TEACHING THE CLASSES on the subject of *Rest*, I told the participants to think of the most peaceful place they could be where they could spend some time in silence. Since Jesus is always present with us, I asked them, when in that quiet place, to realize His presence and to begin just to be with Christ, to abide with Him there.

I warned them that if pictures came to mind, they were to reject instantly, as Satan's doing, any "picture" that was not in accordance with the Scriptures and with the character and nature of Jesus Christ. I asked them to rebuke Satan's demonic forces with these words: "I tell you in the name and by the blood of Jesus to depart." I further instructed them, having quieted their minds from outer and inner distractions and thoughts, to ask the *Holy Spirit* to speak any message or give any pictures that He desired that would enable their practicing the presence of God.

I told them of Leanne Payne, who told those of us listening to her teaching at a prayer conference, to go and be with Christ in the "garden of your heart." At that moment I had immediately seen myself in a garden full of roses. Christ was indeed with me there; I both "saw" Him and sensed His true presence. I remember the great calm and deep peace of just abiding with Him. Nothing more was said or seen. Just being there with Him reached depths in me I had never before experienced.

I now asked my classes to do the same, right where they sat. I asked them to allow the Holy Spirit to show them the special place to be—the garden of the heart. At that point we entered into a time of resting with Christ. We shared afterwards how blessed we had been in those intimate moments, each alone with Him and completely at peace—just being there.

Is the thought of that kind of rest appealing to you? If you've sinned and confessed it and repented of it, then yes, instruction for change must come, but first you need the joy of receiving forgiveness and being restored to fellowship with God and entering into a time of "no hurry no pressure" rest. If we have no sin to confess, then we stay for the sheer joy of *intimacy* with God, and thus *our souls are restored.*

If I have nothing to release, *rest* is still incredibly important for me. After I reach to God, having nothing to release, I then need to stay in the rest, the "Hallowed be thy name" part of the prayer process for awhile, just contemplating the goodness and greatness and wonder of the Lover of my soul.

Rest in Scripture is a huge concept and has many facets. First, though, is the aspect of cessation. If I want to be free of cares and troubles and responsibilities, I seek a time of *rest from* them, a ceasing to consider them, a coming away from them completely. Jesus said to the twelve after their labors of the ministry, "Come aside and rest awhile."

Consider the fact that the Bible contains many words that are translated "rest."

The various aspects appear as we consider some of Hebrew words for rest:

raga: to rest, be quiet;
shaan: to lean or rely on;
shabath: to cease, rest, keep sabbath;
nuach: to cause to rest, also to be at rest;
damam: to be still, keep silence.[5]

All of these definitions have great appeal for me. Yet this resting seems the hardest of disciplines. In this age of action, the quicker the better, the "get it done" mentality dominates us. I feel useless and guilty if I'm not moving to accomplish something. Note the word I used, *feel*; yet the guilt is false. True guilt strikes me when I disobey God. Is He telling me to rest? Why does He command rest when there is so much to be done? And why is it so hard to enter into this resting?

Perhaps the difficulty lies in the aspect of silence. True rest is a quiet thing. *Damam: to be still, to keep silent.* I can silence my mouth by an act of the will, but what do I do with my restless mind? This is the reason that the first step in the Put Off/Put On process is *release*. Only when I have given over all my woes, cares, distractions, rehearsal of responsibilities, and all the other mind clutter to the Lord, only then can I rest down in genuine silence. Solitude helps, but silence is truly necessary, and that means silence within and a cessation of my self-directed thinking. Oswald Chambers spoke of "contagion of His stillness." My husband George describes it as "a cessation of the cacophony of the mind, a surrender to the grace of His silence." A change of focus is necessary.

Perhaps the difficulty lies in the aspect of *waiting*. Psalms 37:7a instructs, "Rest (*daman: to be still, keep silence*) in the Lord, and wait patiently for him..." (KJV). The Hebrew word for wait is *quvah*, defined as "to wait, expect, look for, hope".[6] This same word is used in Psalm 27: 14: "Wait for the Lord; be strong and take heart and wait for the Lord."

When I have relinquished my cares and woes and questions to Jesus, I have yet to enter into rest. This is a choice I must make. Having ceased, I now enter into a sphere of peace, of resting down to *wait* for His direction. Until I do, I do not show that I *trust* Him. If I trust Him, I believe He *will* direct me in His time and in His way. This Biblical aspect of waiting will bring me there.

THE INFINITE/PERSONAL GOD

Probably my greatest need is for a full STOP to hallow the name of God, as Jesus taught His disciples to pray. With whom am I dealing? Are my own thoughts about my problem striving to be heard so that I do not realize the One to whom I am relating? I am fine with the "Our Father" part, but do I fully know Him? I need to continue... "Hallowed be Thy name." This means I will set God apart as the unique Being He is; I will carefully consider all His name reveals of His nature and character.

J. I. Packer has written:

What were we made for? To know God. What aim should we set ourselves in life? To know God.

What is the 'eternal life' that Jesus gives? Knowledge of God. 'This is eternal life: that they may know you, the only true God, and Jesus Christ, whom you have sent' (John 17:3).

What is the best thing in life, bringing more joy, delight, and contentment than anything else? Knowledge of God. "This is what the Lord says: 'Let not the wise man boast of his strength or the rich man boast of his riches, but let him who boasts boast about this: that he understands and knows me'" (Jer. 9:23f).

What, of all the states God ever sees man in, gives God most pleasure? Knowledge of himself.[7]

These words strike me very deeply as I reflect on my life. Do I take time to know Him?

Years ago I read several books written by Francis Schaeffer, founder of L'Abri. Most particularly I remember that he called God the "Infinite-Personal God" –a term that motivated hours of meditation for me. I considered at length all the ways in which God is infinite. God reveals Himself in Scripture as The Ancient of Days—the Eternal One. How can I grasp the fact that He has no beginning and no end? He is the All-Powerful One (omnipotent); the All-Knowing One (omniscient); the Everywhere Present One (omnipresent)—all of them beyond my mind's limited grasp. He is Sovereign over all, who can ever thwart His will? He is Creator. "All things were made by him and for him." He is All-Wise. He is complete, Holy, whole, righteous, Light, Life. I need stretching to know with the knowing that the Holy Spirit provides that God is all this and more in His infinity. Yet if He were only these things, how could I ever approach Him?

I remember being seven years old and gazing into a three way mirror. I was O.K. if I looked straight ahead. But when I looked to the left I saw the reflection of the mirror to the right, so that the images were repeated endlessly. The same when I looked to the right. I gazed and gazed and wondered and wondered how it never ended on either direction. I couldn't grasp it; I began to be dizzy and fuzzy headed just trying to. I am left with that same feeling as I meditate on God's infinity.

But thank God, He did not leave us with only the knowledge of His infinity.

Precious words in Hebrews: "...he has spoken to us by his son, whom he appointed heir of all things, and through whom he made the universe. The Son is the radiance of God's glory and the exact representation of his being...." And John, "...the Word was God...The Word became flesh and made his dwelling among us. We have seen his glory, the glory of the One and Only, who came from the Father, full of grace and truth." And Jesus Himself, "He that has seen me has seen the Father." Now I began to see directly on a scale I could understand. Here is the personal God, coming down to me so that I can understand His *personal* attributes. I could grasp His longing for relationship with the human beings He has created for Himself. In His revelation of Himself in the Old Testament, in the person and work of Jesus in the New, I could see the God of immense love in all its fullness: loving-kindness, care, concern, protection, provision, compassion, tender-heartedness, salvation, redemption, forgiveness—ah, here is a God I could know and relate to.

Yet both His infinity and His personal nature are immensely important to understand if we are truly to hallow His name. If we see only His infinity, He will always be beyond us, too far above us, too awesomely great and strong and eternal and holy to grasp or to want to know. We will fear and stand in awe, but fail to be relational with Him. If we see Him as only personal, we will reduce Him to being merely one of us, our companion and friend, our helper, our doting parent, but fail to realize the Holy Being with whom we are dealing. No, we need to see both sides afresh and fully remember daily (The Lord's Prayer is daily—"give us *this day our daily bread*.") We need to remember the full story of redemption by the Infinite God, how He saved His beloved human creatures in His desire to enter into relationship with each one. We need to remember how God lazer-beams all His infinite attributes into His poured out love on each one of us personally.

I am moved afresh each time I read passages in the Psalms that show this *relational* nature of God, this pouring out of His infinity into His loving-kindness in behalf of man. I relish them. Consider how the greatness, the immensity of God, is joined to His love and caring for you personally as you read each one.

> *You have made known to me the path of life;*
> *you fill me with joy in your presence,*
> *with eternal pleasures at your right hand (16:11).*

Show me the wonder of your great love,
you who save by your right hand
those who take refuge in you from their foes.
Keep me as the apple of your eye; hide me in
the shadow of your wings... (17:7, 8).

He makes my feet like the feet of the deer;
he enables me to stand on the heights (18:33).

Surely you have granted him eternal blessings
and made him glad with the joy of your presence (21:6).

You turned my wailing into dancing;
you removed my sackcloth and clothed me with joy,
that my heart may sing to you and not be silent (30:11, 12).

How great is your goodness ,
which you have stored up for those who fear you,
which you bestow in the sight of men
on those who take refuge in you (31:19).

God speaking:

I will instruct you and teach you in the way you should go
I will counsel you and watch over you (32:8).

I waited patiently for the Lord;
he turned to me and heard my cry.
He lifted me out of the slimy pit,
out of the mud and mire;
he set my feet on a rock
and gave me a firm place to stand.
He put a new song in my mouth,
a hymn of praise to our God (40:1-3).

Surely you desire truth in the inner parts;
you teach me wisdom in the inmost place (51:6).

Cast your cares on the Lord and he will sustain you;
he will never let the righteous fall (55:22).

Praise be to the Lord, to God our Savior
who daily bears our burdens.
Our God is a God who saves;
from the Sovereign Lord comes escape from death (68:19).

From birth I have relied on you;
you brought me forth from my mother's womb (71:6).

Yet I am always with you;
you hold me by my right hand.
You guide me with your counsel,
and afterward you will take me into glory (73:23, 24).

He who dwells in the shelter of the Most High
will rest in the shadow of the Almighty.
He will cover you with his feathers,
and under his wings you will find refuge;
his faithfulness will be your shield and rampart (91:1, 4).

Know that the Lord is God.
It is he who made us, and we are his;
we are his people and the sheep of his pasture (100:3).

Praise the Lord, O my soul,
and forget not all his benefits—
who forgives all your sins
and heals all your diseases,
who redeems your life from the pit
and crowns you with love and compassion,
who satisfies your desire with good things
so that your youth is renewed like the eagle's.
For as high as the heavens are above the earth,
so great is his love for those who fear him;

as far as the east is from the west,
so far has he removed our transgressions from us.
As a father has compassion on his children,
so the Lord has compassion on those who fear him;
for he knows how we are formed,
he remembers that we are dust (103:2-5; 11-14).

There are many other verses, of course, in the psalms and throughout the Scriptures that reveal this personal focus on and provision of the infinite God for each of His children. My all time favorite is Psalm 139. How greatly it has convinced me of the incredible desire for relationship in the heart of my Infinite/Personal God. If you have time, read it now. If not, then soon. Here are a few phrases from it: "O Lord, you have searched me and known me....Even before a word is on my tongue, /O Lord, you know it completely.... Where can I go from you spirit? Or where can I flee from your presence?... your right hand shall hold me fast....you knit me together in my mother's womb....I am fearfully and wonderfully made." Isn't it astounding? Finally, consider the words of Psalm 147:11, "The Lord *delights* in those who fear him, who put their hope in his unfailing love."

This place of rest is also a place of refreshment. Refreshment certainly may happen in the natural because, if one truly rests down, the body has a chance to regroup its forces. I rise refreshed. But how much more is this true in the spiritual realm if I rest with and into the One who longs to give maximum refreshing?

GOD'S JOY AND OURS

In Zephaniah 3:17 the Lord declares to His beloved Israel: "The Lord your God is with you, he is mighty to save. He will take great delight in you, he will quiet you with his love, he will rejoice over you with singing." In the same way, He rejoices over each one of us as individuals and as a family as we abide in His presence. I want to hear His song.

David prayed, "Let your face shine on your servant; save me with your unfailing love" (Psalm 31:16). When I meditated on this verse, I recalled the mother of a new-born; her face actually shone with love as she gazed at her baby. The father's too. I understood that as I sit in stillness in the Lord's presence, I will realize that the His face is shining on me with an even, yes a far greater love. I bask in it.

Consider the marvelous truth of 2 Corinthians 4:6: "For God, who said, 'Let light shine out of darkness,' made his light shine in our hearts to give us the light of the knowledge of the glory of God in the *face of Christ*" (emphasis mine). I ask the Holy Spirit to show me this face of Christ. Is this not God's will for me? Am I willing to let Him gaze at me?

Again, we often do relinquish all our cares and distractions, but do not take time to relish our presence with the Bridegroom, who loves to have us stay in a rested place with Him for the sheer joy of it! The richness of this spiritual experience makes all else seem small and unimportant.

A marvelous book, *The Sacred Romance,* written by Brent Curtis and John Eldredge, looks at the Song of Solomon:

> God does not give us this look through the bedroom window at the love affair between Solomon and the Queen of Sheba just to be voyeuristic. As we turn from the window and look into his eyes, we realize that this is the kind of passion he feels for us and desires from us in return—an intimacy much more sensuous, much more exotic than sex itself.[8]

Rest for our souls is God's *delight* to give. Why do we deny Him delight? Why do we hurry so and deny ourselves what sets all things in order again?

I do not, however, mean to insist that you *must* see a vision of Jesus when you rest. Trying to do so and being unable to would be strain, not rest. But I do know that, when you truly rest, you will have the awareness of *Him.* By faith you will know that He is there, that He is for you, that He is imparting to you His very being. All the fullness of the God of the universe is focused like a beam of light on you. Your awareness of the awesome God pouring out His grace, joy, strength, mercy, wisdom—what can compare? What can set you reeling with fresh awareness of your finiteness, your weakness, your place as mere man, yet simultaneously fill you with an understanding of your preciousness, your value, your purpose and mission? Only a fresh encounter with the infinite God who bends to embrace you.

Jan Karon's book, *A New Song,* has Episcopal priest Timothy Kavanaugh preaching to his congregation:

> "In the storms of your life, do you long for the consolation of His nearness and His friendship? You can't imagine how He longs for the consolation of yours. It is unimaginable, isn't it, that He would want to be near us—frail as we are, weak as we are, and hopeless as we so often feel. God wants to be *with us.* That, in fact, is His name: Immanuel, God

with us. And why is that so hard to imagine, when indeed, He made us for Himself? Please hear that this morning. The One who made us...made us for Himself.

"We're reminded in the Book of Revelation that He created all things—for His pleasure. Many of us believe that He created all things, but we forget the very best part—that He created us...*for His pleasure.*"⁹

It seems a serious thing to deny God His pleasure. It is also our pleasure—and our need.

HE RESTORES MY SOUL

David also spoke of this quality of rest when he said in Psalm 62:

My soul finds rest in God alone;
my salvation comes from him...
Find rest, O my soul, in God alone,
my hope comes from him... (vs. 1 and 5).

I hear the Lord's request: "Come unto me, all you who are weary and burdened, and I will give you rest" (Matthew 11:28). When I need to cease from all that troubles me, and to draw in fresh springs of energy, joy, refreshment, how long must I stay in this place of rest with Him to do so? I believe again the answer is, "As long as it takes."

This silence with Him, this solitude, this resting down, is not a time of meditation on a theme, though thoughts may flow, nor of reflection on the Word, though He may speak to me from Scripture, nor of my petitions, though communication is wonderfully present without a word. It is rather a time, as previously stated, of simply being in the presence of the One I love, of receiving His desire to be with me, to be near me, to hold me, to relish our oneness.

It is also coming to the place of maximum trust in Him, in His intentions, in His character, in His immense love for me that lets me know *He will give me the very best.* This place may be one of trials or blessings. It may be dull days or excitement. It may be mere routine or incredible adventure. But whatever He brings, He knows the way I need to go. He will lead me if I allow it, if I do not run ahead, if I do not try to get it all done but rather rest with Him and allow Him to reveal Himself to me. When I have rested, I am prepared to hear what He will say and to walk out into life with Him.

When Jesus walked the earth in His ministry, we read this about Him: "Very early in the morning, while it was still dark, Jesus got up, left the house and went off to a solitary place, where he prayed" (Mark 1:35).

"...crowds of people came to hear him and to be healed of their sicknesses. But Jesus often withdrew to lonely places and prayed" (Luke 5:16).

"One of those days (after facing the fury of the Pharisees and teachers of the Law for healing on the Sabbath) Jesus went out to a mountainside to pray, and spent the night praying to God (just prior to choosing the twelve disciples)" (Luke 6:11, 12).

Why, when He had so much ministering to do, did Jesus withdraw from everyone and go off alone to pray? Why did He lose sleep in order to talk to the Father? Was He lacking in understanding of what to do and how to do it? He said of Himself: "...I always do what pleases him (the Father)" (John 8:29). Perhaps He went to find out just what that was. Yet I can't help believing He went primarily because He wanted to experience the incredibly close intimacy with His Father that He had always known. One on one, pure essence, no interruptions. Wouldn't you have liked to listen in to their conversation? I would. How did They enjoy each other's presence? How did They converse with each other? What did They say? What an incredible love relationship exists in the Trinity! If *Jesus* needed to seek it when on earth, what do you think you need?

UNABLE TO REST

I have often been unable to enter into this place of needed rest because of my shame. I have released my sin to the Lord. I have accepted His cleansing of my heart and His forgiveness. But I am unable to let go of the shame I feel over what I have done. I feel unworthy to let Him love me. I feel unworthy to serve Him. I feel I simply *must* clean up my act, and then I can come to Him for this kind of restful love.

This was certainly my Jodi experience after I had processed forgiveness of Greg and myself. I was still hounded by a sense of unworthiness.

The Lord really chided me for this, and sent me back to the Release part of the process to relinquish this shame. When it happens now, He reminds me of the death of my Savior and again asks, "Is that enough?" He insists that the forgiveness He gives is complete—it deals with the sin *and* the guilt and the shame. And now I must fully receive His love, and in it all that He is. This giving of Himself is the very nature of God. It delights Him to give. And it meets my need to feel qualified to do His will.

MOTIVATION FOR WORKS

Often we come to the Lord, not for rest, but because we want guidance for ministry. Ephesians 2:10 tells us we have been "created in Christ Jesus for good works which God ordained that we should walk in them." Jesus Himself told us, "I tell you the truth, anyone who has faith in me will do what I have been doing. He will do even greater things than these, because I am going to the Father" (John 14:11, 12). The motivation to do great things for God is a worthy one, but another motivation precedes it.

Jesus said, "Now this is eternal life that they may know you, the only true God, and Jesus Christ, who you have sent" (John 17:3). When the Jews asked Jesus, "'What must we do to do the works God requires?' Jesus answered, 'The work of God is this: to believe in the one he has sent'" (John 6:28, 29). Jesus said , "'Love the Lord your God with all your heart and with all your soul and with all you mind.' This is the first and greatest commandment" (Matthew 22:37, 38). I John 4:19 tells us, "We love because he first loved us." We know that Jesus' thrice repeated instruction on the night he was betrayed was, "My command is this: Love one another as I have loved you" (John 15:11).

My point: Unless we are coming to know God in a personal way, unless we are trusting His marvelous nature because we do know Him, unless we are receiving His love, our tanks aren't full and we are in grave danger of trying to get them full by doing great works so that others will, if not love us, then at least admire us. That's backward. We must open up to and bask in the *person* of our God. We must know how He delights in loving us and receive His love personally, intimately, and freely. First rest. Take in His love. A love response will arise in you.

Those who do not love Him passionately and totally will not be willing to do anything, anytime, anywhere, in behalf of anyone as a *love response* to Him. Nothing short of this love response will give us the pure motivation to hear Him, heed Him, respond to Him, and to walk out in the works He directs and in the power that He gives. I believe there is only one worthy motive for action in the whole of the Christian life, one and one only, and that is *to delight the heart of God.* All true works performed by the Holy Spirit in us and through us spring from this motive.

When we set our wills to love Him in this way, we realize that *our very ability* to love Him is the result of the work in us of the Holy Spirit: "...God has poured out his love into our hearts by the Holy Spirit, whom he has given us" (Romans 5:5). Of this the NIV study notes explain: "the verb indicates a present status resulting from a past action. When we first believed in Christ, the Holy Spirit poured out his love in our hearts, and his love for us continues to dwell in us."

Oswald Chamber explains: "No man on earth has this passionate love of the Lord Jesus unless the Holy Ghost has imparted it to him....He sheds abroad the very love of God in our hearts. Whenever the Holy Ghost sees a chance of glorifying Jesus, He will take your heart, your nerves, your whole personality, and simply make you blaze and glow with devotion to Jesus Christ."[10]

A statement of Jesus in the book of Matthew, chapter 7, verses 22 and 23, strikes terror in my heart: "Many will say to me on that day (the day of judgment), 'Lord, Lord, did we not prophesy in your name, and in your name drive out demons and perform many miracles?' Then I will tell them plainly, 'I never knew you. Away from me, you evildoers!'" It isn't the "great works" we've done that show we know Jesus.

HOW IS REST POSSIBLE?

Prolonged silence and solitude are disciplines I need to practice if I am to be fully rested and to hear God as I need to. But rest in the very middle of my daily life must be possible and practiced too. When can I lay hold of these short times of rest? When can you? It is possible when I move from one activity to another. It is what the working husband needs to choose when there is a work break. It is the state of being mothers must choose when their children are engaged in play or napping or away at school. It is the five minutes the student takes away from study. It is the pastor's habit between appointments with troubled people. It is the fulfillment of the psalmist's words: "He makes me lie down in green pastures, he leads me beside still waters." The Lord would have me turn to Him for a brief encounter, for a renewal of the joy of His presence in case I have forgotten He is there. It gives Him delight to do this. It certainly gives me delight and refocuses me as well.

Many years ago one expert on stress reduction (I do not remember who) recommended that everyone should take three stress breaks a day. At break time, he instructed, one should lie down flat and go as limp as possible, imagining the most relaxing scene one could, whether a beach in Hawaii, a grassy meadow, or a fabulously comfortable bed in a super posh place, or wherever. One should consciously begin with the feet and imagine a warm, slow liquid filling them and then moving up the legs, then trunk, then arms down into the fingertips, and then into the head. If one could maintain this for even a few minutes, his stress level would go down to almost zero. He wouldn't keep pushing it up, up, and up all through the day until he either collapsed in a heap or exploded.

Again, if that is true in the natural, and I found it to be true (and the origin of the power nap, I think), then how much more will it refresh and lighten and empower those who truly rest in the Spirit and with the Beloved?

I recall an old hymn, *O Love That Will Not Let Me Go:*

> O Love that will not let me go,
> I rest my weary soul in Thee;
> I give Thee back the life I owe,
> That in Thine ocean depths its flow
> May richer, fuller be.[11]

When I think of the sweetest of human relationships, I think of watching a sunset with my husband; I think of the times I sat on the couch hugging my daughter; I think of holding my little boy on my lap; I think of sitting with a friend in silence on the bank of a river, just observing the beautiful flow of the water. Where is the intimacy that goes deepest, that union of souls that occurs in silence? "...in thy presence is fullness of joy..." (Psalm 16: 11, KJV).

TIME

So what is your difficulty with all this? Ah yes, time. Too many responsibilities.

Our culture is, as previously noted, increasingly fast paced. And a person is valued according to how fast he can get something done. Minimum time is allowed to drive from place to place. The young driver prides himself that he cut five minutes off the time, no matter that he endangers his life and ours as well. The business man prides himself on choosing the fastest computer with the most efficient hardware. Then he hones his ability to manipulate it to gain the information desired until it is lightning fast. He certainly doesn't have time to just sit. Communication is clipped, clever, to the point. We praise the sound bite. The quick sarcastic quip is most valued. And most wives I know add constantly to their lists of "Things to do." I don't hear of eliminating items.

Do we children of the kingdom of God buy into this? Do you walk in Christ through the door of the kingdom, only to crawl out the window and go back to the ways of the world? I know that as a Christian I am to make the best possible use of my time as a steward of it—but is haste the way to do it?

When I was in my thirties I lived a "hit the floor running" type of life. I remember when I first realized that Jesus' instruction, "Abide in me..." (KJV), meant the sit down, the settle in, Mary listening at His feet—not just being with Him but *in* Him, in His love and peace. I simply couldn't do it! I'd sit down and immediately feel the guilt for sitting down. O. K., I'd release that to the Lord. Next came the distracting list of things yet to be done. O.K., released that. Quit rehearsing it over and over in my head. Then came the agony of anxiety. I just simply felt miserably anxious, as if the world would fall to pieces if I didn't get up and keep it glued together. The longer I sat the more my anxiety grew until I squirmed in my agitation. Everything was getting out of *control*!

But the Lord simply would not give up. He insisted, "ABIDE IN ME!" So I did persist. I'd sit asking Him to enable me to *let go* and become aware of Him. Little by little, moment by moment, over days and weeks, the anxiety began to wane. I got quiet inside. I relaxed. I could make it one minute, then two, then finally five. I sat and enjoyed Him. He was my dearest friend. I sat and enjoyed us. "Be still, my soul" had become a reality. My joy abounded. I began to listen to Him speaking into the quiet. How exciting! We could talk over anything and everything.

In the favorite Psalm 23, I recalled, "He *makes* me lie down in green pastures." I decided that, as one of His sheep, I would certainly follow His leading. That included listening and noticing when He signaled "green pasture" time, a time I came to anticipate and relish.

Yet this is a discipline I have lost and had to replace many, many times since those years. It seems to be the one our enemy would most like to rob us of. But he must not succeed. The Lord's delight in having us come depends on it, our spiritual health depends on it, our joy depends on it—and, indeed, our service depends on it as well.

In the process I have been describing, release is followed by rest and quietness so that I may discern clearly the will of God. The Put Off is to be followed by the Put On.

I ask the Holy Spirit to enable me to sit still long enough to delight the heart of God, to know Him, to fellowship with Him, and to hear Him. I have found nothing but a genuine *all-stop* will provide this. I won't get it by trying. The Holy Spirit shows me the Lord's will when I am quiet and receptive, and not before.

Certainly there are those times of crisis and times of temptation when I must have a flash of the Lord's wisdom to deal with the situation at hand. He gives this grace instantaneously. He knows my need, and has promised to supply it. But in the daily scheme of things my foremost need is to know my God.

How too, do I hear the voice of the Holy Spirit? He speaks with a "still, small voice" we know. If I truly believe the Lord is speaking to me in one of the myriad ways He does, will I be able to hear Him? When I as a parent tried to speak to my child when he was distracted or noisy or totally occupied in his own thoughts or activities, I had no success even when I shouted and repeated and grew totally frustrated. Screaming is not a happy sound.

The Holy Spirit does not do this. He waits for me to be quiet and attentive. I think we'd find the Lord speaking far more quickly if we were more peacefully tuned to hear Him. This *will* take time. Count on it. Is there a better use of it?

FEAR

But perhaps you don't rest because of fear. Perhaps you fear God himself and don't feel comfortable with Him. Or perhaps you fear that you *will* hear Him and fear what He may ask you to do.

Fear of the Sovereign King of the Universe is totally appropriate. How incredible the belief of the world today that He can be ignored with impunity. How incredible to think that the Creator will not have the final say as to the destiny of His created beings. "The fear of the Lord is the beginning of wisdom," wrote Solomon. Reverential fear of the awesome power of God is the height of wisdom, and all other points of view are rebellious, uninformed, or completely misguided.

Nevertheless, when one has entered into the open door provided by His Son, Jesus Christ, to bring *children* to the Father, how wise then to see His immeasurable tenderness towards them. Jesus prayed concerning those who would come to believe on Him: "May they be brought to complete unity to let the world know that you sent me and *have loved them even as you have loved me*" (John 17:23, emphasis mine). How tragic to fail to believe this. How this must grieve the God whose heart of love desires to bless His children. Strange, we feel afraid of Him as the tender Father. Are you afraid of Jesus who picked up little children in His arms? So we come as the children did, for we are. His "Perfect love drives out fear" (I John 4:18b).

PRAISE RISES

It is in times of resting in His love that genuine praise *rises*. It fills me and I overflow with it. Consider this prayer of Paul's in the book of Ephesians:

...I pray that you, being rooted and established in love, may have power, together with all saints, to grasp

how wide

and long

and high

and deep

is the love of Christ,

and to know this love that surpasses knowledge—that you may be filled to the measure of all the fullness of God.

(Ephesians 3:17-19, arrangement mine)

Rest into it!

One day as I sat "resting in Christ" these words came to me:

I Redeem the Time

I redeem the time.
I sit and stare at dawn,
Revel in form and color,
And see Your face
And feel Your arms
And hear You whisper.
Love pours onto an unworthy race
And into me.
Hallowed be Thy name.

I redeem the time.
This is the day You made.
You bring rejoicing,
Anointing me with gladness
In Your presence.
O vast and awesome God,
O dear and tender Father.
Hallowed be Thy name.

I redeem the time.
You place peace on my shoulders
Like a mantle.
My soul, a weaned child resting,
Breast-blessed under Your wing.
You wake my brain to inner sight
And strength pours into me.
I will Thy will be done.
Hallowed be Thy name.

PART IV

PUT ON

Receive, Respond, Rejoice

CHAPTER FOUR

RECEIVE

This is my Son, whom I love; with him I
am well pleased. Listen to him!

Matthew 17:5

PERHAPS YOU RECALL my story of Jodi and Greg in the introduction of the book. I told how that tragedy in my life led to my loss
of faith and to my developing devastating habits of fear and anger
towards men coupled with crippling relationship addiction. I told in Part
I how I returned to the Lord and entered into the process of release and
forgiveness, into His healing of my wounds, into restored joy. I related how
I learned to rest in His love for me, and thus into new fervent passionate
love for Him.

I was given a new beginning. Yet what seemed strange to me during those
years of great renewal of love was that my old habits and patterns were still
there, luring me into sin repeatedly. Though I confessed and repented each
time, and tried very hard to change, I couldn't seem to avoid falling back

into them. I found myself still clutching after what seemed like love. I found myself afraid to speak up to men, unable to confront. I found myself filled time and time again with seething anger and resentment.

I decided I'd better complete preparations to become a licensed Marriage and Family counselor for the state of California, and resumed studies to do so. Perhaps I'd learn ways of dealing with my own besetting habits and patterns. Well, indeed I did learn much about relationships and how they operate, but I seemed no more able to change mine than I had ever been. Instead I tried secular techniques that only led me into deeper bondage. I floundered again in my faith and had to begin all over again— again!

Who, of all people who ever lived, related best to all other human beings? Clearly, Jesus Christ. I was seeking in all the wrong places. My sheer blindness astounded me. I prayed, "Show me, Lord. How is genuine freedom to be found; how is genuine change to be brought about?"

Show me He did—in His actions, in His teachings, by His Spirit. As I studied Jesus afresh, I learned that the Lord wanted me to do more than just put a *halt* to sinful habits. I learned that His Put Off is to be followed by His Put On. I learned to seek Him to put *new* habits in the place of *old*. I learned the *entire* process.

I learned to become aware of the tempting thought or urge when it first occurred, and at that moment to move quickly into the Put Off phase, reaching to Him, releasing to Him, resting in His faithfulness to move me into the Put On. What is the secret of the Put On? It's this—*He* would provide awareness of the new habit He wanted to replace the old. And He would empower me to employ it if I chose to obey Him.

Ah yes, now when I yearned for and was tempted to grab for "love," I sought the Lord immediately. His love for me furnished what I needed, and then He asked me to give that love in specific ways to someone else, freely and with no strings attached.

When I became afraid of a man, I released the fear to Jesus immediately, rested in His opinion of me, and moved out in His courage to do the thing I feared most. I learned to confront. I learned to speak the truth in love.

When I became angry or hurt, I released my feelings to Him, letting them go to the cross. Then drawing on His love, I listened to hear Him tell me what He wanted me to learn from my encounter with the one who had hurt me. Sometimes it was a new approach of confrontation. At times it was an act of love and kindness He wanted from me so that I returned good for evil.

I learned never to "just drop it." I learned never to leave a vacuum. I learned to listen to Him. I learned His life in me is love, moving out into action, the

Putting On that frees. And that is the second part of the process I present to you now.

RECEIVE FROM THE LORD

What do we mean when we use the word *receive*? We who have chosen Jesus as Savior have received a multitude of marvelous blessings: the Father's love and welcome, the indwelling Trinity, the full ministry of the Holy Spirit in us, divine promises, constant access to the throne of grace, full citizenship in the kingdom of heaven, the family of fellow believers, our home in heaven awaiting us—the list goes on and on. Gracious gifts and wonderful.

In this instance, however, I use the word *receive* to mean what we receive from Him for our present growth, instruction, and daily living.

It is well nigh impossible to be *resting* with and in Christ without also *receiving* from Him. That's the way it is. When I am sufficiently rested and quiet, and have forsaken my self-efforts, that's when I hear Him. For in resting into Christ, especially from all our merely natural inclinations, we *are* receiving Him, and in Him we then move. How does this look, this moving out and into action?

THE FILLING OF THE HOLY SPIRIT

We read in John 7:36-39: "On the last and greatest day of the Feast, Jesus stood and said in a loud voice, 'If anyone is thirsty, let him come to me and drink. Whoever believes in me, as the Scripture has said, streams of living water will flow from within him.' By this he meant the Spirit whom those who believed in him were later to receive. Up to that time the Spirit had not been given, since Jesus had not yet been glorified."

Just prior to Jesus' ascension He told the disciples: "In a few days you will be baptized with the Holy Spirit...you will receive power when the Holy Spirit comes on you; and you will be my witnesses in Jerusalem, and in all Judea and Samaria, and to the ends of the earth" (Acts 1:5, 8).

Do you remember how they looked prior to this? These eleven men had been the constant companions and disciples of Jesus for at least three years. Yet at the hour of His arrest and ensuing trial, they all forsook Him. Peter, you may remember, denied three times knowing Him. Though John appeared at the foot of the cross with Jesus' mother, Mary, he had nothing to say. Even after Christ's resurrection and His several appearances to them they were obviously not moving out in boldness to declare the wonderful news. These were still, at that time, men who had only *natural* human love and power to rely on. The Holy Spirit was yet to come in power upon them.

And so they together with other believers, both men and women, waited in that upstairs room as Christ had instructed them. "When the day of Pentecost came, they were all together in one place. Suddenly a sound like the blowing of a violent wind came from heaven and filled the whole house where they were sitting. They saw what seemed to be tongues of fire that separated and came to rest on each of them. All of them were filled with the Holy Spirit and began to speak in other tongues as the Spirit enabled them" (Acts 2:1-4). The outflow of the Spirit had begun.

When Peter preached his first Spirit-filled sermon not long after, he said, "God has raised this Jesus to life and we are all witnesses of the fact. Exalted to the right hand of God, he has received from the Father the promised Holy Spirit and has *poured out* what you now see and hear" (Acts 2:32-33, emphasis mine). Further he instructed, "Repent, and be baptized every one of you, in the name of Jesus Christ for the forgiveness of your sins. And you will receive the gift of the Holy Spirit." And those who did were then baptized, about three thousand of them, and were indwelt by the Spirit as promised.

And what marked their lives now? Very clearly we see great power, boldness, and courage to speak. Peter testified, "For we cannot help speaking about what we have seen and heard" (Acts 4:20).

Did you get that? They couldn't *not* speak! They couldn't contain themselves. *They had to speak of Jesus.* Their passion was enormous, for the Holy Spirit created immense power in them as He poured His own incredible love for Jesus Christ into them.

On the last night before His crucifixion, Jesus had told the disciples: "When the Counselor comes, who I will send to you from the Father, the Spirit of truth who goes out from the Father, he will testify about me" (John 15:26). "All that belongs to the Father is mine. That is why I said the Spirit will take from what is mine and make it known to you" (John 16:15).

In the book of Acts we now see the Holy Spirit in the disciples, pouring forth like a fountain as they testify of Jesus, and in His name preach, teach, and heal. The love of their Lord surges out like a river, irresistible, gathering all in its flow.

Later in the history of the church, when the believers were scattered and began to have their gatherings in homes, the gifts of the Holy Spirit for the building up of the body came into full operation. These many gifts of the Spirit did not now involve only speaking and healing, but also serving, helping, giving, administering. Now they were Christ's hands, feet, and body to each other as well as to a dying world. Now they exhorted and encouraged one another in word and deed. Now they bore each other's burdens. Now they prayed fervently. But all their gifts were to be ministered in and through the Spirit, motivated by the love for Jesus poured into their hearts and then poured out for one another.

When you have been abiding with and in Jesus through the power of the Holy Spirit, that love flow arises in you, and your desire to flow out becomes enormous. You seek an outlet. You realize it is *your joy* to minister in whatever way He directs. Now you are eager to receive instructions from Him.

If you are filled with the Spirit in this way and walk in Him, you will receive from Him His thoughts many times each day. You will desire on-going dialogue with Him. As you hear His voice you will move as He directs and energizes—at rest from the works of the self.

What then is necessary to hear the voice of the Spirit that we may move in His filling? Perhaps one word will do: listen.

LISTENING

I was astonished to see so many listings when I looked up the word *hear* in my concordance. I narrowed my search down to those times when the Lord Himself or His representative (prophet, psalmist, apostle) instructed the people—and you and me—to hear.

Who is not familiar with the *Shema*, Hebrew for *Hear*? (Deuteronomy 6:4, 5) It was given to Israel by Moses as dictated by God (and quoted by Jesus when asked for the greatest law). The NIV Study Bible comments: "It has become the Jewish confession of faith, recited daily by the pious...." The command: "Hear, O Israel: The Lord our God, the Lord is one. Love the Lord your God with all your heart and with all your soul and with all your strength." Awesome command!

Further, God promised incredible blessings to Israel if they would hear and keep the law, as well as clear painful consequences if they did not. And did they listen?

Consider the lament of God in Psalm 81. His heart is in these words; they are filled with incredible sorrow and yearning. Can you hear it?

"Hear, O my people, and I will warn you—
if you would but listen to me, O Israel!...
I am the Lord your God,
who brought you up out of Egypt.
Open wide your mouth and I will fill it.
But my people would not listen to me;
Israel would not submit to me."
So I gave them over to their stubborn hearts
to follow their own devices.
"If my people would but listen to me,
if Israel would follow my ways,
how quickly would I subdue their enemies
and turn my hand against their foes!...
But you would be fed with the finest of wheat;
with honey from the rock I would satisfy you."

(Psalm 81:8, 10-14, 16)

More appeals to listen are found in the book of Proverbs—the father appealing to the son, and Wisdom to whoever will heed. Then very frequently we find the command to hear in the major and minor prophets. For example, note Isaiah 28:23:

Listen and hear my voice;
pay attention and hear what I say.

Or Isaiah 55:2-3:

Listen, listen to me, and eat what is good,
and your soul will delight in the richest of fare.
Give ear and come to me;
hear me that your soul may live.

Then comes Jesus, the Logos, the "radiance of His glory and the exact representation of His nature" (Hebrews 1:3, NASB), the embodied Word! His frequent appeal, "He who has ears to hear, let him hear." His words in Luke 8:18: "Therefore consider carefully how you listen. Whoever has will be given more: whoever does not have, even what he thinks he has will be taken from him." And in John 8:43: "Why is my language not clear to you? Because you are unable to hear what I say." His warnings are found throughout the gospels.

Most poignant to me are the words spoken by the Father when Jesus was transfigured before His three disciples. Peter in his astonishment did what he usually did—he started pouring forth his own ideas. Then came the voice from heaven: *"This is my Son, whom I love: with Him I am well pleased. Listen to him!"* (Matthew 17:5, emphasis mine).

When I finished meditating on the word *hear* found in Scripture, I concluded that the way I listen to God is of extreme importance to Him. I saw that failure to listen will not only bring dire consequences to me (I got what I chose!), but is an absolute insult to Him.

If I truly long to please the heart of God, the foremost way I can do so is to listen to Him. First and foremost, this means to know what He has said in the revelation He has already given—the Scriptures. I establish and steadfastly maintain the discipline of reading, studying, and meditating on the Scriptures daily, being mindful especially of the way the Holy Spirit applies it to me personally. I know there are those who don't want to highlight portions of Scripture, but I personally have to do so, often with the date in the margin. I date it to remember when the Lord first burned this truth into my being. Often I must also journal it with the specific way the Spirit is probing my heart or pin-pointing my sin or giving me fresh insight for growth..

This adventure into Scripture is like a mountain climb. Daily my Lord gives me new and marvelous vistas to behold. He also gives me new instructions for the next part of the trail. I am climbing with Jesus this rugged road of life, and it is arduous. But it is truly thrilling as well.

The Bible is also a gold mine, a diamond field, a grand adventure. It is money to be spent in the bank of my inner being. When I have come to this point of *Receive* in the prayer process, the Spirit hands me the cash, so to speak. The deposit is there; it needs only to be drawn on and applied to the need at hand.

I do not say that Scripture rising from within is the only way the Spirit guides. Yet I do believe it is the foremost way. He has already revealed His will; I am responsible to know it and hold it so He can tap into it whenever He chooses.

I will have more to say on this subject shortly.

Surely, however, He does communicate what He wants us to receive in other ways. This means we stay alert with eyes, ears, and spirit receptive to every possible nuance of His thought or impression. We hear Him in His works of nature. As well as listening to the Scripture that we read, we listen to what is quoted to us by others. We pay attention to visions He may give. We are attentive to His inward whisper. We hear Him in the speakers and teachers He has called as spokespersons. We hear Him in the voices of fellow Christians. We listen to Him in circumstances that arise. We stay attentive to hear *His* voice by *whatever* means He chooses to use to communicate His will to us.

And communicate He will. He doesn't merely give instructions for our obedience. He *enjoys* the fellowship of communication with us. And He wishes us to enjoy Him! This is Life! We travel through this life in the spiritual company of the irrepressible God, and find Him the delight of our hearts.

God forbid that I should break His heart afresh by not listening to Him or by inattentiveness and distractedness. I greatly lament the times I have done so.

HEARING IN DEPTH

When I listen in *earnest* to a person speaking to me, I hear on four levels simultaneously: what does the speaker's *body* tell me—expression of face, posture, gesture, eye contact or lack of it, intensity and tone of voice? What is this speaker's *feeling*—about himself, his content, and about me? What is the speaker's *motivation* in speaking? What *content* do the words convey? With these in mind it seems obvious that to listen well requires that I listen in a total way. Nothing less will tell me all I need to hear. I must go out of myself to the other person; I must give myself away to what I am hearing; I must hold all my responses until I have fully heard. This fullness of listening will require a great deal of practice yet it is one of the greatest gifts of loving that we ever do.

If someone asked you what one thing makes you feel most loved, most intimate, and most cherished, what would your answer be? For the majority the one answer is "to be understood." That means to be truly heard, does it not?

Most of us are pleased to have our words heard. But we are doubly blessed when *empathy* is extended as well. Empathy—that beautiful ability to let go of self and listen *into* the speaker; to discern the emotion and intention there. It is not merely sympathy (feeling with). It is not compassion alone, though this may be present as well. It is stepping inside the other person to hear the inside message. This does not require that the listener take on the emotions of the other person (though he may); rather that he enter into them to *understand* them fully, and in a sense *to be* that other person in those moments of listening. By empathy his heart is then stirred to caring response.

How do you listen to your spouse? To your children? To your parent? To your friend? To the person you greet socially? If my husband is describing his response to a clerk in a store, I know the content is not very significant to either of us, and so maybe I can "coast"; I'll keep on attending my cooking or dish washing. But if he is telling me about that check he bounced, you can bet I am all ears! Of course, if I'm more focused on his content and my responses to it than I am on his person, his feeling, and his motivation, we're probably headed for a fight.

Years ago when my six year old daughter came in from school and began bombarding me with every detail of the entire day, I kept my focus for about thirty seconds before getting back to my potato peeling. An occasional "oh my" or "oooooh" was all that she needed as she told every scissor whack of her cut and paste book building. But when she mentioned a bully harassing her, I tuned in totally. Her few words signaled my need to listen fully and completely.

When a friend comments on the heavy traffic, I may give my usual "uh huh" or now Canadian "oh, yes" response. But when she mentions trouble in her marriage, I know we need to sit down for full face, eye to eye, heart to heart communicating. That means she talks and I listen on all four levels.

All of us listen selectively; we have to. Too much that is inconsequential is coming at us throughout our days. Sometimes we must diligently cut off much of it to stay uncontaminated. But along with our tuning out and our indifference to all the clutter comes the habit of not listening well or fully when we really need to. If someone asks me to sit down and listen, can I do it? Can I change habits? Or have I become so used to "uh huh" and distracted attention that I cannot? Am I even able to give myself fully in listening and in love to the speaker?

Again, this is why learning to rest in and with the Lord is so important. I will miss what He is saying unless I am *fully* attentive to Him. Again, only the filling of the Holy Spirit can provide this listening to Him as well as to others. There may be no body language to read, but I do ask to empathize with His emotions, to hear His intention and reason for speaking, and fully to receive His content. To listen this way takes not only devotion but also practice that only the Holy Spirit can enable. My habits of hearing must change; they must be fully engaged. Indeed, I'll have to learn *to live* in this attentive state so that I don't miss the fact that He *is* speaking to me.

Do you hear Him? If you have spent much time learning of Him and with Him, then you'll know when He is speaking to you. He's your shepherd: you have come to recognize His voice. You have come to know His nature. You have begun to understand His intentions for you.

What do we hear? As previously stated, our need is the intimacy of love. We will hear His words of endearment and cherishing. We will hear His playfulness and laughter. We will hear His companioning. If there has been hurt, we will hear His words of healing. And we will hear His quite definite instructions to us. Certainly when we need guidance, He is pleased to give it—and will. Here is our Savior Friend Lover God before us, with us, and in us, blessing with joy the moments of our day with His communication to us.

HEARING THE PUT ON

What many of us seek to receive, however, is specific direction for changing habits. This is especially true when the Put Off has been completed. Now what am I to Put On? Recall how Paul instructed, "...lay aside the old self....and that you be renewed in the spirit of your mind, and put on the new self..." (Ephesians 4:22-24).

Note that the Scriptures indicate God's will is that I put on the opposite of what I have been doing:

Have done with anger and all its kin—Put on kindness, forgiveness.

Stop stealing—Begin working and giving.

Remove thinking and talking that tears down—Add thinking and speaking that builds up.

What old habit are you dealing with? What specifically are you to cast off? What do you need to put on? The Holy Spirit will direct you very exactly as to what to put on if you ask Him and then listen to His instructions. Recall that between *releasing* and *receiving* comes that time of *rest*, of complete stopping and a fresh filling of Christ's love. This period provides a refilling of the Spirit which empowers you to do whatever He tells you to do.

For example, I have often had women tell me that they had a bad habit of yelling at their children. I had this one myself, so I fully understand what has driven them to this habit. So what is the process? When you first sense the shout coming on, you halt it. Delay doing anything; instead *reach* to God immediately. Tell Him what is causing you to feel this way. *Release* your frustration and anger to Him, and stay to confess that you are trying too hard to be in control (if that is the case). Admit that no one knows how to parent children as He does. Then receive some *rest* with Him if only for a minute or two; allow Him to parent you. Now you are ready for the *Receive.* Ask Him specifically how He would have you deal with this child at this time. What thoughts or pictures come to mind? Do you believe He will speak to you of the action He knows is effective for the child? Wait for it. Do not quickly assume you know. Listen for His instruction, and do not act until you are quite certain your response to the child will be what you are receiving from Him. Then act; if you are obedient to Him, your action will be appropriate.

Please note that you will likely deal with this habit many times. It isn't broken all at once. Take it to Him each time the temptation to shout arises. When you come to the point of receiving His instructions, understand that they will not always be the same as the time before; He will make them specific to the child and that child's need at the moment. Perhaps He will ask you to take time to play with the child. Another time He may ask you to isolate the child to his room or to a corner near you. Another time He may ask you to kneel down and look the child in the eye and deliver the message He gives. He may ask you to simply gather the child in your arms and hold her a while. In this way God teaches us to parent in His Spirit and wisdom.

SCRIPTURE

In asking the Lord how to deal with a specific situation, again consider how clearly the Spirit speaks through the Bible. I have found that He will use that way most often. He wrote the manual of operation, so I couldn't mistake His nature, intentions, and specific direction. I have often asked Him a question only to have the thought quickly rise, "What have I already told you?" Specific application and method follows the general instructions already stated in Scripture.

When we know His words in Scripture well enough, we find them rising in us; we hear Him speaking to us with His inner voice the very words He has spoken in the Bible. It's a delight to have these words rise as choice reminders of His companioning.

Caution. Satan loves to quote Scripture too. Think of his use of it in his tempting Jesus in the wilderness. Scripture alone in our minds is not enough to verify that we are hearing the Lord. If it is the Lord speaking to you, you will be able to discern His motivation, His emotional intention, and His person in it: full listening.

And of course you may often *receive* from the Lord without going through the first three steps of the process. We are in constant need of God's guidance, not just when addressing a habit that needs changing. Jesus, quoting from Deuteronomy 8:3, answered Satan's temptation, "It is written, 'Man does not live on bread alone, *but on every word that comes from the mouth of God'*" (Matthew 4:4, emphasis mine). If we are to live by it, we must take it in.

Back to some more thoughts on taking in Scripture apart from the times of prayer processing. The Spirit instructs us to study carefully and know this Bible. If filled with the Spirit, we crave Scripture and relish it as we do food. We join Jeremiah in proclaiming, "When your words came, I ate them; they were my joy and my heart's delight, for I bear your name, O Lord God Almighty" (Jeremiah 15:16).

Paul writes to Timothy:

> *And from infancy you have known the holy Scriptures*
> *which are able to make you wise for salvation*
> *through faith in Christ Jesus. All*
> *Scripture is God-breathed and is useful for*
> *teaching, rebuking, correction*
> *and training in righteousness, so that the*
> *man of God may be thoroughly*
> *equipped for every good work.*
>
> *(2 Timothy 3:15-16)*

Moreover, the Holy Spirit is able to expose *you* as you read the Bible. He is able to supply the exact thoughts that you need to hear as you read the Scriptures. He brings alive word, phrases, stories, concepts and applies them directly and specifically to your life. Consider the following:

> *For the word of God is living and active. Sharper than any double-*
> *edged sword, it penetrates even to dividing soul and spirit, joints and*
> *marrow; it judges the thoughts and attitudes of the heart. Nothing*

98

*in all creation is hidden from God's sight. Everything is uncovered
and laid bare before the eyes of him to whom we must give account.*

(Hebrews 4:12, 13)

Not only does the Scripture expose us to convict us; it also exposes need so that we may get our needs met. The Lord, as we read His words, builds up, encourages, gives hope, creates fresh faith, gives guidance. How often the Psalmists sing of these precious attributes of God. For instance, take a few minutes to meditate on the very familiar 23rd Psalm and allow the Holy Spirit to apply it to you personally. Meditate on these words from 2 Peter 1:3 and 4:

*His divine power has given us everything we need for
Life and godliness through our knowledge of
him who called us by his own glory
and goodness. Through these he has given
us his very great and precious
promises, so that through them you may
participate in the divine nature
and escape the corruption in the world
caused by evil desires.*

SCRIPTURE AS PART OF PROCESS

Whenever you engage in the process I'm outlining and you reach the *Receive* step, the Lord will often direct you to applicable scripture or to a topic in your concordance. Scripture you have memorized may come to mind. Let me say again, *listen*—listen beyond what you read or remember for His own commentary on it and His application to you personally. I find the Lord absolutely amazing in this regard. What He often turns me to is a complete surprise to me. Just when I think I know exactly what He is going to say, He says something that just absolutely astounds me. It is always awesomely wise and creative and not easy to obey. But if I do obey, I find it the delight and adventure of my life.

This happened to me with Donna (not her real name). We were standing in the back of the church talking before the service began. I asked casually, "How are you doing?" She didn't give the standard answer, "Fine." Instead, she began sharing some of the problems she was having with some relatives that were visiting, telling it truthfully and without judgment. "Bear one another's burdens" leaped to my mind. I listened with total focus. When she finished, I prayed, "Lord, what would you have me say?" Immediately I heard, "Don't talk. Hug." So I just enfolded her into my arms. She began to weep, and we stayed in the embrace for a minute or two. When she drew back she said, "That's just what I needed. Thank you."

How do you think I felt at that time? You know!—I was very joyful to have followed just what the Lord impressed me to do. The union with Him was profound: His arms in me and His love flowing through me. Wonderful.

IN CHRIST

I mentioned previously the joy of *being with* Jesus in His life through the pages of Scripture, becoming thoroughly familiar with His character and nature as He speaks and ministers. I go back in time to do this, and as fully as the Holy Spirit enables become a member of the crowd surrounding Him. I hear Him, I see Him, I respond to Him. As I do this, a sense of oneness with the Lord, of the unity and fellowship, become a reality. I begin to spiritually experience the wonder of being with Christ. Then as I go about in my present life, I may further experience the truth of being "in Christ" and having "Christ in me." Here then is a very much more advanced form of listening, for now I hear the motivation and intention of His heart from *within* as He directs it towards the person I am to serve.

How can this be described?

One day as I was praying I confessed to the Lord a difficulty with a fellow Christian. I told the Lord I didn't know the way to deal with her, and I asked Him to show me how. A picture came to mind. I was standing before the Lord, having just asked Him my question. He said, "Step into me," and with those words turned His back to me.

"What?"

He said again, facing away now, "Step into me."

"How can I do that?" I shot back.

"Just step in," He said.

Feeling foolish, I put one foot into His foot. Oddly it was no problem. I stepped in with the other foot. I was inside somehow; I was looking out through His eyes, hearing with His ears, aware of His understanding and His love for my fellow Christian as He looked *at her*. I then found myself speaking His words of kindness and compassion to her.

"What an imagination! Such fantasies. Left field." O.K. chide me if you will, but this *"envisioning"* was a gift to me. It changed my life. It is priceless to me. It was a visual imparting of the words, "I have been crucified with Christ and I no longer live, but Christ lives in me. The life I live in the body, I live by faith in the Son of God, who loved me and gave himself for me" (Galatians 2:20).

When this is my state of being, I am led continually by it. I do not have to ask for guidance. Isn't this what is meant by "walk in the Spirit"?

ASKING SPECIFIC QUESTIONS

Often, however, I find myself back in my own skin, so to speak, and needing to ask for specific guidance and to listen fully to receive it. Even so, some will object that they have, with the purest motives, sought to receive from God, to be lead, to be informed, to be guided, but have heard nothing and have experienced nothing.

I see two main reasons I personally do not receive guidance from the Lord more consistently. First, I am nebulous in my requests, and second, I demand an answer. Let me deal with the first one, being nebulous. I get confused and beg, "God, lead me." In respect to *what*? What is my specific need? That's the first thing I need to ask *Him*, "Lord, what is my need?" because I often truly do not know. I just *feel* uncomfortable or distressed or fearful, and I want the feelings to go away. But when I make a definite and specific request, I am then focused on a specific answer.

Brian did just this. Here is the account he gave to our Rugged Road class:

> My ex-wife and I have fought over my kids and my support of them for years. She's seemed very vindictive to me and constantly seeking more, more, more. It has made me a very angry man. I stayed angry; it was always there. I would flare up at any little thing.
>
> Well, I found out I needed to release all this to God. So I did. I really poured it on and poured it out. Then I tried to let it go and rest in Him. I had to do that a lot. But I also told Him I was listening. I just asked, "Lord, what do you want me to do?" And He told me. He said I was to

write a letter to my ex-wife and apologize for all my wrong doing during our years of marriage.

So I did that. I didn't hear anything back, so I just left it with the Lord. Amazing thing though, after I did what He said, all my anger toward her was gone.

Another court date had been scheduled, so that morning my lawyer and I walked in. My lawyer was greeted by her lawyer and then was told by him that my ex-wife had dropped her request. She wasn't there at all. Now I wish she'd have let me know in advance so I wouldn't have had to pay lawyer's fees. "But hey," I told the Lord, "who's complaining? You've already done so much in taking away my anger. Now it looks like You've taken away hers too. Now that *is* a miracle!" Fantastic.

Brian had more to say. He'd learned, so he continued:

This listening to God had worked so well in regard to my ex-wife that I asked the Lord if He wanted me to do the same with a past boss who was not dealing fairly with me. I told the Lord if He did to please have my boss call me, and I would apologize to him for my part in our dispute. The next day, my old boss called! I apologized. Silence. Then he sorta cleared his throat—and apologized to me! So then we went on talking about this and that, and then he said, "Hey, I'm hiring right now. Do you need work?" I did, and so guess what—I got a job right then and there. Do you think I'm happy about obeying the Lord?

Ask we must. Has he not told us that we are to do so? Again, is He not glorified when we do so? Consider the following verses and the reasons the Lord gives for asking. I have emphasized some of the words in the verses quoted.

John 14:13-14: "I will do whatever you *ask* in my name, so that *the Son may bring glory to the Father.* You may *ask* me for anything in my name, and I will do it." Note: "in my name" means in accordance with *all* He is, in accordance with His character and purpose.

John 15:7-8: "If you remain in me and my words remain in you, *ask* whatever you wish, and it will be given you. This is *to my Father's glory, that you may bear much fruit,* showing yourselves to be my disciples."

John 15:16: "You did not choose me, but I chose you and appointed you to *go and bear much fruit*—fruit that will last. Then the Father will give you whatever you *ask* in my name."

John 16:23b-24: "I tell you the truth, my Father will give you whatever you *ask* in my name. Until now you have not asked for anything in my name. *Ask* and you will receive, and *your joy will be complete.*"

Matthew 7:7-8: "*Ask* and it will be given you; seek and you will find; knock and the door will be opened to you. For everyone who asks *receives*; he who seeks *finds,* and to him who knocks, the *door will be opened.*"

Matthew 21:22: "If you believe, you will *receive* whatever you *ask* for in prayer."

The apostle John further underscores the Lord's words in I John 5:14, 15: "This is the confidence we have in approaching God: that if we *ask* anything according to his will, he hears us. And if we know that he hears us—whatever we *ask*—we know that *we have what we asked of him.*"

But James warns us, "You do not have, because you do not *ask* God. When you ask, you do not receive because you ask with wrong motives, that you may spend what you get on your pleasures" (James 4:2b, 3).

WRONG MOTIVES AND LACK OF TRUST

O.K. I asked. And I want His glory. I want fruit bearing. I want my joy to be complete. Why am I not hearing an answer?

Joe asked me a question about his marriage. I told him plainly what I believed would help the situation. The look in his eyes told me the whole story: he didn't believe I knew what I was talking about. It's the same way I look at the used car salesman when he tells me this 1986 Dodge has at least another 100,000 miles (or in Canada, kilometers) of great driving left in it before it expires.

When I asked the Lord what to do, I probably heard an answer, but I denied it was the Lord I heard because I didn't trust His instruction to me.

Or I didn't like it. Or I knew what I wanted and hoped He would rubber stamp it.

Again, James nails us: "If any of you lacks wisdom, he should ask God, who gives generously to all without finding fault, and it will be given to him. But when he asks, he must believe and not doubt, because he who doubts is like a wave of the sea, blown and tossed by the wind. That man should not think he will receive anything from the Lord" (James 1:5-7).

And he doesn't. Doesn't hear a thing. The Lord didn't speak; why should He?

But there are those who ask in the way Scripture instructs and with faith, and they do hear. My friend Anna Beketov has written a true story that illustrates this beautifully. Here it is:

A WAR STORY

Len and Frankie had been sweethearts for more than two years. They were "engaged to be engaged", as they used to say. They enjoyed each others company, canoeing, hiking, sailing, tennis—she was as good as he was and just as competitive. And best of all they shared their faith in the Lord and sought His blessing on their activities.

They'd met when he used to drive fifty miles every week with a carload of young people from his small home town (and smaller church)to the big church in the big city of Victoria. Frankie's father was the pastor of this big Baptist church and it was growing encouragingly under his leadership. The expanding group of young people had great times together—basketball games, picnics, hikes and, of course, great Bible studies and fellowship.

Then the war came. The Second World War. Len joined the Royal Canadian Air Force and was posted to an airfield in the middle of Saskatchewan, the bald prairies! It was very hard saying good bye to Frankie. They'd traveled together on the ferry from Victoria to Vancouver so she could see him off on the train. It was a tearful farewell but they both knew there would be the annual furloughs and she'd promised to write often. And she did. Those letters were so important to Len and so eagerly anticipated.

But the leaves seemed very far apart. The first year dragged on and on until the joyful trip home. They picked up where they'd left off and had a wonderful time together. But the time was all too short and then there was another long year to wait. The welcome letters kept coming to Len.

But gradually the time lapse between them lengthened and the tone changed subtly. They became more vague, less intimate. Len worried. He wrote asking what was wrong and telling her how concerned he was but Frankie replied that things were fine. She was working longer hours at her job so was too tired to write as much or as often as she'd done before. He missed their fellowship through the letters and prayed about his concerns. As the weeks went by Len became more anxious and discouraged. Finally, he asked the Lord for help to understand the situation.

His annual furlough was coming up and he wasn't looking forward to it at all. But Len still had one more weekend leave so decided to hitch a ride to Saskatoon. Not far from the airfield an old, broken down farm truck pulled to a grinding halt beside him. "Hop in Sonny," the farmer greeted him. "I always pick up service-men. My boy's in the army. I'm not going far but I'll take you to the next crossroads." They drove in silence, then, "Where ya from?"

"A small town on Vancouver Island, Duncan," Len replied.

The farmer suddenly exploded with enthusiasm. "That's where my Roy is. He's in Victoria! He didn't like it at all at first but now he's met a girl and things are just fine. Would you believe she's the daughter of a Baptist minister!"

Len knew Victoria and he knew there were no other Baptist ministers with daughters in their early twenties. His heart was overflowing with gratitude for the Lord's unusual way of answering his prayer. As he got out of the old truck he thanked the farmer. "You've been most helpful. More than you'll ever know!"

When he arrived home to Vancouver Island, Frankie met him as usual with a cheery greeting. Len's reply to her was, "How's Roy?"

That's really not the end of the story. God had someone much better waiting in the wings for Len. In the years to come he met and married the author of this story—Anna. Now that was a good ending, and Len was incredibly thankful that the Lord had sent Roy along so it would happen that way.

WAITING

But Len had some waiting to do when he asked God just who He *had* intended for him. For a long while there was silence. And waiting.

For me, there are those times when I've asked, believed, listened intently and still heard nothing. Has that ever been your experience? Then I go away peeved at the Lord for the silence, and forge ahead with my own quite adequate rational thinking. And though the Lord does answer through the thoughts He gives—rational thinking—I must be at peace that this *is* the way He is answering me. More often than not, when I forge ahead impatiently, I live to regret it. Why doesn't the Lord answer when I ask and save me all this grief?

When I believe my motives are pure, and still the Lord is silent, I know I must be willing to wait. I need to look again at this concept of waiting. It was very clear to the psalmists who used the word *qavah*, meaning "to wait, expect, hope for," so the word is sometimes translated "wait" and sometimes "hope."

__Wait__ for the Lord;
be strong and take heart
and __wait__ for the Lord.

(Psalm 27:14)

...but those who __hope__ in the Lord
will inherit the land....
__Wait__ for the Lord
and keep his way.
He will exalt you to inherit the land.

(Psalm 37:9 and 34)

I __waited__ patiently for the Lord;
he turned to me and heard my cry.

(Psalm 40:1)

I __wait__ for the Lord, my soul __waits__ for the Lord,
and in his word I put my hope.
My soul __waits__ for the Lord

106

*more than watchmen **wait** for the morning,*
*more than watchmen **wait** for the morning.*

(Psalm 130:5-6)

But why does He insist I wait before He speaks? I want an answer now. I need it now!

Really?

Has it become possible for me to sit silent in His presence, focused on beholding and adoring Him, and not striving to get an answer? How long am I able to maintain such silence? Is my mind still? Am I distracted by outside factors? Inside voices?

Again, what is it I truly want? Am I sincerely longing for the Lord's glory? Am I being pushy? Wanting credit? Wanting answers but not the Lord himself?

Have you ever dealt with someone like Marcia? Marcia called me at 10:30 in the evening. Her boyfriend had stood her up and hadn't called to explain. She had spent the evening smoldering and had now burst into full flames. She raged for a full half hour before demanding, "So now what do I do?" I told her I'd pray with her that she be enabled to release and rest her case with the Lord, and then we would listen together for His direction. She'd have none of it. "No, I don't want to wait. Tell me now what to do!" she insisted. And I wanted to, but it wouldn't have been the answer she was seeking. Telling an irate woman to go take a cold shower might not be a good idea.

But I have to wonder if I ever make the Lord feel that way when I insist on the answer. Now! Not a good idea. Try waiting. Try listening in silence. Try stillness and adoration.

Delphine did just that. She endeavors to stay in very close fellowship with the Lord, practicing His presence in all aspects of her life. She has discovered over and over the faithfulness of God in answering in His time. She shared this with our Rugged Road class:

> I had longed to join our church for several years, but my husband opposed it. I released this issue to the Lord, prayed about it, and left it to the Lord to work on my husband's heart. Every time it came to mind, I released it and prayed afresh and renewed my trust in the Lord to deal with it. I said nothing to my husband.

Not long ago it came to mind again. This time when I prayed I heard the Lord tell me to tell my husband I was going to join the church because the Lord had instructed me to do so. So I considered the opposition I'd get, but I didn't hesitate. I had received the Lord's word, and I would obey.

I went to my husband and said, "The Lord has told me it is time for me to go ahead and join the church now." I expected him to oppose me. Instead he said, "I think I should join too. It is also time for me to become a member." I was astounded and tremendously thankful that I had waited for God's timing. It's perfect.

To recap: ask the Lord a specific question and then listen for His answer. If none is forthcoming, return to the Rest stage and wait, meanwhile enjoying His presence and then going on about the next daily thing you know He would have you do. Continue to come back to Him in prayer with your question, thanking Him in advance that He will provide you the answer in His time and His way. Stay open to the thinking He will give you in regard to it. When you do have His answer, record it and then begin to obey as soon as possible.

LEARNING

I find one of the things the Lord wants most for me to receive is learning. He wants to instruct me as to how to play out a situation when it happens again. Have your ever experienced that helpless feeling of not knowing what to say when a person makes some startling comment, hands you a put-down, criticizes you unfairly, or blasts your Christian beliefs? You are dumbfounded, tongue-tied, aghast.

Drawing a blank, you stare or stammer a vague retort. Or you withdraw or hang your head, knowing that you simply cannot answer in any way. You go away feeling utterly defeated, undone, thoroughly upset, devastated, or angry or all of these together. You may plan a strong retaliation or a noble rebuttal. You may dream of a scathing denunciation or a powerfully overwhelming argument. You feel that you must score a victory over this foe.

What you really need is to engage immediately in the prayer process. When you get to this Receive stage, you can expect the Lord to teach you a new way to handle what you have encountered. You run the whole thing by Him, so to speak, and He rewrites your script. That point where you were thunderstruck—that's where He gives you new insight as well as new words to speak when the same issue or a similar one arises. He may ask you to confront. If so, listen for the words He wants you to use. He may ask you to draw a firm boundary that deals emphatically with the other person's behavior. If so, listen to exactly what this is and how He would have you speak it clearly. Listen closely until you have your God-script completed and then memorize it. Go and deliver it courageously at His chosen moment. You will find this kind of learning from the Lord's Spirit is a powerful experience.

WHERE ARE YOU, LORD?

It is true that we Christians may go through periods when we hear nothing at all from the Lord. Processing anything doesn't seem possible. We don't sense His presence, so reaching up seems useless—who's there?—and there seems to be no one to release to. Rest with Him is out of the question, for He doesn't make His presence known. There is no comfort when there is no one present to give comfort and love. No instructions are forthcoming even when we ask for them. What to do?

Stay the course. Apply your faith. Search to see if there is a sin that needs confessing and repenting of. If not, then trust in what He has already assured you: that He is there even if you don't *experience* Him; that you are to reach to the One you count on is hearing you; that you are to pour out to Him even if your words seem to just fill the air; that you are to trust that you can rest in your faith that He is present even if there is a prevailing sense of His absence.

When you receive no instruction from Him whatsoever—when Scripture is just words with no light, when your spirit hears no internal voice at all, when the words of others seem amiss or inappropriate—settle down and *trust Him.* Engage for as long as need be in waiting. He means this time for your good, even though during it, it is hard to keep believing His good intention. James 1:2-4 tells us something incredible that we are to do at such times: "Consider it pure joy, my brothers, whenever you face trials of many kinds, because you know that the testing of your faith develops perseverance. Perseverance must finish its work so that you may be mature and complete, not lacking anything."

RUNNING AHEAD

I recall another outcry: "You don't understand. I simply *can't* wait. I must have an answer now." Ah, yes. His timing is off, indeed.

Have you read these words in the book of Isaiah?

Who among you fears the Lord
and obeys the word of his servant?
Let him who walks in the dark, who has no light,
trust in the name of the Lord and rely on his God.
But now, all you who light fires and provide yourselves
with flaming torches, go, walk in the light of your fires
and of torches you have set ablaze.
This is what you shall receive from my hand:
You will lie down in torment.

(Isaiah 50:10, 11)

Now that is a promise I don't want to test.

My own presumptuousness in this regard has lead to some very necessary chastening. It has usually been applied by that tool of the Lord called "natural consequences." When I've tried to force God's hand or manipulate or barter with Him, and can't, I've resorted to running ahead and providing my own answer. I often lie and say it is His, that I have surely heard Him. It gets clearer and clearer that the results are neither effective nor joyful. I am left with striving, stress, and ultimately failure. I also have to face the distressing sense that it is my own doing. I am filled with sadness that, rather than delighting His heart, I have saddened it. Why do I deceive myself and insist I've listened and heard when I haven't? How much better to wait for a sure word from Him and the power and joy that accompanies it.

Many times the Lord has had to use His shepherd's crook *again* to draw me back, and it has hurt. I have a permanent scar on my neck from an operation I had in my twenties. It continually reminds me of all the times He's had to hook me and draw me back.

In Jesus' day if a sheep ran ahead or aside too often and couldn't be trained to follow closely, the shepherd would break the sheep's leg, and then carry it. Has He ever had to break your leg? I confess He has had to break mine. I've had much "carry time" to become thoroughly ashamed of myself, and frustrated by the inactivity. But I learned to follow. Usually. How proud and wayward I am!

EXPERTS

I can recall making this mistake in my counseling. I would seek some answer in regard to a client. When the Lord didn't quickly provide it, I would begin to read every expert in the field, and conclude that I needed some new insight. I didn't wait for His leading to do it. When I finished checking the experts, I also had the problem of not checking it out with Him to find out if what they were telling me was indeed *truth*. It was easy to allow theory to replace genuine truth, and so to think that the Bible's wisdom was behind the times. We enlightened moderns needed *new!* When I found what *I* thought would work, I would employ the great new technique. My pride abounded in being at the cutting edge of successful counseling. So I would give this truly marvelous, newest, most effective help which in reality turned out to be very little help at all, even in the natural. It covered the problem effectively for a short while, but didn't truly heal. Sad. A waste of time and energy, followed by the chastening I've described in the previous paragraphs.

I am not saying that we should never consult experts. God is Truth and the author of it in every field. I may very well sense that He would have me read up on the problem at hand. When this is the case, I am very aware that I am not pushing. I have His peace about it, and know it is His guidance. Again I need to ask myself, what is my motive? Is it to please and delight the heart of God, or merely to solve my problem?

Let's say you have a revelation that you have an anger problem. You are touchy and easily upset and angered by little things. Those closest to you can set you off in an instant by their looks or remarks or actions. You know your question for the Lord: "How would you have me get rid of this anger *habit*?" In the quietness of your spirit, you listen. You hear nothing. You research Scripture. You look up every reference that is instructive on handling anger and ask the Holy Spirit to apply each to you. Now ask if He would also have you read further on the subject. Perhaps you need to hear more from a variety of authors. Perhaps He would have you go to an anger management class or to a counselor. One thing is certain: You need to keep listening to Him and seeking His glory and delight until *His* will is clear to you.

Or suppose you know He wants you to set some boundaries in regard to the sinful behavior of a child, a spouse, a boss, a friend. You need expert help on this and you know it. I know of no better books on the subject than those written by Henry Cloud and John Townsend. Check them out, and see what the Lord says to you through their expertise on the boundaries you need to set.

Let me risk being redundant. When I feel I am pushing, in all probability I have not taken time to *Rest*. I've gotten my eyes so much on the problem and on getting a solution, that I have forgotten to seek Him for Himself alone.

I am missing the point. *He wants to produce His life in me.* He wants me to step into Him and walk in the Spirit. He wants me to have His character, His holiness, His power to live out a life without touchiness and anger over small things. He wants to be in me to confront or to set a boundary. He wants me to have His mind, His patience, and His love for the one who angers me and His strength to deal with the one who intimidates me.

Am I pressing this home too strongly? Perhaps. But it seems we Christians think that we must personally strive to improve *our* character, and in doing so we become proud, judgmental, and "holier than thou." Life in the Spirit, on the other hand, is marked by His presence and gladness in us. I'll never develop patience in and of myself. If I improve in that area at all, it will just be the product of natural trying, and I'll take credit for it. Instead I need to realize afresh it is *"Christ in me, the hope of glory."*

In review of the process, when I have finished with the Put Off: Reach to God, Release, and Rest; and I am ready for the Put On. I listen intently and in every way to what God wants to add. I am ready to *Receive* His instruction—what to think, what to perceive, what to do. If it does not come, I thank Him that He will speak when He is ready, and I leave it with Him. I go on to the next thing I know He has assigned me. I do not fret about the Put On. I have found that He will direct me quite clearly in His time. The sense of the Holy Spirit's direction, when it comes, is unmistakable; I don't have to wonder. Rather I find I now must seek to determine if I will *do* as He asks.

RATIONAL THOUGHT

In regard to needing guidance on particular topics, much has been written and I do not hope to fully examine the subject. But I do want to briefly examine one topic: the use of the rational mind. Someone will say, "My need isn't mentioned in the Scriptures. I need a new car, and Scripture doesn't tell me which one to buy. So what's wrong with rational thinking?" This assumes, of course, that you have first determined it is His will that you buy a car.

What is the relationship of the rational mind to the spiritual mind? God certainly is the creator of the rational mind in man. Doesn't He expect it to be used?

Indeed He does, but under His guidance. It is His will that we invite Him to invade all our thinking, to monitor the very thoughts that occur to us. His protection and His guidance come to us in this way. His grace extends to us *through* the rational mind.

Listen to these words from Proverbs 2:3-6, 8-11:

> *...and if you call out for insight*
> *and cry aloud for understanding,*
> *and if you look for it as for silver*
> *and search for it as hidden treasure,*
> *then you will understand the fear of the Lord*
> *and find the knowledge of God.*
> *For the Lord gives wisdom*
> *and from his mouth come*
> *knowledge and understanding...*
> *for he guards the course of the just*
> *and protects the way of his faithful ones.*
> *Then you will understand what is right*
> *and just and fair—every good path.*
> *For wisdom will enter your heart, and*
> *knowledge will be pleasant to your soul.*
> *Discretion will protect you,*
> *and understanding will guard you.*

Several members of our spring class had problems with "control issues." Carmen described it this way: "I have problems with control. Whenever I've faced a decision, my habit has been to think of as many options as I can and to quickly choose one and get on with it. I have learned from this class to reach to God, first, and then to release any of my rational solutions to Him. I rest in Him then and pray that He will direct my thinking to His will. I wait for these thoughts to come to me. If more than one option comes, I pray that His choice will prevail. Then I choose. I have confidence then and peace, and fellowship with Him as well."

Frank added, "I have problems with control like Carmen has. Mainly, I've had to learn that I *can* hear His voice. He *will* show me His will if I'll just expect to receive it and not barge ahead with my own thinking. He really does speak. The thoughts and pictures do come. It's Him, and I know it."

Melinda said courageously, "O.K., I have a problem with control too—I haven't got any. I wake up thinking of all the things on my agenda, and begin 'scatter thinking' in a jumble about all of it. I'm just 'out there' whirling around in space, getting a sense of being caught in the whole mish-mash. I can't seem to get a good handle on anything. I feel lost and overwhelmed. So I just blunder along, just handling it as I go."

"Now I am learning to process each item on my agenda. I am learning to bring each before Him. I am learning not to fly off but to release each item to Him and to wait before Him for His wisdom concerning it. I'm not totally there yet, but I am learning. This gives me so much more peace. I love the fellowship with the Lord. I don't always have to come to Him with my sense of inadequacy and failure. I *start* with Him; that's the difference."

I am reminded of a story my husband, George, has told of his days in the Royal Canadian Air Force. He was a career officer, and after many years of flying and teaching flying, he was transferred to the task of giving survival training to young men. He made many excursions into the Arctic to arrange for camp sites where the men would be assigned for the weeks of survival training.

On one such occasion he and a fellow instructor were in a small hut made of packing boxes and snow blocks that had been built for them twelve miles away from the Cambridge Bay main quarters. The hut housed their cots, a cooking burner, and a small oil burner for heat. They had arrived on this cheery scene earlier on a cold December day. The temperature continued to fall as they went about their assigned mission: to assess what had been done by the previous service team to determine places for building igloos, and to scout out the land for suitable training of the men. By evening it was 48 degrees (F) below zero.

They were alone in this desolate place and would be for three more days until picked up. Ever the optimists and hardy men of the wilderness, they were unconcerned about the possibility of survival or supply problems since the trail back to the main quarters ran along the river nearby. Surely they could find it and walk it back if need arose. They were bundled up in abundant warm clothing, footgear, and gloves. Each carried his indispensable snow knife on his person at all times.

They were glad enough to go into the hut by day's end. After heating and eating their supper of beans, they were ready to tumble into their cots for a long night's sleep.

"This oil burner sure isn't producing much heat," George observed. "Think I'll just sleep with everything on." Cliff agreed, so they removed nothing as they moved toward their cots.

Just as they lay down, George noticed a loud thrumming sound. He knew instantly it was the oil burner. Rushing to examine it, he saw it was red hot.

"Cliff. The oil burner's too hot! Let's go!" he yelled, grabbing his knife and sleeping bag. Cliff dashed out right behind him. They were out in mere seconds and not an instant too soon.

At that moment the hut erupted into flames that shot skyward. The fire roared mightily and devoured their quarters completely. All their provisions were gone in a matter of minutes. The two men stared in shock.

"It's a miracle we hadn't fallen asleep and been burned alive!" George exclaimed. He stood stock still, viewing the total ruin with unbelieving eyes.

Neither had asked anything of God. Neither had prayed. It was the sheer grace of God that had protected them. And they knew it. They were mute in the wonder of their narrow escape.

But then it dawned on them that they were still in immense danger. Cold can kill as well as fire. Now, clearly and consciously, George sought God and asked for His guidance. His heart filled with prayer.

Then the two began to consider rationally all their options:

Hole up in an igloo they must build in the dark of night and remain in it until pick up. No, there was no food now and not enough heat to sustain them, even if they could build in the dark.

Find the river in the dark and walk by it if possible. Was there enough light? The northern lights and the stars made it possible to see the contours of the land, but a light wind blew snow about and obscured their feet and legs. What if they stumbled? What of accidents from falling?

Then George caught a glimpse of a flashing light. It was the beacon at the air field some eight to ten miles away. Rationally they knew they could walk toward it overland, and would likely be more successful at doing so than groping to find the river. At that point George believed it was the guidance of God giving them this sight and these thoughts.

They decided to walk in a straight line toward the light. Staunchly they committed themselves to this rational decision and felt their fears and doubts diminish. Eyes on the beam, they set out at a steady pace.

Every time the wind picked up and blew the snow about, the light was obscured and their concern mounted. But each time the reassuring light reappeared. Each time they proceeded with renewed confidence.

Suddenly again the light was totally blotted out. But this time it did not reappear. They were in a dreaded white out. They could see almost nothing above or below. Snow swirled everywhere. What would guide them now?

Again, George's training came to the fore of his rational mind: watch the *angle* of the drifts, the direction the wind had driven them. These they could see one pace ahead. And this they did, step by slow step. Two men alone on the top of the world in intense dark and cold, possibly lost and likely to freeze—these thoughts were held at bay as they watched for the angle of drift that led each step. Minute by minute, hour by hour, they simply watched and walked.

A mile from camp the beacon light reappeared. They were safe. They would make it. Great relief and thankfulness washed through them and spilled out in shouts and quips. When the camp came into view they headed straight for the lighted kitchen, to food, warmth, and company. And as they entered, George again felt profound thankfulness to God. He praised the God who had invaded their rational minds and recalled their training in order to guide them.

We must be clear that God is not erasing our ability to glean information and to use it. If your need is a new car, it seems clear to me that your need is to *invite Him* to direct your rational processes as *you* study and make the selection. He is enlightening our choices, but He doesn't choose *for* us. In fact, I think, in such a case, we choose according to our preferences, which He created in us, and so He enjoys our fellowship in the process of selection.

Oswald Chambers wrote insightfully on this in *My Utmost for His Highest:*

> What is the sign of a friend? That he tells you secret sorrows? No, that he tells you secret joys. Many will confide to you their secret sorrows, but the last mark of intimacy is to confide secret joys. Have we ever let God tell us any of His joys, or are we telling God our secrets so continually that we leave no room for Him to talk to us? At the beginning of our Christian life we are full of requests to God, then we find that God wants to get us into relationship with Himself, to get us in touch with His purposes....The things that make God dear to us are not so much His great big blessings as the tiny things, because they show His amazing intimacy with us; He knows every detail of our individual lives.[12]

He further introduces another important point in this aspect of guidance:

> If we are saved and sanctified God guides us by our ordinary choices, and if we are going to choose what He does not want, He will check, and we must heed. Whenever there is doubt, stop at once....God instructs us in what we choose, that is, He guides our common sense....[13]

This relationship between asking and not asking becomes clearer and clearer as we spend our days in company with Him. The delight, as Chambers said, is in having God confide His joys to us. Looked at that way, this step of receiving from God flows right out of our rest in Him, and is a continual feast.

CHAPTER FIVE

RESPOND

This is love for God: to obey his commands.
And his commands are not burdensome.

1 John 5:3

S I HAVE PREVIOUSLY stated, many times we receive from the Lord without prior steps in the process. We may be worshipping Him or just moving through our day with Him, and suddenly receive from Him clear words in regard to some matter. Or a portion of Scripture. Or a distinct impression. What a joy this is to me when this happens for I know He is communicating to me, and I hadn't even asked a question. Or knocked. Or even been expecting Him to speak. But He did, and does. For He loves me and He loves my fellowship.

So He speaks, and I hear (receive) and find my *response* is instantaneous. I am full of joy or I am disappointed or I am indifferent. Or I am wary, as is often the case because I am afraid. Or...or....or. Any emotion or combination of them may arise.

If I am wise, I will transparently acknowledge to the Lord what I am feeling, whatever it is. I will release it fully to Him. This is certainly one type of response, and takes me back to the beginning of the process I have been describing. Dialogue with God is to be my constant state of being, so this sort of receiving and responding is the fabric of my communication throughout the day. We walk and talk as the good friends we are.

But my use of the word *respond* at this point presumes I have *received from the Lord* a request to change. What habit have I dropped before it was well formed? Is this a reminder to practice it? Or is there a thought He would have me hold? What new attitude does He require? What new action would He have me take? What would He have me *think* or *do*. It may be to meditate on what I have received from Him. It may be to intercede in prayer. It may be to call a person, to write a letter, to cook a meal. Or perhaps He is asking me to visit the sick, to give a gift, to serve a person in some way. It may be a big request such as to begin a ministry or begin an educational process. How shall I respond to His request? What is *my* will? Is it to do *His* will? If it is an action, I will straightforwardly choose it, schedule it, and do it as soon as I am able.

Perhaps I allow myself to stay dull of hearing because I am reluctant to hear what He may ask of me. What may He request? Will it require sacrifice? Diligent effort? Time? It is so much easier to mellow out with the ballgame, the soaps, a book, magazine, or newspaper. I need to get to my Delete file on the e-mail. I need to do research on the internet. I need to relax with friends and watch a video. I put Him off. If I listen to Him He may instruct me to use the gift or gifts He has given me for ministry. He may expend me and allow tiredness. He may challenge me to risk a new venture.

You may remember Jonah and his resistance to God. The Lord gave specific directions to him to go to Ninevah with a proclamation Jonah didn't want to give. Like Jonah, I know something about this God—He asks me to do things I object to. He asks me to do things that scare me. Sometimes He asks me to do things that embarrass me. Often He asks me to do what I simply would rather not do. It takes too much energy. Too much strategizing. Too much planning. Too much.

I reason that if I don't rest down with Him, totally relaxed and trusting like a baby in a mother's arms, maybe I won't hear anything. Then I can say I never heard Him speak to me. One might call that an easy out. And great missing out as well. But He gives me my choice. And He gives you yours.

When I have heard I often make three mistakes in regard to His request:

1. I immediately think I can handle it with no problem, and proceed to do so in my own natural energy and insight.
2. I see it as overwhelming, far too big for me, and simply not possible.
3. I procrastinate and then forget. I really don't relish the assignment, so I don't outright reject it; I simply postpone it until a "better time." This effectively allows me to excuse myself when I realize I have conveniently forgotten it all together.

The first two remind me of Glenrose, somehow.

Glenrose! The name of that small town always caused rejoicing in my child heart. That was the place my father's family, the ten grown and still living Smith children with their families and a few close kin, held their family reunion each summer. About eighty of us gathered in a large park there to enjoy this festive day Texas style—rowdy and loud, droll and relaxed, and hours of sampling the best of home cooking. I loved Glenrose!

The first order of the morning there was the jump into the big park pool for at least an hour or two. All who did would work up a giant sized appetite for the feasting in the afternoon.

I well remember that I and my brother would jump from the car almost before it stopped moving. We'd rush into the dressing rooms, tear off our clothes, and wiggle into our bathing suits in two minutes flat. Then the mad dash to the counter with baskets, the holding out grimy hands for the pin marked with the basket number. Often I poked my finger attaching it to my suit, shuffling toward the pool all the while. As soon as it was secure, I'd run the rest of the way to poolside and leap with total abandon into the water, loving my creation of splash and crash. I knew when I came up the first thing I'd see would be laughing uncles and frowning cousins. Heaven!

In that pool we children frolicked and played with our fathers and uncles and sometimes each other, and showed off relentlessly to get the ready compliments of the grownups in and along the edge of the pool. And I heard no end of praise and banter because my mom and aunts were the gallery lining the side. They didn't want to get their hair wet. They called and joked and cheered. So did the uncles and dads tossing us about. Child watching, teasing, and extolling were favorite pastimes of all Smiths.

I particularly remember the summer I was seven. I and my brother, Jerry, one year older, were up at the crack of dawn, bolting down cereal, hyperactive and whiny, pleading with our parents to hurry. I was remembering my terrific hatred of my cousin, Ralph, a few months younger than I. He was an expert at mean and dirty tricks, and I'd been the victim of several. (That's another story.) I yearned to best him in all things and I couldn't wait to see what opportunities I'd have at Glenrose this year.

Finally all the food, all the gear, all the kids—my younger brother as well as Jerry and me—and two harassed parents, were stuffed in the old car. We were off! After only two flat tires and lots of sweating and thrashing about, we finally arrived at the Glenrose pool parking lot. I woefully spotted my uncle's car. Oh heck, ol' Ralph, no doubt, was already in the pool splashing and having a merry time.

I moved with lightning speed out of car and clothes, ran helter-skelter to the pool, and made my usual grand entrance, complete with squeal. I came up sputtering and yelling. Aaahheeee! Someone pulled me down from beneath. Up again, I was immediately seized, teased and tossed about by my uncles and grown up cousins. I plunged in and out of the water and almost choked from all the laughter.

I noticed after a time that lots of the boys were jumping off the low board, Ralph included. No problem. I had no fear of water whatsoever, and could dog paddle anywhere. So I lined up and took my turn, and received due praise. Music.

Then cousin J.R., our grown-up favorite, dared the older boys to go off the high board. The boys took the dare of course, and one by one managed their moments of glory. I listened with immense envy to the shouts, whistles, and glad words that greeted them. And Ralph wasn't one of them.

I couldn't stand it. *I* wanted to show that I too was courageous, daring and brave! And I wanted to show up ole Ralph more than anything in the world. I hurried to the line-up by the ladder and took my place at the end. All my boy cousins began to taunt me:

"Whacha think you're doin'?" "You crazy?" "Git outta here, pee wee!" "No girls, dummy!"

I stayed put. One of my uncles noticed me. "Jawee, do you thaink you kin jump off that high board? You a mite young, aint't cha?" I ignored him and kept ooching forward in the line. I could do this. I just knew I could! I'd show them all.

My turn came at last, and I climbed the first four steps boldly and with no hesitation whatsoever.

Then I looked down. Mistake! Fear had a quick birth in me and grew like Jack's beanstalk. Maybe I'd better back down. Maybe I'd just kind of fall off like I'd missed my step. Maybe....

Then I heard my father, "Go on, honey. Show them ole boys. You kin do it!" I heard the delight in his voice. I knew he wanted me to jump. That's all I needed to spur me on. I kept climbing, my muscles tightening and my heart hammering, more slowly with each step. Fear kept growing up but so did determination.

As I climbed the last step and had the view from the platform, I froze. I was so high I could see the entire park! Every eye in the pool and around it was staring at me. My legs were jelly. I knew I couldn't back down and be laughed at, so I knew what I had to do: jump and die.

Again in the silence, I heard my father's voice: "Come on, honey. You kin do it! I'll gitcha soon as you hit the water. I'll be right here." With that, he moved to a spot just beyond the end of the board.

Deep breathing. Muscles thawing. Eyes blinking. Slowly I began to move. Gasping for air, I inched to the end of the board. Standing on the edge I heard Daddy call again. I closed my eyes tight, bent my knees in slow motion, and launched! Hurtling downward, I drew my knees high against my chest, flailed my arms like a dying bird, and felt the momentary sensation of air rushing by.

Then splash! My impact drove me down, down into the depths until I touched bottom, and launched upward. Just then a large hand grabbed my upper arm and pulled me up and out. Daddy, of course. I sputtered and laughed with him, and took in the praise. Lots of voices were shouting it, but right then the only one that mattered at all was his. "Ya did it , honey! That was great! Hooo-eeee!"

Yeah, and my enemy defeated! Ralph, eat your heart out.

I will never forget that moment of our delight together, my father's and mine. My father did not ask me to jump off the board; it was my choice. But it pleased him exceedingly when he saw me on the steps and he let me know it. At that moment I knew he was asking me to do it.

Why did I tell this story? Several similarities in how we respond to God strike me. Please don't misunderstand. I am not saying with this illustration that I get some far out idea, and then expect God to voice His pleasure in it. Not at all. I wait, as I've said before, for Him to make His will known to me. And He does. He lets me know what will please and delight Him. It is totally my choice to respond to Him, or to ignore or refuse Him. But make no mistake, I will in all probability face human emotional *resistance* within myself if I accept the assignment, just as I experienced incredible fear on the high board at Glenrose, and wanted to back down.

The flesh wars against the Spirit, we are told in Galatians 5:17 (KJV), so I expect to sense pride or fear or lassitude or all three. I may start out on my own, with pride in my abilities, as when I started up the steps to the high board. If so, I expect that I may then come to realize how impossible it is for me in the natural to succeed and will engage in rationalization to evade what the Spirit is telling me clearly, just as I did when I became afraid after four steps and looked for ways to back out. Even if He encourages me to go on, as my father did, I expect that fear and a sense of inadequacy may walk hand in hand with faith.

For God is always stretching my capacity. He is always growing me up, and He uses what He asks of me to help me grow. His requests though, if I accept them, bring on incredible adventure, just as did my jump off the high board. And He is delighted, just as my father was.

FOCUS ON ONE

Decades ago my husband and I bought acreage in the Santa Ynez Valley of Santa Barbara County in California. He planted an apple orchard of five hundred trees for eventual commercial production. He continued with his day time job while my two step-children and I tended the new young plants with tender and frequent care as they grew. And grow they did. After three years, I woke one morning to find a sea of white blossoms as I looked out on the orchard. My husband and I had agreed that I would do the thinning. And I just took it for granted that thinning the trees was the Lord's assignment to me. What I felt at the moment I saw all those blossoms was sheer panic.

I knew I had a two month window to do the assigned task. If I didn't do the thinning the trees would bear too much fruit. This would result in overladened branches that would break and the tree would be ruined. It would also mean that the clusters of fruit would look more like large grapes than apples, and would be totally unfit for sale.

We had no money at the time to hire help. In my panic I began to tell God that I simply couldn't do it. Yet with every outcry I immediately began to strategize *how* to get it done. I began to have nightmares.

One morning I ran out to begin my work. I need to explain that this meant trimming each cluster of five or six blossoms down to one or two. The clusters on each tree were so abundant that they seemed numberless. Probably most trees held about one hundred clusters. I felt immense pressure, and began trimming as hard and fast as I could. My panic grew and I began to pray, but this time I also began to listen for God's answer.

"Lord, I'm not going to be able to do this. How can I do this? I know. I'll just focus on one row at a time, right?"

"Too much."

"Oh, I see. Half a row?"

"Too much."

"Five trees?"

"Too much."

"Only *one* tree?"

"Too much."

"One side?"

"Too much."

"Oh, yes, I see! I see! Just one branch, right! Keep my focus!"

"Too much."

"Too much? How much less can I focus on?"

"One cluster."

"Ahhh. Yes." And I meant it. I thereafter focused on one cluster at a time, and joined with Him in wonderful fellowship as I did so. Since it was such rote work, I found that while I cut, He spoke to me of many spiritual things, and my heart sang to hear them. I had wonderful times in that orchard. More than that, in two months I had miraculously thinned five hundred apple trees, and I didn't know how I did it. Unbelievable as it may seem, the whole experience gave me deep joy.

Let me make this crystal clear: God inhabits you to do His work in and through you *one* moment at a time. You will keep the focus on the whole as you begin. He will show you the goal and how to go about fulfilling it. As you then get into the steps leading to the finish, you must keep with Him, one moment at a time. If you insist on reaching the goal too quickly and you fret about getting there, you are trying to take control. If you too earnestly study the past to measure your progress, you risk developing either fear or pride.

Trust Him in the moment, and He will take care of the next. When He wants you to look with Him at the future, He'll let you know. When He wants you to measure the progress, He will let you know that too. He will guide you at the right time to look ahead and clarify the big picture and note the progress of the past. But in the working out, He invariably narrows it down to focus on the present moment. Only as you join Him in the moment do you have the incredible joyful sense of His power and ministry. Don't miss it.

THE RUGGED ROAD TO FREEDOM

MORE OF GLENROSE

Let me say a bit more about the Glenrose experience. Sometimes when I hear what the Spirit would have me do, I am that long ago child beginning the climb up the ladder to the high board. I think, "I can do this! Yes! What grand adventure." I see clearly how it can be done, and I in my self-sufficiency can handle it. If four steps up fear *doesn't* strike, I've learned to beware.

Four steps up and I realize that I cannot possibly do what He is asking. Then I must deal with the enormity and paralysis of *fear*. Unlike the child, I can back down and quit with no problem. No one knows yet. No one will make fun. But He urges me on, as my father did. More than encouragement, God promises to be with me in it. He assures me that "from him and through him and to him are all things" (Romans 11:36). He urges me to step up, *one step at a time*. Is that the same as "in the moment"? Yes and no. I am speaking now not of method (thinning the orchard) but of fear. I must trust God for every single step in the process of doing what He asks of me. I must deal with the fear every step of the way. I may continue to fear as I go, but in faith I proceed.

Sometimes it means a climb all the way to the platform before I truly realize the dimensions of the whole thing. Then the fear nearly overwhelms me. Way too big for me! Way too big! Can't do this! Why is He showing me this? What does He want me to see?

Then He shows me. Duly noted, I then know the next steps to take to complete the mission. I once again have only one step to take—that's all. Then one more. And one more. To the end. Even on the very end of the board, it is only one more step, after all. Then completion. And being caught up in His arms for immense rejoicing. *That's* living!

What is your experience? One thing I know, everything we're not used to that the Lord asks of us requires risk and trust. It is beyond us, even the *small* acts, and we must risk all on His sufficiency, or turn away. Will you reach out and say hello to that stranger? Will you learn to speak with kindness to your spouse? Will you get into the mind of Christ in dealing with your difficult child? Will you risk sincere and deep friendship? Will you persevere in doing your job as unto the Lord in spite of the unfairness of your boss? Will you teach that children's class? Will you take that short-term missions trip? Will you give when it stretches your budget? Will you listen with your heart? Will you make the call, deliver the meal, visit that man in the hospital? Will you write that letter, make that apology, forgive totally? Will you speak to that man on the plane, in the coffee shop, at the beach about your faith? What is the Lord's assignment for you?

EFFECT OF FEAR

When fear is present, but deep down and not fully conscious to me, it is easy at the point of turning away to rationalize that I wasn't really being given this assignment from Him. I convince myself I was just trying to grandstand, and I'd better deal with my pride, quoting Isaiah 5:15, "...and the eyes of the lofty shall be humbled" (KJV), or Psalm 131:1, "My heart is not proud, O Lord,/ my eyes are not haughty;/ I do not concern myself with great matters/ or things too wonderful for me."

And the drawing by the Holy Spirit into great and joyful partnership with God goes unheeded.

Unholy fear robs us. Holy fear furnishes us. We exchange our weakness for God's strength. Our experience of fear is often like a two-sided coin; the fear is the counter-side of adventure. Release your fear to God, flip the coin, and it is "heads up." David had it right again,

> *When I am afraid, I will trust in you.*
> *In God, whose word I praise,*
> *In God I trust; I will not be afraid....*
>
> *(Psalm 56:3, 4)*

In our spring class, Joanne shared this story:

There was a lady in our church who continually moaned and groaned to me about many women in the church. Her criticism annoyed me tremendously and I began to get resentful of her. I bit my lip and said nothing. I began, though, to pour out my feelings about her to the Lord and to release them to Him. I asked the Lord what He would have me do besides pray for her. I heard no specifics at the time.

Then one day the Lord gave me instructions to tell the lady to stop coming to me with the same complaints. It was a bit scary, and I asked Him to do it through me.

The next time she started in again, I said directly but without anger, "Why do you go on about this?" At that moment she flared up at me, but I heard God tell me, "Rest in me," and I did. I didn't give her anything but the one question to feed on. I left it there, and released my fear of offending her to the Lord. I just "shook it off my shoulders" and went into the church and asked for prayer for myself, not giving any details.

After prayer, I went back into the parking lot. I found myself smiling when she came walking towards me. She didn't bring up my confrontation and neither did I. And she never has since that day. But she also stopped her complaints to me.

I rejoice that I stepped into the Lord and saw Him handle this. I praise Him!

GRASPING THE GLORY

In fact, it seems to me that the greater danger is not being afraid. If I continue with my can do attitude, I proceed in my own energy and know-how, I then end up taking the glory. In the Glenrose experience, I as a child did exactly that. I sought the glory and I got it! Am I still immature spiritually and out to get glory for myself?

Purity of motive for the Christian is of supreme importance. God insists that all be done for *His* glory. For He is the only one in all the universe that isn't contaminated by glory seeking, but turns the glory given Him into a way of fellowship and joy. He is the only totally unselfish being in the universe. Not so with man.

Again we check our instruction: is it *from* Him? *through* Him? *to* Him?

If I truly do not know if I have received a request from the Lord, I may ask Him to repeat it. I have always found Him willing to do so. I may confirm it by having two or three with me as we ask the Lord my question and then listen for His answer. When I am sure it is the Lord, I must move into action if I am to be obedient. This is His call to risk taking, to growth, to increased faith, and to joy. For that is surely what His assignments always entail.

PROCRASTINATION

When we truly know what the Lord would have us do, why do we postpone doing it? There may be good reasons: waiting for the appropriate time for all concerned, considering the schedule of the one to whom I am to minister, realizing that the Lord has told me what to do but would have me wait until He tells me when to do it. But usually we postpone because we *choose* to procrastinate: it just isn't to our liking; we are lazy and don't want to exert the effort; other things are more enjoyable and interesting; we are down deep afraid and don't want to take the risk; all sorts of self-oriented reasons. Procrastinate long enough and you will forget the Lord told you to do it, and that is very convenient to having your own way.

Frank, a member of our Rugged Road class, had this experience with procrastination:

Last fall I asked God if there were anything He wanted me to do. He gave me a picture of training a horse, a little gray horse named Dumpling. I wasn't too keen on the idea. I had other things I thought were much higher on the list. A couple of hours later I asked my wife Rhonda to pray and ask God the same question for me. She came back saying God had said to tell me to let Dumpling know I love him. (That meant spending time with him and training him.) I heard but didn't heed.

As fall rolled into winter and winter neared spring, I kept procrastinating. I broke the horse for riding, but only when I found it convenient to ride. I kept saying to myself, "I will really get to training him in the spring when I have more time."

It was mid April after day light savings time was in when God really got my attention. I came home from working at the church (a building project there—much to my liking!) on a Saturday. I found a badly cut horse and a river of blood. It amazed me how much blood could come out of a horse and it still be alive. I knew God and Rhonda were trying to tell me something! We spent the night doctoring the horse and praying that Dumpling be alive in the morning. *I* prayed for forgiveness.

The horse lived, and I thanked God. I'd train it when it healed, for sure. During the next week God spoke to me by impressions of what would happen if I did not do what He said, not only about the horse, but also about getting on into the ministry He had assigned us, to cowboys in the rodeo world. He showed me how boring my life would be—just going to work every day. Life would be easy here, but there would come a feeling of emptiness, a feeling of going the wrong way. God had clearly indicated a big change, and I had been reluctant to accept it.

At that time there came over me a feeling I really can't explain or don't know how to explain. I could just see myself on the way to work doing the same old thing the same old way, and my mind going a mile a minute, wondering why I hadn't just listened to God and obeyed Him. Then I read the homework assignment for our Rugged Road class. The word that jumped out to me in big bold letters: PROCRASTINATION! I then asked God why He hadn't waited until I could read this before allowing the horse to get cut up. He made it clear I wouldn't have gotten half the impact out of reading the assignment if I hadn't seen all the blood that horse shed.

I also remembered a comment I'd made to a friend, Marlene, "I know He's calling us into the rodeo world. But I'm diggin' my heels in." I prayed again for His forgiveness and promised I would become a ready and willing obedient servant. *Now* there is peace and joy in that prospect.

THE DAILIES

The Lord was asking Frank to do a new thing, and Frank was loving his ease too much to do it. The Lord is asking others to be faithful in the same old thing, and not to run ahead of Him into something more exciting.

You may well ask, "What of the 'dailies'? Life can't always be exciting, can it?" Certainly some of it is sure to be drudgery. You may be thinking you already know the tasks He has set before you; you know clearly the work He has given you to do to earn money, or you know the tasks you must do as a homemaker, mother, wife. Or as husband, son, daughter. You know what He expects from you as a church member or teacher. You know His assignments as a pastor or leader.

Some of these tasks can easily be done in a rote manner. They are routine, boring and often unpleasant. You can work by habit and without thought. The "can do" isn't even conscious. You may not even want it to be conscious. Often as we do our dailies, the Lord's presence is missing completely.

Have you read the wonderful classic by a seventeenth century monk, Brother Lawrence? In *The Practice of the Presence of God* this unusual man tells of his fellowshipping with God as he washed pots and pans in the kitchen. He *willed* his awareness of God's presence in those most mundane times, and found incredible companionship with the Lord when he did so.[14]

After reading this book, I determined to stay aware of the presence of the Lord with me in the dailies. Not only with me, but *in* me as well. So I often found myself asking Him, "Lord, do you peel carrots?" "Lord, do you scrub floors?" "Lord, do you go grocery shopping?" For it isn't the energy expended, nor the skill required that's in question as I do these things. It is the spirit in which I do them that matters. Is it in His Spirit? And is it in His fellowship? Am I living, or just performing? Does His presence, as I do these things, increase our intimacy? Our enjoyment of each other? And am I drawing on His love flowing from me as I do them?

Paul instructs, "*Whatever* you do, work at it with all your heart, as working for the Lord, not for men, since you know that you will receive an inheritance from the Lord as a reward. It is the Lord Christ you are serving" (Colossians 3:23, 24, emphasis mine). Part of that inheritance is present now. It is His very presence with us and in us. He washed feet. Now with Him and in Him we serve each other. We figure bills, diaper babies, prepare meals. We play with children, talk on the phone, repair the car. We go off to the job, serve on school committees, clean toilets. We mow the lawn, do the laundry. We also give cups of cold water, clothe the naked, comfort the suffering, befriend the lonely. We visit the prisoner, feed the hungry—as if it were Him we are ministering *to* as indeed He says it is. Again: *from Him, through Him, to Him.*

One of our Rugged Road class members, Kurtis, a young man, blue eyes sparkling, with a mind for missions and service shared this:

> I was really discontented with my work. I had a really bad attitude about it and groused a lot. I also knew I had some hard feelings towards my dad who is also my boss. I decided to reach to God and release my feelings about it to Him. I saw my attitude as sin and confessed it as that. I told the Lord I wanted to trust Him in regard to the whole thing. I gave myself and all I am over to Him. Right then He spoke to me very clearly from the Scriptures: "Whatever you do, work at it with all your heart, as working for the Lord, not for men....*It is Christ you are serving*" (Colossians 3:23,24). That really hit me. I'm serving *Christ!* How would I do my work for my dad if I actually believed it was Christ giving the orders? Christ I was serving as I obeyed? It changed everything! I was really able to do my work gladly from then on.

> So I also decided to release to the Lord my desire to go on a short term missions trip. I didn't ask my dad for time off. I didn't say anything to my family about it. Not even hints. I just left it with the Lord and went on being joyful in my work. One day not long ago, my dad said to me, "Aren't you going to fill out an application for that short term mission trip?" God is awesome!

THE SMALL THING

When we are dealing with a habit He wishes to replace, we will move many times through the Put Off half. So often that is all we do. We continue in our sense of freedom and forget that there is a Put On side. "Cast off...put on." If we move into the Put On, beginning with listening and expecting His instruction, we hear. We then have to implement what He asks of us. We have received instructions, now will we do them?

As I have said before, I am often amazed at what He asks of me. Many times it is a small thing, perhaps even a usual thing, but clothed with a new attitude—His. That changes the doing of it altogether.

I sometimes miss out on intimacy with Jesus when doing something mundane for another reason: my sense of entitlement. Why is it that I assume that life is going to be richer and more exciting than it is? Why do I assume that the Christian life I am living, if I am obeying God, will always be to my liking? Why do I judge everything I am going to do on the basis of whether it will contribute to my happiness or ease or sense of fulfillment, somehow believing that I have a right to all these things? When I truly believe I have been given a direction by God, why do I weigh it out, rejecting it if it doesn't offer the adventure or comfort or fulfillment I want?

Did David like being hounded by Saul and his army? Imagine how he liked living in that cave with all those who came to him: "All those who were in distress or in debt or discontented gathered around him, and he became their leader. About four hundred men were with him" (1 Samuel 22:2). That's how God prepared David to become king of Israel. You think you have it bad, having to deal with the disgruntled people in your life? Try four hundred of them!

Did Paul enjoy those months in prison, being confined at Ephesus under house arrest, not free to come and go at will? Yet he wrote, "...for I have learned to be content whatever the circumstances. I know what it is to be in need, and I know what it is to have plenty. I have learned the secret of being content in any and every situation, whether well fed or hungry, whether living in plenty or in want. I can do everything through him who gives me strength" (Philippians 4:11-13). I find that amazing. Can I say that? Can you?

In *My Utmost for His Highest* Oswald Chambers expresses what he believes God is saying in reference to our sense of entitlement: "'I reckon on you for extreme service; with no complaining on your part and no explanation on Mine.' God wants to use us as He used His own Son."[15] I somehow find, rather than deflating me, those words promise a zestful effort and challenge to my life, rather like a player listening to the coach effusing his players with the stamina and will to win.

FIVE MISTAKEN RESPONSES

In essence, I keep seeing life now as a pilgrimage I am on with Jesus. He is instructing me in the way to go and in what to do along the way. There are five ways I can leave the path and distress His heart in my leaving.

First and most frequent for me personally, I can run ahead of Him and try to show Him shortcuts, and expect Him to praise me for doing so. I have felt His shepherd's crook pulling me back more often than I care to tell, as I have already said.

Second, I can lag behind, refusing to keep pace, whining that it is all too hard for me. He lets me trudge along in my lonely and self-chosen misery, missing the zest of it all.

Third, I can fall headlong into the pit of fear on the left side of the path. There I remain paralyzed and thoroughly distressed until I call on Him to lift me out, and trust Him to do so.

Fourth, I can gaze off longingly to all the pleasures and distractions that lure me on the gentle, downward slope on the right. Sometimes I bolt, run down and snatch them. I forget that He is a good God Who often makes rest and refreshment stops of His choosing for the two of us. These are far superior to baubles and circuses and sin carnivals that so attract me. These pleasures of the sin center enervate and eventually kill. His refreshments revitalize and invigorate—they give life. Seen this way, I am totally convinced again that I must look to Him, hold His hand, enjoy His fellowship, and go on persistently and steadfastly as He directs. When the going is arduous and I'm getting sweaty and tired, I remember that rest and recreation *will come* when He chooses and at the perfect time.

Is this not freedom—to walk only on His path, to hear only His voice, to have only One to obey?

Fifth, there are other voices calling. I may listen to these other voices and follow them along their trails instead of staying on the path with Him. How many other voices are you listening to? What trails do they lead you along? What is the outcome? What is the destination? How many bring you under their demands and stress you out? How many create unconscious resentment in you? It is a huge step into freedom to narrow all voices down to only *one*. And to realize that this is the One who yearns to give you life more abundantly.

GOD'S EVALUATION

If knowing, loving, and walking with God is the goal of my life, how much does *He* value my obedience? To be certain, He values the good deed that will be accomplished, or He wouldn't ask me to do it. But more significant, I think, is that when I am yoked with Him and dwelling in Him when I do the good deed, I come to know His heart more and more fully. I am brought more and more into His conforming me to His image by having Christ living in me as I obey. But whether I realize these things or not, I can be certain that instant obedience to His will holds incredible dividends.

There is manifestly an effort of the will required to live the Christian life, but even at the moment of exerting my will to obey Him, I sense in myself a genuine gladness that He makes my life count for something. John 15: 5: "I am the vine; you are the branches. If a man remains in me and I in him, he will bear much fruit; apart from me you can do nothing." When do I experience the "much fruit"? What a joy when I see it has appeared through His life in me, and is ready for harvesting. It delights me. It also delights Him.

Are you glad that He offers you the privilege of being of service and value, even though suffering and sacrifice and stress are involved? Above all are you glad that He gives you the joy of delighting His heart?

I had an experience on a camping trip that triggered my thinking. I sat at the edge of a small still lake at twilight. As I gazed at the incredibly reflective water these thoughts came:

Mirror Lake

One evening twice
One above, one below
A mirror lake.
The twilight glow
Delaying night.
Balm of release
In doubled light
Bathes all in peace.

I would in stillness
Mirror be
Of beauteous God.
In depths of me
His lovingness reflect,
Strong, full, and tall.
His hands, my hands,
His face, my face,
Twice blessing all.

Have you ever asked your nine-year-old to take out the garbage and had him do it willingly and without complaint, not lagging or messing up? Remember how you wished that would always be the case? You were delighted, and your face and words clearly revealed it. He knew it delighted you, and you watched his grin spread and his chest expand.

Isn't my Father like that as a parent, and I the happy child? Indeed, and this brings us to the subject of rejoicing.

CHAPTER SIX

REJOICE

Come and share your master's happiness.

Matthew 25:33

I'LL CALL HIM Jack. Jack irritated me every time he spoke. Every word he said brought up judgment against him in me. I bristled at every opinion he expressed. If he sighed, I ground my teeth. My discernment of his every motive was that it was shot through with, at best, self-deception or, at worst, self-enhancement. I detested what I believed was his false humility. Every time I came in contact with Jack, I had the urge to hide. When I saw him in church I immediately engaged someone in earnest conversation. If I saw him in the grocery store, I bee-lined into the next aisle, and studied the boxes of cereal intensely.

But it wasn't possible to avoid Jack. I had to work with this man.

I did have the grace to realize that my whole attitude was sin. All of it. No rationalizations. "It's me, it's me, O Lord, standing in the need of prayer," says the old song. And I sang it. And I prayed. I poured out my irritation to God, and then confessed my sin every time I encountered Jack, for I always needed to. I told the Lord I was thoroughly ashamed and wanted desperately to change. I knew I was grieving the Lord, and that grieved me.

But every time in my processing I reached the Receive stage, I told the Lord that I was well aware already of what I was to put in place of my irritation and my tearing down. I knew the Scriptures on this subject; I was to love him, to build him up, to encourage him, first in my mind, and then in word and deed. I said I would. And I tried. *That* was the problem—I thought *I* knew just what to do and *I* tried. *Nothing* changed.

One day I was at it again. This time, however, when I reached the Receive stage of my prayer, I admitted that I knew nothing and that I felt hopeless.

In desperation at last I asked the Lord, "What would You have me to do?"

This thought came immediately: "Be cheerful."

"Be cheerful? That's it?" I was astounded.

"Be cheerful. Be joyful. Be rejoicing. That's it."

"I can't!" I wailed. "It's Jack!"

"Of course not."

At last I realized that *my* trying availed nothing. "Then let Your joy be in me, Lord. I am willing." I knew my emotions weren't in line with this. My faith that anything would change was very weak.

But it did change. As long as I called on the Lord to come through in me in Jack's presence, things were totally different. I kept sensing and then expressing the Lord's good cheer and joy in me; I sensed His gladness and His laughter. I rejoiced in His joy!

When I slipped back into the natural, my irritation emerged again immediately. I knew I needed to process through release and confession, resting in His love, remembering the instructions I had received from Him, and responding again by stepping into His joy. I set my will to it, even when my emotions weren't in-line with His. Fairly soon, they were.

What a change this made in my day! I enjoyed His joy so much that I just stayed there.

Our God is a God of *joy*!

FREEDOM IN REJOICING

I have been writing about a process, a way to change habits, to remove what the Lord wants removed (Reach to God, Release, Rest), and to add what

He would have us add (Receive, Respond) and now we come to the last step: Rejoice. If we have received His instructions and if we have responded by obeying His will fully, we can hardly avoid rejoicing.

Yet I have found some people I have dealt with so eager to "get on with it" that they forget to rejoice and thank God. Remember the healing of the ten lepers? Following their request that Jesus heal them, they went to the priest as Jesus told them to. As they went, they were healed. What a cause for rejoicing! Yet only one took time to come back and thank the One who had preformed this miracle. Are we like that, realizing incredible blessing, but so on the go that we do not take time to thank Him and rejoice with Him? Do we know what it means to enjoy His joy?

You need to take time to rejoice with and in Him, whether when you've finished the process, or just because you remember how absolutely wonderful our God is.

Shout with joy to God, all the earth!
Sing the glory of his name,
offer him glory and praise...
Come and see what God has done,
how awesome his works in man's behalf!...
Praise be to God
who has not rejected my prayer
or withheld his love from me!

(Psalm 66:1, 5, 20)

FREEDOM

Why would the ability to rejoice be a way to *freedom*? It is very much like listening to only one voice, God's, and disregarding all others. I consider the natural way my mind tends to jabber and chatter to me, how it tends to focus on problems, duties, difficulties, and negatives in general and then to comment endlessly about them. Then I think of the ability given by the Holy Spirit to step into God's joy, and into all that which is a cause of His celebration—that ability is a real liberator from all clutter of the negative mind content.

It is an ability the Holy Spirit is more than willing to provide. We never need force rejoicing. We've only to ask that He fill our hearts and minds with it. Again, even if we are in the midst of trial, sorrow, or pain, there is *always* that for which we can rejoice: first, in God Himself; second, in all He has created and done.

So what is my mind on at present? Today war rages, the stock market is plunging, a pipe in the back yard watering system broke and will have to be replaced, the house tax bill arrived with a considerable increase for this year, and soon I will have to decide what to cook for dinner. For me, eating is cause for rejoicing, but cooking isn't. None of the other items are either. I see clearly that *now* is the time for the freedom of focusing on the Lord and rejoicing again in Him, the treasure of life. Now is the time to participate in His joy, to join Him in seeing what gives Him joy.

GOD'S GLORY AND REJOICING

Do we think of God as a Being of joy, of happiness? In John Piper's fine book, *Desiring God*, he states, "God's ultimate goal is ...to preserve and display his infinite and awesome greatness and worth, that is his glory....God would be unrighteous...if he valued anything more than what is supremely valuable. But he himself is supremely valuable....For it is right to take delight in a person in proportion to the excellence of that person's glory."[16]

Therefore, God delights in the glory of His person, in His Son, in His Spirit, but He also delights in His creation, both nature and persons. "God loves to behold his glory reflected in his works. So the eternal happiness of the triune God spilled over in the work of creation and redemption."[17]

I'm sure I don't fully understand what I have just quoted, but this much I do conclude: God has immense happiness and joy within Himself. He is by nature an incredible giver, so He created us and then redeemed us so that He might give us this joy in Him.

Piper states further: "We praise what we enjoy because the delight is incomplete until it is expressed in praise. If we were not allowed to speak of what we value, and celebrate what we love, and praise what we admire, our joy would not be full. So if God loves us enough to make our joy full, he must not only give us himself; he must also win from us the praise of our hearts—not because he needs to shore up some weakness in himself or compensate for some deficiency, but because he loves us and seeks the fullness of our joy that can be found only in knowing and praising him, the most magnificent of all Beings."[18]

I find these truths wonderfully and overarchingly presented in the first chapter of Ephesians: He has blessed us with "every spiritual blessing in Christ." He chose us, predestined us, and adopted us as his children. In His glorious giving, He has provided redemption, the forgiveness of sins, and lavished His grace on us. He has made known to us the mystery of His plan to bring all thing together under Christ. I'm just highlighting the tops of gigantic waves of blessing, given by the great Lover. All, all He has done "to the praise of his glory"—this phrase is repeated three times in those first fourteen verses. Incredibly He has caught us up to see this glory of His and to enable us to share it. That's the highest He can give. Read and rejoice!

We therefore experience His glory when we rejoice in Him and His works for us. Our God obviously loves our rejoicing. He is the God of joy. Read further of His delights. I have emphasized several words.

"The Lord your God...will take great delight
*in you...he will **rejoice** over you...."*

(Zephaniah 3:17)

*For the Lord takes **delight** in his people:*
he crowns the humble with salvation.

(Psalm 149:4)

*the Lord **delights** in those who fear him,*
who put their hope in his unfailing love.

(Psalm 147:11)

*"I will **rejoice** over Jerusalem*
*and take **delight** in my people."*

(Isaiah 65:19)

And listen to Wisdom, a characteristic of God here personified, speaking when the Lord was creating the earth and mankind:

"Then I was the craftsman at his side.
*I was filled with **delight** day after day,*
***rejoicing** always in his presence,*

rejoicing in his whole world
and delighting in mankind."

(Proverbs 8:30, 31)

ISRAEL'S REJOICING

If God were not the God of incredible joy, why would He so often command it of His chosen people, Israel? Yet He did, and even ordained three special holiday feasts and celebrations for them. In late spring, they were to celebrate Pentecost—"a festival of joy...and thankfulness for the Lord's blessing of harvest." In the fall they were to have an entire "week of celebration for the harvest; living in booths and offering sacrifice." And then in winter, Purim was to be "a day of joy and feasting and giving presents, to "Remind the Israelites of their national deliverance in the time of Esther."[19] There were other observances, of course, but these three were assigned days of riotous celebration, rejoicing in the goodness of their God and His blessings.

In regard to these feasts, God instructed Israel to celebrate—*sachaw*—"*to laugh, deride, play, rejoice."*[20] What a descriptive word! They were to joy in Him as their God. They were to joy in their work, their eating, their harvests, indeed in "all good things" (Deuteronomy 26:11). What motivates me to laugh, play, rejoice as they did?

When Israel obeyed God, they had much to rejoice in as reflected in their songs, the Psalms. Another Hebrew word used to define rejoicing is *gil—to spring about.*[21] I love the picture that creates in my mind. And what motivated them to such springing about? They rejoiced "in the Lord" (32:11); "in his name" meaning the totality of all He is (89:16); in His salvation (13:5), in His strength (21:1), in His deliverance from their enemies. (118:24) What is there about the Lord and/or what He has done for me that causes me to spring about with joy?

Another word, *sis—to enjoy, rejoice*[22]—called forth full enjoyment of the Lord Himself (40:16; 70:4), of His rescue of them (35:9), and of Him as burden bearer (68:19). David found enjoyment "under the shadow of your wings" (63:7). God's "unfailing love" (90:14) brought this form of rejoicing. What do you enjoy in God and from Him that brings rejoicing to your heart?

I have given you only a few instances. Several other Hebrew words are used to mean rejoicing. In many Psalms the full story of the cause of rejoicing is not just named but fully described. Consider Psalm 100 where Israel rejoices

140

at being the "sheep of his pasture." All Psalm 119 rejoices in the law, in the words of God. (See verses 14, 62, and 162 especially) What do you go on and on about, extolling and describing in your appreciation of God and His works?

ISRAEL'S REJOICING IN PAST EVENTS

In many places in the Psalms, righteous men of Israel remembered past glorious exercises of God's might. Picture the Exodus. Can you see the fear and trembling on the night of the first Passover? Can you sense their relief and rejoicing when they realized they remained alive? Can you see those thousands and thousands and thousands of people following Moses out of Egypt? I guess I am remembering "The Ten Commandments" with Charlton Heston as Moses, but I am envisioning it, and as I do, I understand why it was the great event told over and over at the annual celebration of Passover, passed on from generation to generation. It served to bring rejoicing year after year. Can you picture the parting of the Red Sea and Israel's deliverance from the chariots of the Pharaoh? Can you see the crossing of the Jordan River as Joshua lead them into the Promised Land forty years later? Further rejoicing over past events had the writers recalling the conquering and settlement of Canaan, the establishment of David's reign, and the building of the temple. In all these events and many more they rejoiced in their God who had "done marvelous things." Have you memories of His marvelous doings in your life? Does it bring rejoicing?

REJOICING IN PRESENT BLESSINGS

At all times the "righteous" were to be found seeking their God (40:16), experiencing refuge in trusting Him (5:11) and His love (32:7). In these things they rejoiced day by day. What do you find to rejoice about specifically in regard to God and His present encounters with you? Does it ever seem like the Lord does really specific things just for you? I remember many of these in my life, but one especially stands out that I'd like to share.

Many years ago my family and I and several relatives made our way in the dead of winter to the Grand Canyon. We had been travelling from Texas to California, and felt we just couldn't miss out on this opportunity to see most canyon at a time when, it was said, the air is clearest and the colors most vivid. We arrived there after dark and quickly sought and found places of rest, greatly anticipating the wonders we would see in the morning. We woke to incredible disappointment—there was a complete white-out of fog. Total. Out in it I could hardly see my hand in front of my face. The two inches of snow on the ground and trees would have been beautiful to see, but who could?

We all agreed we could afford to wait awhile, but we'd have to leave by ten thirty if we were to make it home by a reasonable hour. About nine we inched our way to the museum display, peered about, and then listened to the ranger's lecture. His talk made us even more eager to see the wonders of the canyon.

It was now nine-thirty. We were champing at the bit, and frustrated. The white out continued. I minced through it slowly to the canyon's edge which I found when I bumped into the fencing. There I peered into the fog, above, below, ahead. White.

"Oh, Lord," I prayed, "I'd so love to see this canyon You carved. Would You just move this fog out of the way?"

Still solid white everywhere. So I made my way back and trudged into the souvenir store that had now opened. The whole gang was there, moseying about, examining this blanket and that bird carving, mostly killing time. About ten fifteen one of them said, "We might as well go. We're never going to see anything today anyway."

"Could we wait just a bit longer?" The wistful tone was in my voice and hope in my heart, though it was weakening. Everyone went back to milling around. I went back to the canyon's edge again.

"You heard that, didn't You, Lord? They want to leave. Please now, could You part this fog?" I stood still for a few minutes, staring into the white. Then I saw it—a slight rift in it seemingly only a few feet beyond where I stood. As my excitement mounted, the fog cleared as though a shaft of energy had carved a column of light from the top of the fog down 5000 feet to the bottom of the canyon. And there was the river below, the mighty Colorado, just a ribbon of slate green shinning clearly in the morning light. Then the canyon walls began to appear. Their colors glowed, blues and reds and tans, russets and grays and yellows. I marveled.

I suddenly remembered the others and hurried into the store shouting. "Come see! Come see! You can see it!" At that moment I had the sense that God had done this for my own personal delight and His and as a way for me to call others into it.

"Thank you, Lord, thank you. How wonderful!" I felt I shared that time of ecstasy with Him.

The store owner came out to see and told us if the fog was lifting here, it would already be clear on the west wide. We hustled into our cars and made our way west along the rim, moving cautiously, tensely, slowly through the white. Suddenly we drove into the clearing. All of us tumbled out the doors and ran to the fence. Before our eyes the white continued to retreat, as if a mighty giant hand was pulling back a curtain. The full panorama spread there before us. We were spellbound. Silent. The depths, the contours, the magnitude—it was beyond comprehension and utterly magnificent. Etched forever in our memories. I know I have never forgotten the wonder and beauty, nor the sense that God *delighted* in delighting us.

NOT NOW BUT LATER

Sometimes the Israelites didn't rejoice. They wandered. They sinned. They rebelled. And God administered the punishment He had promised until it was completed and then forgave them. The prophets heralded these times of great rejoicing when the punishment ended and the people were brought back from captivity into the land (Zephaniah 3:14, 15; Jeremiah 31:3, 4, 13), when the land was restored (Joel 2:21 and 23; Zechariah 2:10; 4:10), and when Jerusalem was again a place of joy. (Isaiah 66:10,14)

Hear their song in Psalm 126:1-3:

> *When the Lord brought back the captives to Zion,*
> *we were like men who dreamed.*
> *Our mouths were filled with laughter,*
> *our tongues with songs of joy...*
> *The Lord has done great things for us*
> *and we are filled with joy.*

Yet God Himself was so great, so faithful, and so good, even when chastising, that Habakkuk rejoiced even in the midst of devastation:

> *"Though the fig tree does not bud*
> *and there are no grapes on the vines,*
> *though the olive crop fails*
> *and the fields produce no food,*
> *though there are no sheep in the pen*
> *and no cattle in the stalls,*

yet I will rejoice in the Lord,
I will be joyful in God my Savior.
The Sovereign Lord is my strength;
he makes my feet like the feet of a deer,
he enables me to go on the heights."

(Habakkuk 3:17-19)

What is your experience of God when you are undergoing chastening? Where is rejoicing then? Move through your prayer process until you come into the prayer of rejoicing in your God.

NATURE'S REJOICING

Israel was also led to see that God's creation rejoiced. They knew the declaration of David: "The heavens declare the glory of God; the skies proclaim the work of his hands" (Psalm 19:1). What kind of declaration was this? The psalmists revealed that God caused even nature itself, as it were, to rejoice: "when morning dawns and evening fades, you call forth songs of joy" (65:8); "the meadows are covered with flocks and the valleys are mantled with grain; they shout for joy and sing" (65:13); "Tabor and Hermon sing for joy at your name" (89:12); "Let the earth be glad...sea resound...fields be jubilant...trees... sing for joy; they will sing before the Lord, for he comes, he comes to judge the earth"(96:11-13); "Let the sea resound...rivers clap their hands...mountains sing together for joy...for he comes to judge the earth" (98:7-9); "All you have made will praise you, O Lord" (145:10). It brings incredible joy to me to sense this expression of nature praising the Maker. I'm remembering my Grand Canyon experience all over again. Many other scenes of beauty, past and present, rejoice my heart. You have your albums as well, I dare say.

THE WAYS ISRAEL EMPLOYED IN REJOICING

I am intrigued and blessed to learn of the all out, full, and total expressions that Israel was told to employ when rejoicing. They were to "sing joyfully... make music...sing him a new song; play skillfully and shout for joy" (Psalm 33:1-3). "Clap your hands...shout to God with cries of joy" (Psalm 47:1). Again, "Shout for joy...burst into jubilant song with music...with the harp...singing... trumpets and the blast of the ram's horn—shout for joy before the Lord, the

144

king" (Psalm 98:4-6). And "let them praise his name with dancing..." (Psalm 149:3). No preserving dignity at those times. It makes me wonder if we are too reserved in our worship today. Is our God not worthy of outrageous joy? Indeed He is.

NEW CAUSE FOR REJOICING

Even though the Israelites rejoiced in this fashion, most of them knew God only as the Most Holy One. They were not allowed, nor would they ever dare to approach Him personally. They were incredibly blessed as the chosen nation, but their attitude toward God was awe and great fear. Theirs was a system of sacrifices for the removal of sin. They dealt with priests who offered it for them. They stayed remote from God. This system remained until the coming of Jesus Christ, the Lamb of God, the once for all complete sacrifice for sin. Now we, after the cross, can enter into an intimate, *personal* relationship with the Holy One of God who has made *us* holy by His blood. I don't know about you, but I know I am very glad God chose me to be born after Jesus came, rather than before. What a cause for rejoicing! He desires to forgive my sins. He yearns to have me personally. He longs for an intimate relationship.

In John 1:14 we read, "The Word became flesh and made his dwelling among us. We have seen his glory, the glory of the One and Only, who came from the Father, full of grace and truth." Envision that close intimacy beginning with the disciples. John wrote in 1 John 1:1, "That which was from the beginning, which we have *heard*, which we have *seen* with our eyes, which we have *looked at* and our hands have *touched*—this we proclaim concerning the Word of life."

Does it astound you that Jesus Christ, the Son of God, left heaven to take on human flesh to make our relationship possible? Every Christmas I am amazed again to realize the truth of God in human flesh, the babe in the manger. Even more astounding to me, though, is to realize what motivated God to do it. "Let us fix our eyes on Jesus, the author and perfector of our faith, who for the *joy* set before him endured the cross..." (Hebrews 12:2).

When Jesus spoke to his disciples that last night with them, He told them plainly, "If you obey my commands, you will remain in my love, just as I have obeyed my Father's commands and remain in his love." What could ever be closer than the relationship between the Father and His Son? Yet He wants each of us to be that close to Him! "I have told you this so that my *joy* may

145

be in you and that your *joy* may be complete" (John 15:10, 11). Good news! The blessings simply *flow* to us from the grace His sacrifice provided: "From the fullness of his grace we have all received one blessing after another. For the law was given through Moses; grace and truth came through Jesus Christ. No one has ever seen God, but the One and Only, who is at the Father's side, has made him known" (John 1:16-18).

JESUS REJOICES

We have the account in Luke 10:1-24 of Jesus sending out seventy-two young disciples to all the regions of Judea. He gave them power to heal the sick, to cast out demons, and to give the message: "The kingdom of God is near you." This sending did not include the twelve disciples, the permanent members of his band, who had already done a similar going out many months earlier into all the region of Galilee. Now these young and zealous new learners of the Master Jesus were given their commission and sent on their way. They must have met with great receptivity, for they told Jesus on their return, "Lord, even the demons submit to us in your name" (Luke 10:17).

What really captures my attention is Jesus' response: "At that time Jesus, full of joy through the Holy Spirit..." (Verse 21). Different translators of this phrase render it in different ways, trying to capture in a few words the fact that Jesus was ecstatic: "exuberant," "filled with gladness," "filled by the Holy Spirit with rapturous joy," "inspired with joy." Envision that dance of joy!

Further, He voiced His joy in exultant prayer. *The Message* (Eugene Peterson) expresses it this way: "I thank you, Father, Master of heaven and earth, that you hid these things from the know-it-alls and showed them to these innocent newcomers. Yes, Father it pleased you to do it this way."

Recall the parable He told of the three servants (Matthew 25:14-30). "Again, it will be like a man going on a journey, who called his servants and entrusted his property to them. To one he gave five talents of money, to another two talents, and to another one talent, each according to his ability" (Verses 14, 15). The first two went right out and put the money to work. Focus on these two obedient ones. When the master returned, he strongly commended the two faithful servants, using the same words to both: "Well done, good and faithful servant! You have been faithful with a few things; I will put you in charge of many things. Come and *share your master's happiness*" (Verses 21, 23, emphasis mine).

Jesus is full of joy.

THE BREAKOUT OF JOY

In view of the wonder of our salvation, Our Savior, Our God, His nature, His character, His grace, His love, the believer comes to rejoice in the Lord *at every moment* of awareness. Indeed we are told to do so very clearly: "Rejoice in the Lord always. I will say it again: Rejoice!" (Philippians 4:4) Especially when I have spent time enjoying Him intimately, a unique joy fills me. Praise rises, and I must worship, I must sing, I must dance.

Even though I have been discussing a process and even though I am discussing rejoicing as the last step in that processing, it certainly does *not* occur *only then*. Rejoicing *breaks out* every time my heart is filled by the Holy Spirit with the wonder of my God.

Mark Buchanan, our gifted pastor at New Life Community Baptist Church, also authors books and magazine articles. The October 7, 2002 issue of *Christianity Today* contains an article he wrote entitled "Dance of the God-Struck." In it he describes King David as that exuberant young man brings the Ark of the Covenant into Jerusalem. It is a time of incredible worship, praise, and joy for the king. Here's a part:

> ...David dances....Choreographed by yearning and wonder, this is the dance of the God-struck, the God-smitten. This is the dance of the one who dances in fire, at cliff edges, on high wires, in the midst of mortal peril, between death and barrenness.

> David dances, alive, fully alive.

> Occasionally we get glimpses of Deepest Reality, intimations of what remains after all else has been shaken out and burned up.

> Glimpsing it, that Deepest Reality, can make you do funny things. You can become stony still. Or giddily happy. Or chokingly afraid. It can calm you with uncanny peace, or disrupt you with implacable dread. It can make you, simultaneously, not yourself and fully yourself. It can make kings dance.[23]

Kings must dance for joy. So must we. The psalmist tells Israel in Psalm 149:2:

> *Let Israel rejoice in their Maker;*
> *let the people of Zion be glad in their King.*

But note especially verse 5:

Let the saints rejoice in this honor
and sing for joy on their beds.

What? Yes, anytime! Day, or the middle of the night (Psalm 42:8). Ah yes, "songs in the night" (Job 35:10).

MANY OTHER ASPECTS OF JOY

Moreover, what great joy it can give the believer to contemplate all that God has planned for the future in heaven. That certainly deserves several books, and many have been written. If you are not well acquainted with these coming marvels, I urge you to read the Scriptures in regard to them as well as the many good books available on the subject.

In addition to all the ways in which we are tuned to rejoice and to express gratitude to God for our great and complete salvation, there are also a host of blessings that are showered on us mortals by His hand. "Praise the Lord, o my soul, and forget not all his benefits...." (Psalm 103:2) Each of us has past and present blessings that we would do well to contemplate and to give thanks to our merciful, giving God. Gratitude should fill our days. Past memories of His goodness should trigger again and again our thanksgiving.

There is the joy of remembering my own past. I'm provided by God's grace with lovely memories of home, family, happenings, and everyday blessings. No, not all memories are happy ones, but so very many are. I have stored memories of wonderful encounters with the Lord and with our family in Christ, as I'm sure you have. I find it a great blessing to recall these (and by now, after seven decades, they are cramming the brain shelves). It is especially delightful when they just rise unbidden and bless me afresh.

A special one for me is etched indelibly on my mind. It occurred amid great sorrow. I remember particularly a phone call in the middle of the night. It was January, 1971. My brother broke the news to me that our dad had suffered a massive heart attack and was not expected to live. I booked the first plane I could get out of Santa Barbara, praying as I went that I would make it in time to see my dad, to say the all important good-bye. The plane landed in Dallas about 2 A.M.

Weary beyond belief, I made my way to the exit. There at the bottom of the ramp were two tall, handsome, stalwart men—my brothers. They smiled up at me, and I knew I'd arrived in time. I smiled back and made my way down. As I reached them, they each took hold of an arm and lifted me right off the floor, carrying me for several yards. I was delighted. We laughed and hugged and were comforted. This memory always brings joy to me. It also triggers a joyful idea—many times I've thought of how I seem to have the Father on one side and the Son on the other, carrying me along through difficult times. I am blessed, and I rejoice.

Another great joy is to gather with the congregation, our spiritual family locally, and to enter into worship: to sing praises, to exalt Him, to pray together, to rejoice in His mercies to us, to hear His word proclaimed.

The list could go on and on, couldn't it? As I think of my life now, and my days, I am reminded of the old hymn, "Count Your Many Blessings." It is a constant state when we are walking in the Spirit. In fact all the stages of processing are constant when we are walking in the Spirit: I don't have to reach to God because I am there; I am in a released mode, flowing out in His life; I am at rest from myself and indwelt by Him; I am aware of His leading and of my glad following of it; I am filled with the joy of His fellowship so that rejoicing and gratitude accompany all we do.

PROCESSING

However, our bondage to habit has been my theme. There is some measure of joy in every phase or stage of the prayer process.

First, I realize the *Reach* stage of the process—communion with Him—is in itself a joy-filled privilege, and I relish remembering all He is to me as I come to His throne. Here I know that I am in the presence of the One who welcomes me and delights to have me come.

The second phase of the process is *Release.* Now I am almost certain that you feel as I do when you unburden your soul to the Lord. Casting your cares on Him, letting it all be relinquished—ah, that feels good. How do you feel after you've confessed fully and received His forgiveness? We not only experience cleansing and freedom and peace, but a wonderful gladness of heart.

Then *Rest.* You might wish to reread that section at this point. That's when we receive the joy of further intimacy with Him. That's when we experience companioning and His poured out love personally—our Lover. That's when we can reveal the deepest desires of our hearts and be fully received and understood—our Friend. That's when we can engage in true play with Him, as a child with a parent.

When you have practiced processing each time you feel pressed or stressed, you will find it becomes very quick to move from releasing your stress to God into that wonderful sense of peace and rest in Him. At that moment you experience a quick gladness of heart that the Holy Spirit gives, even as you realign yourself in regard to what you were doing. Immediately you are enabled to do it "in the Spirit" and with joy.

How wonderful the *Receive* step! I am joyful to be listening and actually hearing His voice. It is also my joy to Respond, to obey in the strength the Spirit gives and in the company of Jesus. The completion of the assignment then brings celebration. I Rejoice.

WHAT IF

"But what if...?" I've heard many sentences that begin this way. Probably the most frequent is in regard to something the Lord asked of a person. Let's call him Mike. Mike did just what he heard the Lord tell him to do, and he did it with right motives and in the strength of the Holy Spirit. Great! Therefore Mike should by all expectations succeed magnificently, shouldn't he? But he didn't. The project, barring some small good, was a decided failure.

Now Mike is depressed and immobilized, although he can't see what he could have done differently. Underneath his other feelings is disappointment with God that He didn't bring about the great results Mike expected.

Mike, please consider: The Lord sent prophet after prophet to Israel, and none of them succeeded in bringing about the repentance and lasting change the Lord desired.

Consider Jesus. During His years of ministry, His own brothers didn't believe in Him. In His hometown of Nazareth He was thrown out of the synagogue. On His last visit there "...they took offense at him. Jesus said to them, 'Only in his hometown, among his relatives and in his own house is a prophet without honor.' He could not do any miracles there, except lay his hands on a few sick people and heal them. And he was amazed at their lack of faith" (Mark 6:3-5).

What more could He have done to win the hearts of the Jewish rulers and people of Jerusalem? Yet hear His cry, "O Jerusalem, Jerusalem, you who kill the prophets and stone those sent to you, how often I have longed to gather your children together, as a hen gathers her chicks under her wings, but you *were not willing.* Look, your house is left to you desolate" (Matthew 23:37, 8, emphasis mine).

Even God Himself cannot escape sorrow over the hard hearts of men who reject His will. He gave man free choice and He will not rescind it, though it rends His heart. God is "not wanting anyone to perish, but everyone to come to repentance" (2 Peter 3:9). Well, then why don't they? But they don't; they *choose* not to. In getting men to choose *His* will, God is a failure—so to speak. He sorrows, and if you are intimate with Him, you sorrow with Him.

Yet we know that our God is always full of joy, having opened the gates of heaven to the redeemed. All heaven rejoices over one sinner that repents and claims redemption. See Luke 15:1-7, Jesus' parable of the shepherd who leaves the ninety-nine in the fold to go rescue the one lost sheep.

It is Easter week as I write. I think of all Jesus said to His disciples that last Passover. I think of His agony in Gethsemane. I think of the ordeal of the arrest, and the trials. And then the cross—eternal and blessed mystery of how He bore our sins and sorrows there. All His suffering would bring us down to despair except for Sunday morning. Resurrection! I think that moment He came forth from the tomb must have been the most joyful moment He had ever known! The Father and Spirit too. All heaven and all earth as well. And the joy continues eternally, and spreads to all who believe. "...who for the *joy* set before Him endured the cross..." (Heb. 12:2). "But now is Christ risen..." (1 Corinthians 15:20, KJV). Rejoice!

So *simultaneously*, Mike, you may sorrow over the indifference of many to your efforts, yet still rejoice first *in Him* and all He has done for you. Second, you can rejoice that you did as the Lord asked you, and were fully obedient to Him. The results belong to Him.

Think of the ministry of the Apostle Paul. How did his various missionary endeavors end? With riots, floggings, being thrown into prison, given forty lashes, stoned, let down in a basket, constantly hounded by irate pursuers. Did he fail? He eventually ended in prison, and there wrote the book of Philippians. The introduction to the book by NIV contains this note: "It is outstanding as the NT letter of joy; the word 'joy' in its various forms occurs some 16 times."[24] Paul was the man who was "sorrowful yet always rejoicing."

It seems to me that Christians are the only people on earth that can know sorrow and joy simultaneously.

MY LESSON

Almost thirty years ago, I learned a very valuable lesson. I was teaching a women's Bible study each week. Our group began the year in September with about a hundred women. Three weeks later, our numbers were down to sixty. I was despondent and distraught.

"Lord, what am I doing wrong? Where am I not hearing You? What would You have me do?"

These words came to mind quite clearly, "How many did I win when I walked the earth?"

I had no definite numbers of course, but I knew the answer was "Very few."

"If *I* couldn't win them, who do you think you are?"

It seemed a harsh answer but it was not said harshly. Forceful and arresting, that's what it was. I was learning not to have a personal vested interest in the assignments of the Lord, measuring the success of them as man does. I was learning to be fully obedient and to leave results to Him.

This didn't and doesn't negate the requirement that I give Him all I am and have and operate in Him. "Whatever you do, work at it with all your heart, as working for the Lord, not for men" (Colossians 3:23). The Lord is not pleased with shoddy goods or half-hearted efforts. He wants A+ endeavor. But it is *His* heart and His alone that I long to please, whether the project seems to succeed or not.

"No personal vested interest in outcomes? Surely not! Aren't we to measure our success?" Again, not in mere natural assessments. Review all before the Lord, and accept His judgment on your effort. If He shows you areas for improvement, make them, and rejoice in the opportunity for improvement. If He shows you none, rejoice in His delight in your obedience.

SORROWFUL, YET ALWAYS REJOICING

We too must truly learn to be "sorrowful, yet always rejoicing..." as Paul was. We've just recalled the many, many trials, pains, and sorrows he endured in fulfilling the Lord's commission to him. Yet let me call to your mind again that Paul is the one who wrote, "...rejoice in the Lord....Rejoice in the Lord always. I will say it again: Rejoice" (Philippians 3:1 and 4:4).

Perhaps this is a time of trial for you. How are you to rejoice in the midst of it? First, consider why you are suffering. If it is because of your faith in Christ, you need to recall Jesus' words in the Beatitudes: "Blessed are those who are persecuted because of righteousness, for theirs is the kingdom of heaven. Blessed are you when people insult you, persecute you and falsely say all kinds of evil against you because of me. Rejoice and be glad, because great is your reward in heaven, for in the same way they persecuted the prophets who were before you."

Also Peter's instruction, "But rejoice that you participate in the sufferings of Christ so that you may be overjoyed when his glory is revealed. If you are insulted because of the name of Christ, you are blessed, for the Spirit of glory and of God rests on you" (1 Peter 4:13, 14). Consider that—participants in Christ's sufferings.

But maybe it isn't that you are being persecuted because you are a Christian. Maybe it is just a trying time. Maybe you are in a blue funk. Or you are sick. Or there is a crisis in your family. Maybe there are personal problems: you haven't been heard, or you are truly misunderstood. Or...or. Peter also has words for times such as these. He speaks of "the coming of salvation that is ready to be revealed in the last time. In this you greatly rejoice, though now for a little while you may have had to suffer grief in all kinds of trials. These have come so that your faith—of greater worth than gold, which perishes even though refined by fire—may be proved genuine and may result in praise and honor and glory when Jesus Christ is revealed" (1 Peter 1:5-7).

"Very well," you may say, "I'll have plenty to rejoice in when He comes again. But what about *now*? I'm hurting right now." Keep reading—1 Peter 1:8,9: "Though you have not seen him, you love him; and even though you do not see him now, you believe in him and are filled with an inexpressible and glorious joy, for you are receiving the goal of your faith, the salvation of your souls." Does it help to realize your growth in Christ is happening? Your faith is being tested and strengthened. You are getting to know Christ in it. These are causes for thanksgiving, even if you cannot *feel joyful.*

Accept the mixture: sorrow and joy. Stress and joy. Trial and joy. Joy because you know the Lord is with you in it. "Consider it pure joy, my brothers, whenever you face trials of many kinds, because you know that the testing of your faith develops perseverance. Perseverance must finish its work so that you may be mature and complete, not lacking anything" (James 1:2-4).

THE DAILIES AGAIN

Moreover, we need to celebrate frequently in the moments of our days. I find the Lord delights to point out beauties and treasures. He seeks laughter with us; He brings us heart-stirring moments. See that child's incredible look of discovery. Fathom that gleam in your friend's eye. Listen to those words of cherishing. Admire the beauty of a stranger. Hear the soul splitting song. Relish the singer's range. See the thankfulness on the face of one you have listened to with love. Delight in the brilliance of a great thought. Stroke the head of your faithful dog. Taste the fresh prawns. Accept a gift that is "just what I wanted." Share an incredible Greek lunch. Listen to the awesome beauty of a symphony. Watch the strength of a horse as it runs. Gaze at a waterfall. "God of wonder..." right here, right now.

I am also struck by a phrase in 1 Timothy 6:17: "...God, who richly provides us with everything for our enjoyment." I sometimes wonder if He isn't disappointed with us that we don't pause to do so, that we don't take it in and thank Him accordingly. I am not speaking of the world's lure to destructive pleasures. Nor do I think we should be claiming our rights to "a little fun," selfishly insisting on what we think we must have to experience happiness. I am speaking of the amazing array of the things *God* has provided for our enjoyment. Do we take time to enjoy them with Him?

I long to relish His daily beauties and special moments as fully as a child does. I remember myself as a little girl of four. My family at that time was neighbor to two spinster sisters approaching old age, two lovers of beauty who cultivated vibrant roses of marvelous hues. There were none in our yard, my parents being incredibly hard put to find time for all the difficulties of those Depression years and with no time to cultivate flowers. Little Joy, however, was fascinated by all flowers, especially roses.

So I slipped away in the early morning, unnoticed by my mother or the dear neighbors, into the rose garden. I went very quietly for I wanted to have my discovery all to myself. The roses were fresh with morning dew, the sunlight creating small round prisms of color, pearls on velvet. The rose petals, softly rounded, whorled out and open. I was mesmerized by them, gazing long at first one and then another, time forgotten, fear past, just me with roses. I had to smell them, and drew close and breathed deep. Their rich perfume was to me as wine to Bacchus. Now I had to touch them. I stroked one petal with one small finger, and knew the inexpressible happiness of sensation. I gathered several fallen petals and put them in my tiny pocket so I could enjoy the sight, smell, and touch again and again. By the end of the day, I'm sure I'd had them in and out a dozen times or more. I know I have been a devotee of natural beauty ever since and now relish with Him all the "party decorations"!

As the years have fled by, I have come more and more to rejoice in this companioning with Jesus even in very small ways: the aroma of morning coffee, the fragrance of fresh laundry, the smoothness and smell of a baby's skin, the radiance and warmth of a fire, the e-mail from my sister, the sound of my son's voice, the taste of my Mexican casserole, the twinkle in my grandson's eyes, the voice behind me singing in church, my daughter's "Hello Mama" on the telephone, my husband's wide smile as we dance together. I am reminded of a hymn, "I am His and He is Mine," that expresses this well, the second stanza especially:

> Heaven above is brighter blue, earth around is sweeter green,
> Something lives in every hue Christless eyes have never seen.
> Birds with gladder songs o'reflow; flowers with deeper beauties shine,
> Since I know, as now I know, I am His and He is mine.[25]

What is your experience of sharing beauty and activity with Him, even in the dailies? You will sense that He is asking you to linger and look deeper, to relish the aroma, to taste the goodness, to touch the fineness, to hear the melody. To participate in His joy. All this happens when we are at home with the Lord, though we may be very active indeed.

A FINAL LOOK

No wonder we are instructed, "Rejoice always" (1 Thessalonians 5:16). And surely one day we shall. Picture this worship service:

> *"Then I heard what sounded like a great*
> *multitude, like the roar of rushing waters*
> *and like loud peals of thunder shouting 'Hallelujah!*
> *For our Lord God Almighty reigns.*
> *Let us rejoice and be glad*
> *and give him glory!*
> *For the wedding of the Lamb has come,*
> *and his bride has made herself ready.'"*

(Revelation 19:6, 7)

Let's practice rejoicing. In our future home we're going to be doing a lot of it.

PART V

APPLICATIONS

A GAIN I WANT to stress that the six stages in the Put Off/Put On process of being conformed to Christ's image are not to be applied rigidly. This is not a lock-step technique, In fact, you can't technique it at all.

Each stage or step has its own realm of freedom. But these stages may not always be processed in the order given. And not all steps are always required in dealing with habits, though they frequently are. All, however, are ways of *encountering Christ* and coming to love Him, to receive His love, and to fellowship with Him. This is the goal, as I have said frequently—our love *relationship* with Christ. He orchestrates the process He chooses to use with you. Each phase or step is His, is with Him, and is applied to you personally, and results therefore in increasing freedom for you and personal intimacy with Him. Each stage will take encounter and direction from the Holy Spirit every step of the way.

The following are some composite case studies and instructions to enable you to see how the Lord deals with habits you may have. Also please consider if the Lord is asking you to minister to others—praying with them and helping them engage in this process toward freedom that will greatly increase their fellowship with the Lord. Welcome their ministry to you as well.

CRITICISM

Janice couldn't look at another person without a negative thought arising. She was very proficient in "categorizing" and prided herself on it. Sometimes she voiced it quite spontaneously with a tinge of cleverness in her pronouncement. And she could spot a phony or a hypocrite a mile away. She often passed it all off as humor. She felt very clever.

She became aware that her thoughts were criticism, not discernment. She learned about the Spirit-filled heart: the believer who discerns weakness or sin in another is instantly filled with sorrow, compassion, and pity for the person. Anger and grief at the sin and its effect fill the believer's heart as well. She knew that the discerner turns immediately to *pray* for the one discerned.

Her critical heart, on the other hand, habitually denounced or felt superior or both to the one she observed. She became acutely aware of this habit, one she slid into frequently.

She then realized that she had learned this habit in her family of origin. Her mother especially had been a very critical person. Janice dealt with the anger she felt toward her mother for modeling this habit. She forgave her mother, and also sought the Lord's forgiveness for taking up this habit herself.

Then she turned to the habit itself. She learned that she must turn to the Lord immediately with the *first thought* of criticism and confess it as sin.

She began to ask the Lord to make her aware of her first thought. At that moment she would reach to God immediately with it. She also became able to internally verbalize her thought to God only, followed by full confession and release of her sin to the cross. She felt incredibly shameful as she faced this sin, time and time again. Yet she sought the Lord's forgiveness each time, and accepted the fact that He did forgive her.

She learned to accept a new beginning and to seek a time of rest in her relationship with Him. It was always joy to relish His company and dialogue with Him. Abiding in His love became practice, not just theory.

When her mind became joyful and quieted and she was aware of the filling of the Spirit, she asked the Lord what He wanted in place of her criticism. She knew the Scriptures that told her to be kind, to forgive, to encourage, and to build up. She set her will to do His will as she recalled these Scriptures. Then she listened for specific acts that the Lord brought to mind, and either did as He asked immediately or as soon as indicated.

Her joyful obedience gave rise to more rejoicing with the Lord. Fellowship with Him became a habit. And joy as well.

It took many weeks of processing in this manner for Janice's habit of criticism to fade, but fade it did, and at length she realized that even her first thoughts of others were no longer critical. Discernment with compassion had replaced them.

As with Janice, when you find this habit of criticism in yourself, you will know the moment you turn to God and ask to be searched, that this criticism in you is sin. You too will need to release fully, especially your thoughts and the accompanying attitude, in confession to God. You will need to ask for His forgiveness.

Often you may think that is the end of the matter, but at this point you would do well to enter into a time of extended rest—focusing on Christ and His presence, and further allowing Him to search you for the *root* cause of your criticism. Receive whatever He shows you. It may likely be your sense of your own imperfection and unworthiness based on what you were told about yourself as a child or in comparisons to others. Either of these can be healed only by basking in the love of Christ, whether you know the origins of such a sense of low value or not.

Take time in the rest stage to allow the Lord to search you out in this way. When He does, let Him heal the hurt of your heart if you remember being criticized as a child. If such a memory comes, become that child again. Invite Him to come to you and to tend to the hurt, to comfort, soothe, and to give *His* opinion of this wonderful being He has created.

If you find such root wounds, you would do well to spend some "counseling" time with Him daily, inviting Him to bring up whatever painful memory of put down that He chooses. After the recall of the painful experience, invite Him to come in after it to heal you of the hurt. Linger to experience His parenting of you in regard to it. It will help to journal what He says and does. If you find this difficult to do alone, invite a trusted Christian friend to pray along with you. Make appointments with your friend for a "session" or two each week. Keep them, even if you feel afraid. Jesus *will* meet you and free you. Trust Him.

Perhaps the root cause of your habit is not the criticized child. Another root cause of criticism is pride. You are proud of your giftedness and your accomplishments. This pride can only be eradicated by standing in Christ's awesome presence until you know absolutely that you have nothing of your own efforts to bring to Him that is not sin-stained and worthless. "...and all our righteous acts are like filthy rags..." (Isaiah 64:6). Therefore, stay in the rest stage with Him for His further revelations to you. You may need to see things from your past that He will bring to mind. Then you can release these and confess them, item by item, to Him.

Recall again the Put On: receiving, responding, rejoicing. Remember to ask Him what He would have you put in the place of your criticism. Accept any scriptures He brings to mind. Ask Him how He would apply these specifically. Would He have you spend some time in prayer for the one you have criticized? For others? Write a note or letter of encouragement? Make a phone call? Whatever it may be, you are to hear it and to do it as quickly as possible. Then the rejoicing with Him comes.

161

Each time your criticism comes, repeat your process, remembering not to hurry through the rest stage where He may have further insights for you about your habit. Remember, your goal is primarily to know Him and to do His will.

ANGER

Bart had an incredibly quick temper, especially on the baseball field. He played in a soft ball league, and loved the game. But he wasn't in his left field position for two minutes before something the pitcher or a teammate or the coach or a member of the other team did that sparked his anger. Condemnation gushed from him in furious words that in turn infuriated his teammates and sometimes invited the donnybrooks that ensued with the opposing team. Nothing good ever came from his temper outbursts. Quite the opposite.

He made vows galore, but found no amount of will power would end his tirades. They spewed like hot lava. He managed to bite his tongue a few times, but only for a minute or two while the anger continued to build. He could not convince himself that his indignation was justified, though he tried. Down deep he knew it wasn't and that he was bringing dishonor to the Lord he loved by this habit.

In counseling I taught him how to use the prayer processing steps to deal with his anger. It helped him tremendously on the field to reach to God immediately and begin to voice out internally the rage he was feeling the moment it began. He would grit his teeth and rail inwardly for several minutes, knowing he intended to release the anger to God, not to build it. He could always tell the moment the Lord asked him to "let go" as an act of the will. He confessed the angry thoughts as sin and asked to be forgiven. All the while he kept playing, saying nothing. He had purposed in his heart beforehand not to speak.

Following this he focused on the Lord being right there with him on the field, enjoying with him the fun of the game, and then also receiving any specifics the Lord brought to mind. He found himself shouting out encouragements and words of cheer, rather than "blastin' the guy." This felt great, until the next "offender" goofed. Then he had to do the process all over again. This happened many times in each game. But little by little, the anger habit weakened.

I had asked that after each game he review it with the Lord, and ask for further insight. In time he was able to invite the Lord to search him out for the origins of his anger, and found he had quite a bit of processing to do in regard to his father and how he had handled life through anger. Bart also engaged with the Lord in the healing of memories when his father's anger had been directed at him. These came forth in his counseling sessions with me when together we asked the Lord if there was any memory He wished to bring up. Bart did the same later in daily sessions he held alone with the Lord. His fellowship with Jesus became paramount as his freedom and rejoicing increased.

Have you that trigger quick reaction of anger to people and/or situations: the driver who cuts in, the frustrating situation that you can't control, your wife's coolness, your husband's inattention, the needless bureaucratic tangle? Whatever sets you off, you find yourself inflamed and sending out sparks. You say the hasty nasty words. You move too quickly, putting yourself and others in jeopardy. You grit your teeth and burn, charring your insides and releasing toxic smoke into the atmosphere.

Whatever the result of your anger, it isn't righteousness. This isn't holy anger, and you can no longer tell yourself that it is. No good comes of it, either for you or for those affected by it.

The moment you feel such sinful anger, *reach* to God in prayer immediately, and begin to *release*—pour out to Him why you are angry. Tell Him the fault of the one who brought it on as completely as you can. Scream if you must, pound your pillow, run around the block as you vent, get it *out*, but only for a few minutes. Then choose to release it to Him, and *let it go!* Say and mean it, "That's enough."

Now *stop.* Come to a complete halt. Realize it is *your* habit—this allowing inappropriate anger. Confess it as an indulgence in emotion, one that you need to be rid of. Tell the Lord you know you are helpless to stop. Seek His grace and forgiveness.

Now you need to *rest.* It is time to spend awhile just looking to Him and enjoying His company. Become aware of His presence and His attitude toward you.

Notice His incredible peace. Dwell in that peace. Settle down and be at home in it, in Him.

In regard to the current anger, having released and entered rest, you will know when you are ready to ask Him the questions: "Lord, what would You have me put in place of my anger habit? What do you want me to *receive* from You?" Listen. What comes to mind after a moment or two? You may hear one or more passages of scripture. I usually hear, "The wrath of man does not work the righteousness of God." If it did, I could feel righteously angry, such as over injustice, and God would utilize my anger to energize the actions He would dictate to curtail it. That most surely is very infrequently the case.

Usually you will hear a specific new habit to put in place of your anger. *Respond* to Him—do what He tells you to do as soon as you possibly can. He usually asks me to perform some act of service for the one who "inspired" my anger. I am always asked to pray in His Spirit for the "instigator". Then of course, I can *rejoice* with Him in the doing of it and can keep on rejoicing when it is done.

You may find yourself needing to repeat this process many, many times before your anger habit fades. If your anger springs from something deeper— and it usually does—you need to pray Psalm 139:23, 24: "Search me, O God, and know my heart...." Ask Him specifically, "What is the source of this anger, Lord? I am ready to have You show me." Again this invites the recall of painful memories, one at a time. After you go back to the hurtful encounter and experience it, remember to invite the Lord to come in, and to heal your hurt before it turns to anger.

If you remember that a person aroused great fear in you, you may also realize that it has turned to anger. As you recall the time this person incited fear in you, let the scene unroll before you. Stop at the time you felt fear most deeply and invite the Lord to come to you at that moment in the memory. Stay in the age you were then. Invite the presence of the Lord. Retroactively release the fear to Him fully. Then, being in the age you were at the time of the fear, rest with Him—stay with Him for the full healing and the joy of His presence. In every deep healing session the Lord will ask you to forgive the one who sinned against you. Be absolutely certain that you forgive and let it go. Again, ask the Lord to forgive you for turning the fear to anger. Now you can return to the present and to the Put On part of the process.

CONFLICT

"We *have* to move to Phoenix. I have to live there. We should have moved there right after we graduated from college. We stayed here in Santa Barbara because of your family, so you could be close to them. Now it is time to move to Phoenix so I can be close to Dad! You know how hard this will be for him with Mom gone." Alice realized she was shouting at Todd. She crumpled, sobbing loudly, and tumbled onto the couch.

Todd and Alice had been married three years when her mother died. Alice was devastated. Although she had been with her mother when she died, Alice had felt great remorse and guilt for not living in closer proximity and being with her more, and now, two months later, she had edged deeper into depression. Her outbursts to Todd were very disturbing, though he tried to comfort her but found he couldn't. He felt helpless and resentful. He couldn't understand her need to move. She'd been fine about living and working in Santa Barbara. He was enjoying his work as a junior high math teacher—he really liked the kids. He'd thought she enjoyed her work as a high school English teacher just as much.

Alice had, in truth, spent many hours on the phone to her family in the past three years, especially her mother. They were extremely close; Alice depended on her mother's understanding, sympathy, and advice. They discussed everything, sometimes even before Alice shared her thoughts and feelings with Todd. Now motherless, Alice called her dad almost daily, often crying and telling him how much she wanted to be in Phoenix with him.

Todd finally became exasperated and told Alice to forget moving. He did not want to move to Phoenix. He did not intend to give up a good job he liked, and he did not think Alice's insistence was in line with God's will. He was adamant. He wasn't going.

Their arguments increased in volume, frequency, and intensity. Finally they sought counseling, each hoping the counselor would choose his/her side and support its validity.

When Todd and Alice came into my office, I told them this issue was deeper than it seemed. I spent several sessions with each separately to bring each one out of dependence on their "family of origin" and worked at length with Alice to enable her to release her anger toward God for her mother's death, and then to grieve out her sorrow to Him. In doing this I had each of them relate more and more fully to God as parent and comforter. I spent hours listening as each poured out pent up feelings to God, encouraging a full and complete outflow. Following release times, I invited each to relate deeply to Jesus in a rested state and to drink in His love and care.

In further sessions, I brought each in prayer to release hurt feelings toward the spouse and to extend full forgiveness in prayer. I found this is effective only when prayed out to the Lord personally and individually, not just said to each other. At length I asked them to come to a session together and to extend forgiveness to each other, praying it out in the Lord's presence.

We still had the conflict to deal with. Now I asked each of them who they most wanted to please. Both showed some confusion. I asked them to wait before the Lord with this question: "Who do *You* most want me to please?" It only took a few minutes of quiet before Him for both of them to answer, "The Lord. He wants me to please Him."

"Where does the Lord want you two to live? Let's now ask Him that in prayer and listen for His answer. Will you each go home, and hold that question before Him in prayer for this week? Do this separately. If you feel your own desires coming back to provide the answer, release these fully to Him, relinquish them, rest in Him, and then ask the question again, 'Lord, where would You have us live? I long to please You.' Don't discuss the answer with each other. Come back and we will talk about it here."

That next week two quiet, subdued people came in together. I asked Alice to remain in the reception room while I talked to Todd. "All right, Todd," I said, "What did you hear from the Lord?"

"I know Alice won't like this, but I felt His leading to stay right here. I couldn't get past it. I tried to see us in Phoenix, but I just couldn't sense His blessing on that at all. I know I'd be willing to move now if He wants it, but I honestly don't think He does. I'm afraid to say this though."

"Just stay with what you think the Lord is telling you, Todd. You wait outside now please while I talk to Alice."

Alice came in smiling. I didn't even get my question out before she said, "I couldn't believe it, but the Lord said clearly that we are to stay here! The funny thing is, I know that's right! I really feel good about it now. I realize *He* wants to be the one to comfort and sustain my dad. That's not my job. He wants to show me how to be a good *wife*. I am to "leave and cleave" He told me. I guess I really haven't wanted to grow up. Now I do."

Needless to say, both were delighted to hear the answer the other had received.

In some cases of conflict, the background problems are not as deep as in this case, and the two involved can go straight to the Lord for the answer— that is, if they have cleared their motivations of any "I want's" and truly long to hear what the Lord wants. He makes His will clear when we are willing to hear him. Only in rare instances has the "we agree to disagree" been the "final" word. Even so, coming before the Lord in humility and genuine willingness to hear His will has produced loving attitudes, each towards the other, even if differing answers prevail.

The following are a few examples provided by the class I taught in the spring of 2003. I have changed some of the names to protect confidentiality of those who requested it.

WORRY AND CONTROL

Shirley's story:

I have a son who is forty-six years of age. He has an ex-wife who left him five years ago, and five children ages nine to twenty-one. Theirs is a story of money mismanagement to the ultimate. He worked and still does as a mechanic, taking home a fair salary. Yet year by year in the past he sank deeper and deeper into debt. He knew little of household financing, and his wife had complete control—such control that when she left their home of twenty-two years, all utilities were due to be cut off. My son never took control of this and it spun out of his reach. All of a sudden his wife was gone, he was ready for bankruptcy, his appliances were in total ruin, and he couldn't manage his children, his house, nor his bills. He sank into a deep depression.

Our family members were afraid of what measures he might take. We did all that we could for him financially, physically, and emotionally. It wasn't enough. I worried so much that I developed insomnia. I couldn't depend on a night's sleep for months on end. I who resist medication took sleeping pills twice and knew that wasn't the answer.

In desperation I began asking God if He would just help me through the night so I could get some sleep once in a while. I prayed for Him to cradle me in His arms and rock me to sleep.

Finally one day after I had begun this course and learned about Release, I was at another class, my women's Bible study, and I just couldn't take any more worry about my son. Now his back was out and he had just started a new job! I was totally downcast and I came to the class in a daze. I didn't absorb much of the lesson because I kept praying for God to help my son.

At the end of the class our leader asked me what was wrong and the flood gates opened. I poured out my worry, and then gave my son to God. I lifted him up and handed him over. I said, "Lord, I can't do this any longer. Take him. He is yours to deal with."

I was relieved after this happened and I felt a wonderful warm peace flood over every inch of my body. I felt comforted. I heard God say, "You are finally letting go of what only I can do." After that I waited. I knew in my heart I was to do no more for my son. I am his Mom, but I am not his fixer of all things. I was to replace worry and fret with prayer for him.

His back healed remarkably fast. So fast, as a matter of fact, that I could hardly believe it. I told him this was the Lord's work and that I and my friends were praying for him. From this I received reassurance that God is in control and that He is the only one that can change things. He loves me, He wants me to rest in Him, and He will get things done.

My response to this is I must learn to trust Him and not go around fixing everything and everybody. It kind of reminds me of retirement. I didn't know it could be so good until I gave up and retired. I rejoice in the wonderful gift the Lord has given me and my son. I just pray that one day he will really come to understand the power of the Great Physician!

GOAL ORIENTED; PRESSING

Carolyn's story:

It has been revealed to me that I am very goal oriented, and that I focus all my energy on getting things done and over with. The problem with this is don't take time to enjoy the journey with Christ, and I often miss out on relationships He wants me to have with others because of my task orientation. Also, I miss opportunities for spontaneity and fun along the way.

God revealed that He wants to break into this habit, and bring more joy and play into my life. I had just completed a major project—writing a paper in which this whole habit was revealed. I felt good about finishing: "Yeah! It's done!" and I immediately thought, "What is the next thing I have to do?" Then I remembered. I had to organize the Spring Fair at my kids' school.

Right away the anxiety and stress of the next task started to build, but then I decided to release it to God and to rest in Him. I asked Him to help me *enjoy* the planning of the fair and asked Him how that was to be done. He gave me the name of a young mom who is often eager to help and seems like a fun person to be around. So I phoned and asked her to help me organize. She was delighted.

And so I continue, ready to "enjoy the journey."

HURT FEELINGS

Ruth's story:

I had a negative experience with a person. She hurt my feelings and angered me with her harsh words and her questioning of my motives. I spent a couple of days quite annoyed with her until I realized I needed to fully release it to God. As I released and went into rest He gave me a picture of her, showing me that He wanted to give her a "garment of praise". But He first had to remove a cloak of heaviness that was on her. I saw she had on a dark brown, heavy, old worn leather coat.

As He lifted it off her, her whole countenance changed. Where there was anxiety, worry, and stress lining her face, as He lifted off the heaviness, a lightness and joy radiated from her. The Lord gave me a couple of words to go with it; the first was "expectancy." This indicated there was nothing she was to try to do. God was going to do it, but she was to wait expectantly. The second was "let go"—she was to let go of the old coat, not hang onto it, but let it go completely.

I e-mailed this picture and the words to her and told her I was praying for her.

Praise God! Not only was my message received well, but God has answered in an incredible way. This is a cause to rejoice!

A PRACTICAL MATTER: TO MOVE OR NOT TO MOVE

Audrey's story:

This is first of all a story of a question I asked the Lord: "Should I sell my home at Shawnigan Lake and move closer to the church?" My church was in Duncan, about twelve miles away. My children were grown and gone and I lived there alone. My yard was a lot of work. It took me one and a half hours to mow the lawns, plus tend to all the flower beds, rockery and my fenced in rose garden. Although I could still handle it, sooner or later I would need to let go. But when?

I had no idea what I preferred. I told the Lord, "I have no idea what to do, but I am going to trust you to open and shut doors for me. If I am to stay as I am now, that's fine, but if I should move, that's fine also. Just let me know and do Your will."

Soon after in late March I contacted a realtor and began to look at condo units and patio homes. All the while she told me I was doing this backwards. I should sell my home first and then look for one to buy. I knew I didn't want to sell and have pressure to panic buy, so I told her, "No, I'll find a place that touches my heart, put an offer on it, subject to the sale of my house. If it doesn't work, that's O.K. because I will just stay where I am." I was trusting the Lord and I had peace about the whole process.

I looked at many choices of homes, but none of them were right for me. Then there was a *me* issue: I had said for years, "I'll never live in Duncan." Never say never when you've left it to the Lord to open and shut doors because He has a sense of humor.

When I looked at a lovely condo unit, #57, in *Duncan*, I became excited. It was very near my church. And it felt so right. But it was complicated—an estate sale with renters. The law required they be given sixty days notice, after completion of the sale. This would make the sale of my home a problem in timing since most buyers want early possession.

I showed the place to my family of three children and spouses and all of them felt it would be a good move for me. So the following day, Monday, I signed the purchase agreement and listed my house for sale at 1:00 P.M. At 5:30 P.M I received word from my doctor's office that polyps I had had removed from my colon were cancerous! (a second story but very mixed in with this one; it's next.) Would I have thought of moving if I had thought this would be the report? I think not!

I decided to pray and release it all to the Lord. I believed He wouldn't have had me make these commitments, just to have to undo it all and stay at Shawnigan Lake.

My offer on #57 was accepted, pending the sale of my house, which sold in nine days! And the possession date was no problem, as the young couple that bought it were living with family and could wait. The deal was concluded for only $500.00 less than I had asked. I praised the Lord.

A few weeks later after sorting and packing and preparing to move, I arrived home to receive a phone call from my realtor telling me that the couple that bought my house had separated, and could back out of the deal and forfeit their deposit. I could end up with two houses! Then what would I do? I admit I began to worry.

I awoke the next morning with the song, "This is the Day That the Lord Has Made" running around in my head, and I had never needed it more.

My cancer scare was still looming, and now all this with houses! I decided again to trust the Lord, and I released it all to Him again.

Later the realtor phoned to say that the male buyer's mother (of the couple who bought my house) was going to take it for herself, renovate it, and resell it. How the Lord was caring for me!

The move, August 3, went so smoothly that I was simply amazed. The packing, sorting, and slugging it out were over. And I now have a love for #57 that I have never had for any of my homes (and there were many, several of higher quality). But this home is "OUR HOME"—the Lord's and mine. He blessed me every step of the way.

ILLNESS

Audrey's second story:

At the time I was looking for a home with my realtor, I went in April for a routine checkup to my doctor. Tests results showed colon polyps. It looked like they were cancerous! I was terrified.

After a few days I went to the Prayer Ministry group at my church. I would have to have the polyps removed to see if they were cancerous. I asked the group to ask the Lord what He had to say to me in regard to the polyps. After the group bowed in silent prayer for several minutes, each one shared with me what he or she had received.

I was given much encouragement from the Lord through them, but the one that gave me the most courage and release was this: Jeremiah 29:11-13 "For I know the plans I have for you...plans to prosper you and not to harm you, plans to give you hope and a future. Then you will call upon me and come and pray to me, and I will listen to you. You will seek me and find me when you seek me with all your heart." I was astounded. These were "my verses"—given to me years before by my cousin in Washington. I was six feet up in the air in my heart. I released all my concern to the Lord.

The following Wednesday, April 24, I was to go to Victoria for the polyps removal. That morning when I woke an old chorus was running through my head, "Give me oil in my lamp, keep me burning...." I couldn't remember that chorus as one I had ever sung, but the Lord put it into my heart that morning. My daughter, Beverlee, picked me up. I asked her if she knew the chorus, and she did. We sang it together as she drove.

Afterwards I was at peace about the chance of the polyps being cancerous as the surgeon felt they were not. And I remained at peace in the days that followed.

Then came the message on May 6. That was the day I signed to purchase my condo and sell my home at 1:00 P.M. At 5:30 my doctor called to say that the polyps that had been removed were indeed cancerous. I had truly believed the results would be negative. What now? I felt caught up in fear. My thoughts were torturous, my night a nightmare. The next morning I turned to prayer, poured out my fears, and then fully released to the Lord both the cancer and the real estate commitments. Now I could rest. Again He asked me to trust Him, replacing fear and worry with assurance of His mercy and grace. I was to continue with the things on my date book.

I was waiting for a booking to have a Sigmoscopy, a procedure where the surgeon planned to "tattoo" the area where the polyps were removed in case I required surgery. He would also take sample tissue from where the polyps were removed, to see if there was cancer remaining or if it had all been removed.

While I waited I anticipated my move and began to prepare. Also, I antici-pated the wedding of my granddaughter on June 8th. It was to be a very big wedding with six bridesmaids, showers, the works. I knew the Lord wanted me to be part of it all and to give all the love and service He directed, so I continued to leave all my worries in His hands.

The booking I had waited for was scheduled for June 17th. Prior to that, on June 14th, the Lord gave me Isaiah 60:1—"Arise, shine, for thy light is come, and the Glory of the Lord is risen upon thee." I cherished it for the waiting was becoming difficult. That evening, I had been working in the yard, and as I was putting away my garden tools, a breeze came up. Then I heard on my wind chimes the melody of my favorite hymn, "Blessed Assurance"—just those two words. I wept.

On June 17th, I chose to drive myself to the Jubilee Hospital; somehow I wanted to be on my own with the Lord. I prayed and committed it all to Him again. The test went well, and I arrived home to learn of the problem with the sale of my house. I was lamenting that it had been a very bad day. But at bedtime the Lord gave me, "Expect things above all you ask or think. The Lord is able to give thee much more than this. Ask largely." And "Thy God will be a kindly giver unto thee." What a comfort. So I set my mind to do as He had asked.

By June 26th I still didn't know the results of the Sigmoscopy. And that morning a sales person came from the moving company to price my move.

Was I moving? Yet the Lord gave me Psalm 91:15,16: "I will be with him in trouble, I will deliver him and honour him, with long life I will satisfy him and show him my salvation." Again, I released all to Him and continued with my day.

I awoke June 27th feeling peaceful, believing that the Lord is in charge. What a change from the last few days. Then came the call from the doctor's office. The results of the tissue taken from the area of the polyps: NORMAL. I found it hard to take it in at first. Then my heart melted. I phoned my children and friends so that they could rejoice with me. I had already invited two of my best friends to tea previously, not knowing, of course, that they would be coming on the very day I received my great good news! What perfect timing, Lord! Such a glad ending to this chapter of my life.

REBORN EXPERIENCE

In our fall 2003 class Karen shared her thinking. Speaking of the process, she wrote:

This link with the Lord is constantly amazing me. I have been a Christian for years yet I feel reborn. It began with praying over and over Psalm 139:23 and 24. This led to realizing how much I do in a "take control" manner. I had no idea I was constantly doing things my way with no thought given to what the Lord thought. I never thought to ask for His consideration nor His help. I was brought to realize the enormous love the Lord has for me. One night the final sentence He wrote me was etched in the sky—a sunset and cloud formation that was simply dazzlingly awesome; it reverberated with the Lord's "I love you!"

Now I eagerly look forward to the day and sharing it all with Him. He is constantly showing me "miracles"; it is hard to believe I feel so light hearted. It is so easy to laugh now. This new life style has revolutionized my walk with God.

FINDING TIME

Annette, a member of our fall class, shared:

My road to freedom developed some potholes. It has to do with obedience. I knew what the Holy Spirit was requesting me to do. For some time now He has laid it on my heart to arise before my children so that I can spend time reaching to Him before we start our day. I'm not a morning person. I would rather stay up late and sleep in to at least 7 A.M. My bed is just too warm and comfortable to get out of. I know God would like me to get up though; He even confirmed it upon my request. I asked one evening for verification. Around 5 the next morning the fire alarm went off for no reason and I haven't had a problem with it since.

I started to wonder as I wrote this why I preferred to stay up late in the evening and rise late in the morning. I now see that I am trying to escape the chaos of my life. I am having trouble parenting my two boys. I imagine releasing them to God by shooting them into outer space!

Having been given this assignment has made me take action. I asked God again to wake me and told Him that this time I truly would get up. It happened for me this morning. Yet I again resisted until I heard my son get up at 5 A.M. I jumped out of bed to let him know that he could return to his. I now realize that if I have the boys get up at 7, I can get up at 6, and that way I can spend an hour with Him. I feel good about this. I know I need to be consistent and make it a new habit! I am confident He will enable me to do so.

JOB LOSS

A bit of background to this story. Colleen and her husband, Greg, moved shortly over a year ago from Ontario to Duncan, B.C. because of a job offer he had from a nearby Christian camp. He had served for several years as a pastor, but now both Greg and Colleen believed God was calling them to Vancouver Island for special purposes. He accepted the job offer. They left everything behind and struck out on the grand adventure. After several months of work, he hit a snag and was asked to come to a job review.

Colleen's story:

> When my husband had a probation review of his job, it was decided by both parties that he wasn't quite the right fit for the job. That meant his employment would come to an end. I heard the news with mixed feelings. What had God called us to by bringing us all the way here to end the job so soon?
>
> Time to process! Reach up to God—Help, Lord! Now what? I then poured out all my concern and anxiety and left it with Him, choosing to release the future fully to Him. I chose to Rest in Him, relishing His love and care for us. He knew we had no income. I would trust Him.

Then I did ask Him this question: "What now, Lord?" I had peace in asking it, but thought I'd have to wait to hear the answer. Instead I was surprised when this thought came clearly to me, "You will know by Sunday. Just wait and trust me."

That was Wednesday in mid-November. At our church the Servant Leadership Team (elders) met for their monthly meeting the next evening. One of the associate pastors had resigned and was leaving in January. The leadership team voted that night to ask Greg to become Interim Pastor for one year, and then to be reviewed for a possible permanent position at the end of that year. One of the SLT members was assigned to go to Greg and ask if he would be willing to serve. Amazingly, Greg and Colleen had planned a social evening with this member and her spouse that Saturday night. When she asked Greg the question at the beginning of the evening, he and Colleen were astounded and couldn't stop being amazed at God and His timing. The four of them gave out some great shouts of joy amid numerous hugs. The entire evening was celebration.

The next morning the Chairman of the SLT, Stewart Bradshaw, approached Greg in the church hall for his answer. Greg and Stewart were ecstatic over the big "YES!!" And so was Colleen. She had certainly had her answer by Sunday. Her words: "That Sunday when we heard that his new job was confirmed, let me tell you, did we rejoice! God is amazing."

FEAR OF MEN:

A member of our fall class shared this story of using the process:

I loved my Dad but I also feared him greatly. He was authoritative. Every time I was around him I was afraid. All my life since then, when I am around strong, authoritative men, I feel nervous, tired, and threatened. That is, until I took this class.

This was certainly the way I felt when my husband's boss asked to see us in his office. This boss was certainly an authoritative man. When I heard about it I cried all day. I thought, "Why? What for?" I praised God that I had some time to prepare. So I sat with God each day for five days and kept going through the process. The *releasing* the fear and anxiety was the best part for me. I kept releasing and releasing all that fear and I put it on Jesus and asked Him to take it from me. Then I rested in His love, and I knew I was to receive His peace to accompany me as I went about the day's assignments. And I was able to experience the peace and to rejoice in it.

The day of the meeting came. I didn't even feel nervous or afraid. I was amazed at myself. Going into the office, sitting down, I was on guard but still at peace. The boss spoke. I listened. It appeared he desired to know each of us better and on a personal basis. I didn't say much but I answered any question he asked me, asking God in my mind to help me, guide me, tell me what to speak. I left the office feeling unscathed, not threatened or condemned or attacked. What a change—the new had replaced the old! I was filled with joy and thanksgiving.

HURTFUL CHILDHOOD MEMORIES

Bev, a member of our fall class, wrote of her experience:

I wanted to share with you a picture I was given in my mind a few months ago when I was dealing with some hurtful childhood memories. The picture is Jesus holding a little girl of about seven to ten years old. Jesus has His arms totally wrapped around the little girl, and her arms are totally wrapped around Jesus. Her ear is pressed against His chest. When I received this picture it spoke volumes to me. Afterwards I went off by myself and felt inspired to write these words:

The child's ear is pressed against Jesus' chest.
She hears His heart beat; that heart beat is His
Love for her.

The heart represents the love God has for you.
His love for you can never change no matter
What you have done. He is the same yesterday,
Today, and forever.

He calls you MY BELOVED.

The little girl in the picture represents the
Little girl in each of us who have been hurt,
Violated—physically or emotionally—by others.
Jesus holds that little girl in us. He wraps His
Mighty arms around her and heals, comforts,
And becomes her all in all. The one who will never

Leave her nor forsake her. Jesus tells her I AM
Your comforter, your love, your healer, I affirm you, I accept
You, I have confidence in you, I am your security. Now
That I have healed the little girl in you,
You can become the woman who walks in
Freedom and be a woman who runs after my own heart.

Ephesians 3:14-19.

Many other instances could be cited to show how the process had been applied in actual cases, situations and lives. My appeal is that you apply it to yours. Spend enough time relating to the Lord Himself in this process, and you will find not only the answers to your questions, but more wonderfully by far, you will come to know Him who is Himself the Answer. And you will learn the true meaning of freedom—the liberty of living in Jesus Christ. Your pilgrimage with Him is always on the rugged road.

I pray too that many of you who read this book will assist others in this prayer process. Many will be too weak in faith to complete the process alone. Pray with them, expressing your faith as the Lord directs.

Others will have deep issues, and may require frequent prayer sessions and encouragement to stay with the processing. Some of you may need to refer the person you've been meeting with to a professional Christian counselor. Yet for most of those in need much can be done by willing prayerful believers. May God enable you to become a prayer mentor who comes along side to give needed encouragement, insight, and perseverance in prayer.

There will be those who cannot seem to get started. They feel themselves inadequate to the task and fear to enter in. Help them. It is your privilege and joy to see God set captives free as you pray.

Free us, Lord to be with You for adventures on the road.

THE STUDY GUIDE

THE RUGGED ROAD TO FREEDOM—
BEGINNINGS, OVERVIEW, AND CHAPTER 1

Study and Reflection Questions:

1. Do you agree that changing habits is an arduous process? If not, why not? Have you ever succeeded in changing a habit by will power? Describe.

2. What is your motive as a Christian for changing habits?

3. Recall the four directions our defensive habits take us. Did you find yours? Which one or ones? How does it operate in you?

4. Have you ever bartered with God? Where did it get you?

5. Do you genuinely encounter God when you read Scripture? How?

6. Explain the distinction between the *natural* person and the *spiritual* person.

7. What has been *your* experience of moving into the new realm of the spiritual and letting go of the natural? What leads you back into the natural? Are you aware when it happens?

8. See Oswald Chambers' comments on page 34. Do you agree or disagree with what he says? Explain.

ASSIGNMENT: Read all of Chapter 2. Record in your journal your thoughts as you read. Note what you question.

Practice the concept of Release to God. Record either the release itself or a summary of it in your journal. Also consider how you felt about it. Record that as well.

THE RUGGED ROAD TO FREEDOM—CHAPTER 2

Study and Reflection Questions:

1. What do you "stuff" by habit?

2. Have you ever been a volcano or a flood? What was the result?

3. Do you sometimes (or frequently) give "a piece of my mind"? What is the result?

4. "If He knows all my thoughts, why do I try to hide them, or even to clean them up before telling them out to Him?" Do you agree with this sentence? Why or why not?

5. How do *you* release? Do you have a scream or cry location? time? Or do you release more effectively in writing?

6. Would you be *willing* to pray daily Psalm 139:23 and 24? Would you then listen for what God brings to mind? How much time are you willing to give to this?

7. Consider these words of Jesus (John 16:33 KJV): "In the world you <u>shall have tribulation....</u>" (underlining mine). Are you offended with God that He does not prevent *your* tribulation (sickness, pain, financial difficulties, anxiety, grief, stress, etc.) on this earth? Recall the last time you experienced tribulation. How did you feel? Toward whom?

8. How do you *forgive* those who have sinned against you?

9. When are you truly able to rebuke in love and for the sake of the wrong doer? What is needed for this to be possible?

ASSIGNMENT: Read all of Chapter 2 again, especially focusing on the second half. Again, make notes on your thinking as you read.

Record any difficulties, conflicts, or arguments with the text. Be willing to address these in your group.

Study and Reflection Questions:

1. What do you do with guilt and shame that reoccurs?

2. Explain what you do with self directed thoughts and goals.

3. How much have you stored up in your "closet"? How are you going to deal with it?

4. How do you practice release when it is needed in the moments of your day?

5. Is coming to God as a little child really necessary? If so, when? For how long (repeatedly)? What happens when you no longer need to come as a child?

6. Explain the relationship of letting go of emotion and letting go of "fixing it."

7. See James 5:16. Here we are told to confess our faults to one another. Explain when you believe this is necessary.

ASSIGNMENT: Read all of Chapter 3, Rest. Again, make notes as you read. What do you find difficult? With what do you disagree? Question? Be prepared to discuss with your group.

Are YOU able to rest with the Lord? What hinders? When are you able to rest? What are your feelings when you do? What do you want in this regard?

THE RUGGED ROAD TO FREEDOM—CHAPTER 3

Study and Reflection Questions:

(Note: All questions about <u>rest</u> have to do with a time of spiritual entering into rest with the Lord.)

1. What is the first aspect of *rest*? How do you obtain it?

2. Of the Hebrew words for "rest," which is your favorite definition and why?

3. Is rest a difficult spiritual discipline for you? Why or why not?

4. What does silence have to do with rest? Can't a person rest without silence? Explain.

5. Explain how waiting relates to rest. What does trusting the Lord have to do with it?

6. Is seeing the Lord's face important during rest? Why or why not? What other senses might be engaged during rest?

7. How **deeply** do you get into rest with God? What happens during that time?

8. What hinders you from entering into rest with God? Into abiding?

9. Are you able to have "rest breaks" with the Lord during your day? Why or why not?

10. Practice resting. Set aside time for at least one period of resting daily. After several days, list several significant benefits of resting with the Lord. Explain how you personally experienced each.

ASSIGNMENT: Read all of Chapter 4. Use your journaling to record your responses to what you read. Be sure to note any questions and objections to what you read as well. Consider the ways YOU have "received" from the Lord. Record some of these to share with your group.

THE RUGGED ROAD TO FREEDOM—CHAPTER 4

Study and Reflection Questions:

1. What does the filling of the Holy Spirit have to do with receiving instructions from the Lord?

2. How important is our listening to God *to God?*

3. How do you listen in depth to others? When? When do you listen in depth to God? How?

4. When processing and you reach the "receive" step, discuss how the Lord uses the following means to instruct you:
   a. Scripture
   b. Stepping into Christ
   c. Specifically communicated guidance (asking a question of God, then listening for His answer

5. Why do we sometimes have to "wait on the Lord" to receive instructions? What do we do in the meantime?

6. What are the dangers of
   a. Running ahead?
   b. Consulting experts?

7. How does God provide guidance through rational thought (training, skill, common sense, etc.)?

ASSIGNMENT: Read all of Chapter 5, recording responses and thoughts as you go along. What do you particularly respond to? Why? What do you wish were added to this chapter? What subtracted?

Are you continuing to practice your *Put Off?* Do you now Reach to God many times during your day? Do you practice complete Release? Have you learned to Rest in and with the Lord following Release? Do you then move into the *Put On* and expect to Receive from Him? Record the process as you move through it. Now add the Response you make. What is it? What are your difficulties with it?

THE RUGGED ROAD TO FREEDOM—CHAPTER 5

Study and Reflection Questions:

1. What is your usual response when the Lord asks something of you?

2. What is your response if you don't *like* what He's asked you to do?

3. In regard to responding to God's instructions, three "sins of the flesh" are named: pride, fear, and lassitude. Which if any do you find true of you? Do you know why? Explain if you do.

4. What can you expect "in the natural" if you do accept and respond readily to God's assignment?

5. Read the section "More of Glenrose" again. With what do you agree? Disagree? Why?

6. What is your motive for doing the assignment God gives?

7. Do you find your daily tasks difficult or boring? How can these become enriched and enlivened?

8. Do you have a sense of entitlement? Describe it if you do. What is God's attitude towards it? How do you deal with it?

9. Read the "Five Mistaken Responses" again. Are any of these yours? How can you eliminate them?

10. What does God want from your obedience?

ASSIGNMENT:
Read carefully and reflect on Chapter 6. Make notes as you read, using the text to spur journal entries of your own. Bring to class those things you are moved by. What do you have to share?

This is the last step in the process: rejoicing. You now have all six steps— three to *Put Off;* three to *Put On.* Are you using the process? To what are you applying it? Ask the Lord to give you the habit of thought, emotion, impulse, or behavior that He desires you to change. Pray that He would take you through the process in regard to it. Find out from experience if this process brings you into closer fellowship with and obedience to Him.

THE RUGGED ROAD TO FREEDOM—CHAPTER 6

Study and Reflection Questions:

1. How do you see God as a God of joy? In what respects? How does His joy relate to His glory.

2. Note the many ways Israel was commanded to rejoice, as well as their occasions for rejoicing found in the Psalms. List these. Compare these with ways the church of Jesus Christ rejoices today. What similarities do you see? What differences? What conclusions do you draw?

3. What gave joy to Jesus Christ in His life here on earth? Meditate on these.

4. In what way is rejoicing an accompaniment to every step of the processing presented in this book? Why is rejoicing particularly the last step?

5. How is it possible that Christians can experience sorrow (or sadness or stress) and joy simultaneously? Do you? Why or why not? Do you expect to?

6. Scan the chapter. Consider the sources of joy presented. What are *your* sources of joy as a Christian? Do you see any others of which you have been unaware?

ASSIGNMENT:
Read all of Part V. Write out your own testimony. Be prepared to share it with your class or group the next time you meet.

ENDNOTES

1 Oswald Chambers, *My Utmost for His Highest* (Grand Rapids, MI: Discovery House, 1963), 23.

2 John Ortberg, *The Life You've Always Wanted* (Grand Rapids, MI: Zondervan, 1997), 126-127.

3 Words by Joseph M. Scriven, music by Charles C. Converse, "What a Friend We Have in Jesus," *Hymns for the Family of God* (Nashville, TN: Paragon Associates, Inc., 1976), 466.

4 Oswald Chambers, *My Utmost for His Highest* (Grand Rapids, MI: Discovery House, 1963), 42.

5 Robert Young, *Analytical Concordance to the Bible* (Grand Rapids, MI: Wm. B. Eerdmans, 1971), 811.

6 Ibid.

7 J. I. Packer, *Knowing God* (London: Hodder and Stoughton, 1993), 35.

8 Brent Curtis and John Eldredge, *The Sacred Romance* (Nashville, TN: Thomas Nelson Publishers, 1997), 161

9 Jan Karon, *A New Song* (New York, NY: Penquin Putnam Inc., 1999), 394.

10 Oswald Chambers, *My Utmost for His Highest* (Grand Rapids, MI: Discovery House, 1963), 184.

11 Words by George Matheson, music by Albert L Peace, "Oh Love That Will Not Let Me Go," *Hymns for the Family of God*, (Nashville, TN: Paragon Associates, Inc., 1976), 404.

12 Oswald Chambers, *My Utmost for His Highest* (Grand Rapids, MI: Discovery House, 1963), 155.

13 Ibid.

14 Brother Lawrence, *The Practice of the Presence of God* (Grand Rapids, MI: Christian Classics Etheral Library)

15 Oswald Chambers, *My Utmost for His Highest* (Grand Rapids, MI: Discovery House, 1963), 353.

16 John Piper, *Desiring God* (Portland, OR: Multnomah, 1987), 38.

17 Ibid., 33.

18 Ibid., 37

19 Kenneth Barker, General Editor, "Old Testament Feast and Other Sacred Days," *NIV Study Bible* (Grand Rapids, MI: Zondervan, 1995), 174-175.

20 Robert Young, *Analytical Concordance to the Bible* (Grand Rapids, MI: Wm. B. Eerdmans, 1971), 803.

21 Ibid.

22 Ibid.

[23] Mark Buchanan, "The Dance of the God-Struck," *Christianity Today*, October 7, 2002.

[24] Kenneth Barker, General Editor, *The NIV Study Bible* (Grand Rapids, MI: Zondervan Publishing House), 1803.

[25] Words by Georges Robinson, music by James Mountain, "I Am His and He Is Mine," *Hymns for the Family of God* (Nashville, TN: Paragon Associates Inc., 1976), 590.

Printed in the United States
56657LVS00003B/193-213

9 781894 667722